Wounding the West

Wounding
the West
Montana, Mining,
and the Environment

DAVID STILLER

University of Nebraska Press : Lincoln & London

© 2000 by David Stiller

Manufactured in the United States of America ⊚

Library of Congress Cataloging-in-Publication Data

Stiller, David, 1947–

Wounding the West : Montana, mining, and the environment / David Stiller.

p.   cm.   Includes bibliographical references and index.

ISBN 0-8032-4281-6 (cl : alk. paper)

1. Mineral industries – Environmental aspects – Montana – Mike Horse Mine Region.

2. Mike Horse Mine (Mont.) – History 3. Water – Pollution – Montana – Blackfoot River.

4. Hazardous waste site remediation – Montana – Mike Horse Mine. I. Title.

TD195.M5 S75 2000 363.739'42'09786 – dc21 99-048939

For Jean

who encouraged my efforts,
tolerated my stubbornness,
and reminded me constantly
to write also about people,
not just things

Contents

List of Illustrations   ix

Acknowledgments   xi

Introduction   1

1 Beginnings   9

2 Discovery   17

3 Hard Times and Early Signs   35

4 Rebirth   45

5 The Dam   63

6 An Open Portal   87

7 Planting Fish   105

8 When Giants Die   125

9 Cleanup   149

10 The Divide   175

Notes   183

Index   207

Illustrations

PHOTOGRAPHS

1 Kornec boys and the Kornec family's second home   40

2 Mike Horse Mining and Milling Company, looking south toward the portal   48

3 Mike Horse Mining and Milling Company, old campsite and mill   49

4 Mike Horse Mining and Milling Company, main camp   55

5 Mike Horse tailings dam and impoundment at the mouth of Beartrap Gulch   67

6 Mike Horse tailings dam following 1975 flood   76

7 Close-up of breached Mike Horse tailings dam following 1975 flood   77

8 Mike Horse Mine main portal shed   92

9 George Kornec in the Kornec's Sammy K. tunnel in upper Beartrap Gulch   151

10 ASARCO's pretreatment pond   170

11 ASARCO's artificial wetlands   171

12 Upper Blackfoot River drainage   177

MAPS

1 Montana and the upper Blackfoot River drainage   xviii

2 Mike Horse Mine and Blackfoot River headwaters   18

Acknowledgments

IN LATE 1994, I found myself wanting to know more about the history and related environmental consequences of hardrock mining in the American West. Having lived my entire adult life in the region, I already knew that mining was the West's first lifeblood. Evidence of its historical dominance is everywhere. But rather than assimilate and digest statistics, I sought to know one mine well, a decision that led to identifying just one of the hundreds of mines in the mountains surrounding my home in Helena, Montana, and then seeking out its environmental history in detail. I chose the Mike Horse Mine.

I had no plan to write a book when I began. Indeed, my quest commenced as little more than random mountain walks and some library research. But as the story of the Mike Horse Mine unwound and information accumulated on my desk, what began as a modest personal interest grew beyond all reason. Ultimately, this book came of it. And as audio tapes, references, maps, notes, and fragments of manuscript gradually overwhelmed my desk and diffused throughout my office, I realized how dependent I was on the good nature and generosity of those I asked for help. Nearly everyone I queried could point me toward those with astute and functioning memories, locate lost or obscure references, and otherwise make my search possible, even pleasurable.

Now the job is done, and I thank them. It is no overstatement that this book would have been impossible without their assistance.

Fairness dictates that I point out four individuals whose special knowledge, generosity of spirit, and enthusiasm boosted this project along at various stages. George and Dan "Rosie" Kornec breathed human life into my initial queries by sharing with me their family's history concerning the Mike Horse Mine. Had I not followed some very good early advice and introduced myself to these brothers, I would still be wandering through the district's canyons and lodgepole forests. They have become friends as much as ready sources of oral history. Colorful characters in their own right, their door was always open, the coffee hot, and the conversation spirited and fun.

Judy Reese, oversight manager of the Mike Horse Mine's cleanup for Montana Department of Environmental Quality, ensured that agency files were open to me. Anyone who has ever attempted to make sense of or pull together an industrial chronology from government files will understand how absolutely indispensable her assistance was. Judy also reviewed an early version of a chapter and in the process pointed out errors and politely suggested that I be more circumspect when describing Montana's hazardous waste statutes. Judy cares deeply about the Mike Horse and the health of the upper Blackfoot River. I hope Montana's taxpayers recognize that in her they have a dedicated and knowledgeable employee.

On the other side of the regulatory fence, Chris Pfahl professionally represented ASARCO's interests in the district. In every way, Chris was Judy's equal in helpfulness. He readily dispensed candid, technical information about the mining industry and the mine whenever asked. From our first contact, he made ASARCO's files available to me in a way that I would never have imagined, especially on a rainy winter afternoon when he left me to my whims in ASARCO's Wallace, Idaho, records building. In retrospect, I realize it was vintage Pfahl. Openness is his nature: he looks you in the eye, tells it like he believes it to be, and dares you to discuss and disagree. Chris never equivocates about the history of mining in the American West or its demonstrable environmental impacts, although he is assuredly among those in the industry who wish to mine cleaner and safer in the future. Chris likewise commented on an early version of a chapter.

Other persons similarly pushed, pulled, and prodded my efforts. Those who read all of the early drafts—in some cases more than once—and who offered appropriate comments and guidance, include my good friend Brace Hayden, as well as Philip Hocker, Scott Slovic, and Peter Carrels.

Additional friends and associates also read and critiqued selected chapters: Dick Bailey, Stan Bradshaw, Paul Browne, Owen Hughes, Kellie Masterson, Don Saunders, Ted Schwinden, Liter

Spence, and Pat Van Eimeren. Where my language was stilted or my facts or interpretations fuzzy, they never hesitated to set me straight. Sometimes, they only encouraged me to continue, in itself an appreciated response.

Past employees of the now-defunct Anaconda Copper Mining Company, and its several historical iterations, helped me along by answering what must have seemed strange phone calls at odd hours about obscure events long past. Bob Dent, in particular, fleshed out Anaconda's activities along the upper Blackfoot River during the mining giant's declining years. Jack Harvey, Martin Hannifan, and Frank Laird Jr. also were kind enough to answer questions.

Details about Anaconda's involvement along the upper Blackfoot River in the 1960s were extracted from the Anaconda collection, housed in the University of Wyoming's International Archive of Economic Geology. There, Bradford Burton, manager, and Jennifer Sanchez, archive assistant, helped immeasurably. In particular, Jennifer plucked clean the archive's computer database so that I might access long-buried Mike Horse Mine maps and reports. Certainly, some of the uncovered material was available through no other venue.

Montana Department of Fish, Wildlife and Parks employs a multitude of astute professionals; some provided sound advice along the way and others helped me interpret obscure agency reports and files. All endeavored to educate me in the way of trout and clean water. Wayne Hadley, Chris Hunter, Howard Johnson, Don Peters, Glenn Phillips, and Ron Pierce are included in this group.

Montana Department of Environmental Quality also employs many dedicated scientists and engineers who likewise answered my questions, nudged me along the path to veracity, and explained the nuances of Montana's mining and hazardous waste statutes. Carol Fox, Gary Ingman, Bill Kirley, John Koerth, John North, Mike Pasichnyk, and Tom Ring all provided timely assistance. Monte Mason, of Montana Department of Natural Resources and Conservation, also assisted my research at a particularly critical period.

From time to time, numerous others rescued me, and they deserve a sincere thanks for helping me locate, research, and comprehend a wide range of seemingly unrelated scientific, regulatory, and statutory details and history. It would require another chapter to delineate which subjects each assisted with, but I nonetheless thank Shirley Ashby, Dorothy Bradley, Douglas Dollhopf, Pat Farmer, George Furniss, Steve Gilbert, Terry Grotbo, Brian Hansen, Kevin Keenan, Scott Mason, Johnnie Moore, David Newman, Douglas Parker, Jim Posewitz, Dick Rogers, Paul Roos, Koehler Stout, Bill Thomas, John J. Thompson Jr., and Charles Van Hook. Frequently, they had little idea why I was calling or what I was after; indeed, I did not always know myself.

Washington DC's Mineral Policy Center, an environmental watchdog of the hardrock mining industry, provided data on the historical extent and modern remnants of hardrock mining in the West and directed me to many useful scientific and engineering references. Alan Septoph, in particular, calmly answered my several phone queries.

Employees of Helena National Forest provided background information concerning the Heddleston Mining District's geology, mining history, forests, and headwaters trout fishery. Thanks to Jack Kendley, Vicky MacLean, Bill Straley, and Len Walch.

Sundry other state and federal agencies furthered my investigation by responding to requests for information. Although I did not always note individual names, I hope those who read this will nod knowingly and remember with compassion the chap asking strange questions in random fashion. I specifically applaud Montana's Secretary of State Office and Department of Transportation, the Western Governors Association, Colorado Department of Natural Resources, federal Office of Surface Mining, and the now-defunct U.S. Bureau of Mines. All provided data, information, and answers when I called or visited.

Tracing the names of miners in Montana's early mining camps and the Heddleston district, as well as the history and status of the district's many mining claims, was no simple task, yet two very capable professionals with the U.S. Bureau of Land Management, Ardella Berzel and Bill Wetherley, made it look easy.

Lory Morrow and Bonnie Morgan, from the photograph archives at the Montana Historical Society, located photographs of the Mike Horse Mine from the 1930s and 1940s. Thanks to them, we know what the mine and mining camp looked like more than a half-century ago.

Likewise, I must not ignore the always-helpful staffs at the Lewis and Clark County Library in Montana and Norlin Library at the University of Colorado in Boulder. Everyone I asked seemed to know just what I was after and where to find it.

Finally, I thank the editorial staff at the University of Nebraska Press for assisting in my headstrong efforts to write about a topic sorely in need of greater public recognition. Their steady encouragement has been much appreciated. I especially wish to thank Kristin Harpster for an editor's keen eye for detail and healthy appetite for accuracy. Her efforts added considerably to the text's accessibility to the wide audience I attempted to reach.

To those whom I have inadvertently neglected to mention, I offer my sincere apologies. I hope that you know who you are and will accept my gratitude even if I fail to acknowledge you individually.

While I am the grateful recipient of so much help, I cannot and will not hide behind this assistance. The simple fact is that though I believe this history to be accurate and fair, it is still my interpretation of events. I will be astounded if anyone agrees completely with all that I have written. In the end, any factual errors, misinterpretations, or misstatements are mine alone.

Wounding the West

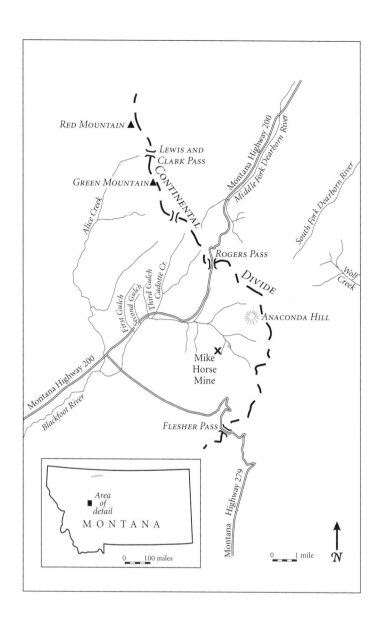

Map 1. Montana and the Upper Blackfoot River drainage.

Introduction

Of all ways whereby great wealth is acquired by good and honest means, none is more advantageous than mining. —Georgius Agricola, *De Re Metallica*

Without knowledge of the past, the way into the thickets of the future is desperate and unclear. —Loren Eiseley, "The Last Neanderthal"

IN THE FIRST HOUR OF DAYLIGHT I climb fifteen hundred vertical feet, switchbacking up a slope strewn with frost-shattered boulders and ragged spruce. I am breathing hard from the ascent but consider myself lucky. It is February in the Northern Rockies, and the slope is bare and dry where the snow should be several feet deep.

Leaning into a gusting wind, I pause to catch my breath and look back at my truck parked alone and far below. No traffic approaches the highway turnout from either direction. Opposite my truck, sandwiched between the pavement and a cliff of muted olive drab and purple rock, a wind-weathered, gray and brown forest service sign announces both the summit of Rogers Pass and the Continental Divide—or simply, the Divide, as Montanans call it. The pass lies more than fifty-six hundred feet above sea level, although as passes go it is little more than a highway notch bulldozed through a rock-ribbed ridge.

I continue climbing and soon reach a promontory where the Divide levels out to a broad, nearly treeless ridge that rolls and snakes for miles to the southeast. Above its far end the sun continues its morning climb, its light razor sharp. Above me the atmosphere is an inverted bowl of cloudless pewter. I tilt my head back and stare straight up, but my eyes have nothing to fix on, and I cannot tell if I am looking one hundred feet up or to the far edge of creation.

For the most part, the Divide threads a sort of natural compromise through western Montana. When it approaches Rogers Pass, however, for no obvious reason, it abandons its north-south course and bends eastward, straying to the very eastern edge of the Rockies, or the Front. From where I stand, the Front's ragged skyline stretches northward until it warps beyond the earth's curvature. The Front is the most abrupt geologic transition in North America.

An abused metaphor offers the Rocky Mountains, extending as they do from the Yukon to Mexico, as North America's spine. I dislike this analogy, for a true spine lends skeletal support to the body. The spine comes first, not last. Yet for all their impressive topography the Rockies do little but hang onto the older and more stable continental mass. In fact, the Rockies are geologic newcomers to North America.

Still buffeted by forty-knot winds, I proceed toward a timbered rise named Anaconda Hill. The wind is too brutal for me to tarry, or for that matter to be without a fleece jacket zipped to my chin, an anorak, and a snug cap. February in Montana can be only so mild.

Wind defines the Divide, and this wind-raked ridge brags a climate so severe that the vegetation is limited largely to sparse clumps of sun-bleached, wind-bent bunchgrass, broken occasionally by knots of shin-high dwarf juniper and ground-hugging kinnikinnick. The kinnikinnick hides beneath the spreading juniper. Even in midwinter each shrub bears visible berries. Juniper berries are indigo and the size and shape of peas that have been dusted with powdered sugar. In vivid contrast, the larger kinnikinnick berries are cheery red. The shrubs squat together in kaleidoscopic confusion among outcrops of red and green bedrock.

Farther on, I crouch in the lee of several gnarled conifers to munch on a sandwich. These evergreens are head-high, more like shrubs than trees, but I realize that I am stooping behind mature pines. I did not expect them in this harsh environment. At seven thousand feet I expect spruce or fir. The needles of these stunted pines are too short for the ubiquitous ponderosa pine common to lower and more temperate elevations. Through wind-watered eyes I count five needles to the bunch and recognize the whitebark pine, a natural for this site. Telltale fragments of purplish brown cones surround me, suggesting that Clark's nutcrackers have already consumed the edible nuts.

I turn slowly and see what has encircled me all along: runty whitebark pines in twisted clusters and wind-blasted, stand-alone individuals. Their gnarled shapes exemplify the German term, *krummholz*, or "crooked wood." The tallest specimens have only one or two remaining branches. The others have been stripped by wind-driven snow where their trunks protruded from snowbanks. Although their existence here is tenuous, I admire their adaptation. The whitebark pine must be stubborn even to survive. Farther west, in California's Sierras, naturalist John Muir spent a storm sheltered in a patch of these pines, during which he counted 426 annual growth rings on one specimen's trunk that measured only six inches in diameter.[1] Such tenacity must be respected.

Above the western horizon, airborne moisture hangs in a blue-gray haze. Beneath this haze sit row upon row of thick-timbered mountains. Their steep eastern prows face me head-on. Meanwhile, over my shoulder, much of eastern Montana is so dry that farmers rely upon irrigation or rotation cropping instead of growing-season rainfall. Except for wheat fields, the prairie appears sun-swept and wind-blistered. It is baked in summer and hard frozen in winter. The ready evidence is that water does not stay; puddles and snowbanks are short-lived.

Whereas western Montana's valleys are mild and well timbered, extreme temperatures characterize the state's sprawling, sparsely populated eastern counties. Summer temperatures commonly exceed one hundred degrees, while just several miles from where I stand, in January of 1954, the coldest temperature in the contiguous forty-eight states was recorded: seventy degrees below zero. Today's temperature lies happily near the midpoint of these two extremes.

A shadow darts across the earth in front of me. I freeze but quickly recognize the overflight of a large bird. Looking up, all I see is a winged outline banking deftly against the sun. The bird's colors and distinctive markings are invisible and, seeming to prefer it that way, it holds its position against the sun. Still, I know it is a golden eagle; its size and swept-back wing tips tell me. Golden eagles are more common in this corner of the West than its fish-mongering cousin, the bald eagle.

Two miles to my west, the Blackfoot River is born from the confluence of Beartrap and Anaconda Creeks. After a spectacular westward dash of about a hundred miles, it joins the Clark Fork, which continues across western Montana, becomes the Pend Oreille in northern Idaho and eventually joins the Columbia River near the Washington–British Columbia border. Now, two thousand feet below me, hidden in the bottom of thick-timbered canyons incised into a jumble of mountains, the headwaters creeks are frozen in midwinter lockstep.

An Indian name for the Blackfoot River is *Cokalahishkit*, which means, "the river of the road to buffalo." Two hundred years ago, the peaceable Salish, Kutenai, and Nez Perce tribes of northern Idaho and Montana's western valleys traveled this trail to the plains and the buffalo. Their forays were frequently disputed by the more territorial Blackfeet, who lived along the Front north and east of here. These enemies battled over access to the buffalo until smallpox epidemics of the 1830s decimated most plains tribes.

In the summer of 1806, Meriwether Lewis advanced up the Blackfoot River on his way home after crossing the continent and wintering at the mouth of the Columbia River. Had I been watching from the Divide on that July day I might have seen his small band leave the river and ascend Lander's Fork to cross the Divide over what is now known as Lewis and Clark Pass, six miles to the northwest. In January of 1854, during a reconnaissance for transcontinental rail routes, the Stevens Expedition approached closer to the Blackfoot River's true headwaters. Lt. Grover ascended the river and crossed the Divide at Cadotte Pass, just two miles away.[2] After the Stevens Expedition, the only non-natives seen for decades in this remote and harsh region were small bands of prospectors.

The gist of this historical recounting is that until the last few decades of the nineteenth century, humans merely passed through this piece of the American West. There is no evidence that natives regularly wintered or summered along the upper Blackfoot. The river valley seems little more than a passageway joining their homes with their hunting camps.

The Divide is considerably more crowded today than it was during the first half of the last century, although if every person within my line of sight lit a smoking fire I doubt I would see as many plumes as I have fingers and toes. Nonetheless, humans have become a predictable component of the landscape, and the principal resulting nicks to the landscape are obvious: wheat fields to the east and clear-cuts checkerboarding timbered mountains to the west.

Arguably, one of the most lasting scars is the Mike Horse Mine. Below me, the mine bleeds into the headwaters of the Blackfoot River. Its acids and metals, carried in a thick, red soup, have rendered the river almost barren for several miles downstream. There were other mines around here, too, like the Paymaster, the Anaconda, and the Carbonate. All found beginnings as silver and lead mines in the final decade of the nineteenth century. Although serious mining has not occurred near here since the early 1960s, the Mike Horse was, and remains, the heart of the Heddleston Mining District. It produced the most ore over the longest period, generated the most wealth, and provided the greatest number of jobs.

Among Montanans and the West's environmental cognoscenti, the Mike Horse has a uniformly pernicious reputation, one that provokes cringes of disgust, or, at best, resigned shrugs. It sits away from paved roads, invisible to anyone unwilling to leave the highway. Its infamy rests on its organic tie to the Blackfoot River, a ribbon of trout water made memorable by Norman Maclean's novella, *A River Runs Through It*. This single mine remains the source of most of the pollution still cursing the upper reaches of this mountain valley and the river that drains it.

I turn around and look down into the headwaters of the South Fork of the Dearborn River. Two miles off, a pair of ruts slips across a barren hillside. They constitute a remnant of a wagon road that originates at the Mike Horse and descends the Blackfoot River for several miles before it turns away from the river, ascends Rogers Pass, and crosses the Divide. After traversing into the South Fork drainage, the road crosses into the Wolf Creek watershed before continuing downstream to the community of the same name. Early in this century, horse-drawn wagons may have hauled Mike Horse ore over this road to the railroad at Wolf Creek. I write *may* because no one knows anymore. The few remaining memories are uncertain.

The wagon road is abandoned now—has been for decades. In most places it is little more than parallel ruts. On topographic maps a meandering dashed line seemingly connects nothing. The railroad remains, however, as does the town of Wolf Creek, which is split by Interstate 15, a winding blacktop strip that links Great Falls and Helena, and Canada with southern California.

For all this scenery and history, a piece of the Blackfoot River is missing. Its highest waters are decidedly unfriendly to trout and aquatic life for a mile below the mine. Decades of mining and milling turned lower Beartrap Creek and the upper Blackfoot River into a lethal brew flowing across a narrow, unvegetated plain of mixed stream gravel and broken mine waste. For the next mile or so, fish habitat improves as the river begins to meander among the willows and conifers that shade the river banks, but the water remains deadly. The few trout that manage to survive do so in the lower reaches of tributaries like Anaconda Creek or Pass Creek. They have learned to avoid the river.

For the next eight miles trout fishing remains an exercise in optimism. Water quality improves, and there is evidence of a struggling trout fishery, but the river is neither what it was nor what it could be. This near-dead reach of once-dazzling mountain river is the Mike Horse Mine's primary legacy.

As much as anywhere else in the West, this is mining country. And the Mike Horse story, a human history wrapped in a remote mountain environment, is as typical as it is spectacular. The nearby mountains, streams, and forests were eons in the making, while hardrock mining has been around for only a century or so. Mining created jobs and wealth for Montanans and others but left behind disturbing eyesores and acidic waters that sustain little life.

Far below me, dark crags and lone pines throw lengthening shadows onto canyon walls. As I begin retracing the day's steps, the wind gains muscle and a familiar shadow sweeps across the ridge before me. I do not need to look up to know that the same solitary eagle, still floating between me and the sun, spins and glides over the Divide.

Like most forgotten and derelict mines, the Mike Horse is known by few. Until the 1970s, neither activists nor government functionaries realized the nature and extent of its harm. Still, the story behind this one mine is like thousands of others that have simmered for decades, reflecting tales of justification, corporate wheeling-dealing, and gradual, meaningful environmental loss. Mining in the West began in defiance of nature with the belief that we could never exhaust any resource. Today, the ubiquity of abandoned mines, acidic wastewater, and barren waste dumps, and their cumulative effects on the environment, say otherwise.

It is hard to grasp the significance of hardrock mining in the American West by reading mind-numbing statistics, snippets of history, one-sided economic studies, and aged corporate reports and newspaper accounts. Looking closely at one mine is a way through broad-brushed histories. This is the story of the Mike Horse, the individuals and companies who owned and worked it, its physical environment, the geology and engineering that created it, and the business decisions and science behind its current standing in Montana and the West.

1. Beginnings

The use, abuse, and preservation of natural resources is, I believe, the most discernible trail across the mountains and through the deserts of the West. —Philip L. Fradkin, *Sagebrush Country*

[O]nly in America has the word "claim" come to mean a parcel of land. That single word expresses a revolution in attitudes. The historian who remarked that America's whole history could be read as one continuous real estate transaction was not too far off. —Wallace Stegner, *Wilderness*

IT IS RIGHTLY STATED that the West's first genuine mining fracas began in January of 1848, far from Montana Territory, when gold was discovered in the gravel of California's American River. The telegraph was years from linking the coasts, and weeks passed before news of the strike reached the rest of the country. Transcontinental railroads had yet to be constructed, so for those who would not cross the continent by foot, horse, or wagon, there were two sea routes: by ship to Panama, across the isthmus on foot, then by ship up the Pacific coast, or by ship around the tip of South America and Cape Horn. The latter balanced the speed and relative comfort of ocean travel against the ravaging storms of the Magellan Strait. In spite of these primitive modes of transportation, an estimated one hundred thousand would-be forty-niners made their frantic way to California in the first few years following the initial strike at Sutter's Mill.[1]

It is too simple, and largely incorrect, to describe the West's subsequent mining boom as a sequential list of strikes radiating from California, although prospectors certainly fanned outward from the new Gold State in concentric waves. The greater truth is that gold-seekers were knocking about the frontier decades before the California strike. After 1849, however, prospectors seemed everywhere at once. Other strikes followed within a decade. Colorado's Pike's Peak and Nevada's Comstock booms, both in 1859, were followed by Colorado again in the 1870s and then by South

Dakota's Black Hills gold rush (which indirectly led to Colonel Custer's ignominious demise at the Little Big Horn). Arizona was later yet.[2]

From the mid-1860s on, mining so dominated the economies of the West that it would be difficult to overstate its significance. One academic noted that at least 25 percent of the residents of Nevada, Idaho, and Montana were working miners. Of course, mining's employment impact was far greater than the numbers of miners. The industry also required assayers, equipment manufacturers, and teamsters as well as suppliers of clothing, housing, and entertainment.[3]

In Montana Territory, the first prospectors appeared in the 1820s and 1830s, about the same time that wagon trains began following the Oregon Trail. At least one historian credits Francois Finlay with discovering the first gold in Montana Territory, in 1852, near Gold Creek, forty miles west of a yet-to-be-settled mining camp called Helena. Others credit the Stuart brothers and Reece Anderson with this achievement six years later. Regardless of who made the discovery, little came of it. Today, Gold Creek is a modest mountain stream running through rangeland, scrub timber, and piles of weed-smothered, worked, and reworked placer gravel.

The Gold Creek strike was soon overshadowed by major placer discoveries a hundred miles to the south, on Grasshopper Creek, in 1862. Within months, Grasshopper Creek and its mining camp, Bannack, put Montana on America's map. A year later, nearby Alder Gulch lent new meaning to *boomtown* in Montana Territory, with the founding of Virginia City.

Before the news filtered eastward about Bannack and Alder Gulch, "back east" hardly knew Montana Territory existed. The territory's non-native population likely numbered fewer than ten thousand. No one knows for sure—there was no census—and in any event, easterners were far more concerned with the hostilities between North and South. Still, for those hardy and optimistic individuals who left eastern and midwestern farms and families and made their way west, mining offered promising alternatives. History would prove that the majority simply made a living, but for many, gold was an excellent excuse to avoid the bloodbath of civil war.

By July of 1864, as the Civil War entered its fourth year, gold fever in Montana Territory expanded with the discovery of shallow gold placers in Missoula and Dublin Gulches, minor tributaries to Silver Bow Creek. These gold strikes were quickly exhausted, but by 1866 silver lodes were discovered in surrounding hills. These, too, eventually played out, followed promptly by the prospectors' realization that the future of the just-formed Butte Mining District lay in copper.

In the same month that gold was first discovered along Silver Bow Creek, four prospectors struck another gold placer on Last Chance Gulch, fifty miles to the northeast. This strike spawned Helena, another nucleus from which still more prospectors scurried into the surrounding mountains. The find occurred along what is modern Helena's main city street, still called Last Chance Gulch by tourism boosters.[4]

The establishment of each new mining camp was a step toward increasing civilization. If the surrounding mines demonstrated staying power, a mining district was born. Mining districts were, in effect, the beginning of government where none existed. Created by neighboring miners and prospectors, the primary purposes of a mining district were to define the included geographic area—a delineation typically based upon the proximity of a cluster of mines and nearby strikes—and to act as the administrative vehicle for organizing mineral survey claims filed by the district's prospectors and miners. Realizing that someone had to keep track of ownership and record sales, and generally keep tabs on the district's claims and mines, elected or appointed officers established the protocol for staking, recording, and organizing the district's mineral survey claims. Montana Territory would not become a state until 1889, but in lieu of the administrative benefits of statehood, Montana's first rough-hewn miners created more than two hundred such districts.[5]

Official histories of Montana's mining industry prior to 1900 fail miserably in their quantification of the mineral wealth extracted from its first mines. The U.S. Bureau of Mines did not begin compiling meaningful records until 1904, and accurate state records from before the turn of the century are generally unreliable. Production estimates that do exist are limited to approximations of the monetary value of mineral production.[6] In 1902

Montana's inspector of mines estimated the total value of Montana's mineral production prior to 1901 to have exceeded one billion dollars—the rough equivalent of seventeen to eighteen billion dollars in the mid-1990s—a significant amount when one considers that there were no income taxes at the time and that metal prices were much lower than they are now. The same report concluded that gold was the dominant metal produced in Montana between 1862 and 1881, followed by silver's dominance until 1896, after which Butte's copper took the lead.[7]

In the final decades of the last century, what and how much a mine produced was no one's business but the owner's. Estimates of the mineral wealth produced from Montana's mines during that era remain speculative. One droll observer noted, "The early goldhunters were not remarkable as historians."[8]

Western prospecting and mining were straightforward activities in the nineteenth century because nobody contested miners for the land. To be sure, the land and minerals were federally owned, yet the lack of a strong federal presence in most of the West made ownership of the land a technicality largely ignored by the miners and their industry. Most prospectors and miners did not concern themselves with who "owned" the land, for the land, to their eyes, was still empty. Montana's population in 1900 was less than a quarter million, and most of that was concentrated near the mining centers of Butte and Helena, the timber town of Missoula, and along the state's two major transcontinental railways.[9]

An 1866 act of Congress declared the West open to minerals exploration, subject only to existing state and territorial laws and the rules of local mining districts. The same act outlined procedures by which a claimant could obtain a patent, the legal document transferring title to a discovered mineral deposit and surrounding land to a private person or company. These congressional declarations were little more than primitive affirmations of what western miners had asserted and practiced all along. Still, the declarations fired debate on the federal role in mining and western mineral ownership. That debate ended, at least temporarily, with congressional enactment of the General Mining Law of 1872. Signed by President Ulysses S. Grant, the 1872 law remains the most significant federal legislation controlling hardrock mining in the West. Under this law, nearly three million acres have been transferred from public to private ownership.

The primary point of debate up to that time was never whether to open unclaimed federal lands to minerals exploration and mining—this was generally agreed to by the majority of members in both houses of Congress—but whether to sell the land outright in order to pay off remaining Civil War debt and to finance future government obligations. In opposition, a strong and organized block of senators from western states argued that legal title to both the minerals and land should pass as early as practicable to those making a discovery, without meaningful or continuing financial obligation to the federal government. These senators ultimately had their way.

The 1872 law limited the size of lode claims to fifteen hundred feet along the vein and three hundred feet on either side of its center line, an area encompassing slightly more than twenty acres. Provided that the claimant performed one hundred dollars of labor per year on each claim and that the claim ultimately proved to bear a valuable mineral commodity, a patent could be obtained for five dollars per acre. A pittance in the 1990s, such a sum was considerable in 1872, when agricultural lands sold for about $1.25 per acre. Moreover, if a miner was less than totally persuaded about the worth of his "discovery," he still legally controlled and could mine the land without having to "proceed to patent." Hundreds of prospects and mines never warranted patenting and were operated without the property leaving the federal domain.[10]

That the federal treasury and taxpayers never received much in direct payment for thousands of acres of mining claims or billions of dollars of minerals is the result of a conscious policy adopted by Congress shortly after the Civil War. Congress wanted to settle the West, and however wise or shortsighted the manner it chose, the 1872 law did much to achieve this objective. Although most nineteenth-century mining camps eventually disappeared, some survived. A scattering grew and thrive to this day. The presence of mining camps stimulated nearby transportation hubs and agricultural centers that, in turn, provided necessary freight links and food to the miners.

The environmental consequences of this nineteenth-century congressional largess remain far-flung and significant, primarily in the form of abandoned mines and mineral processing sites on both patented and unpatented mining claims. Cumulatively, hundreds of mines like the Mike Horse continue to seriously impact the West. Open shafts and adits swallow several unsuspecting hikers every year. Thousands of acres of waste-rock dumps and forsaken tailing ponds remain unvegetated and contribute metal-laden sediments to waterways. Acids still drain from hundreds of mines to render streams and rivers lifeless.

By one authoritative estimate, more than 557,000 abandoned hardrock mines remain unreclaimed and troublesome in thirty-two states, mostly in the West. These relics possess fifty *billion* tons of untreated mine waste and pollute 12,000 miles of waterways and 180,000 acres of lakes and reservoirs. A 1988 General Accounting Office study concluded that more than 424,000 acres of unpatented federal lands remain affected by abandoned hardrock mines. Again, most of these are in the West.[11] Another source contends that Alaska and the eleven states west of the one hundredth meridian account for nearly a half-million abandoned mines, waste dumps, and deserted smelters and mill sites, occupying more than 468,000 acres.[12] This amounts to more than 730 square miles. Stitched together, the mess would blanket the District of Columbia ten times over.

Most of these half-million sites are relatively benign. Throughout the West, mining's nicks and scratches are visible from the highways and interstates as multihued pockmarks scattered across seemingly diseased mountainsides. Their essential defining characteristic is ugliness. The modern Bureau of Land Management still attempts to manage 1.1 million active, yet unpatented, claims throughout the West, located on twenty-five million acres.[13] As many as fifteen thousand of these deserted sites create very real public health and safety problems and relentless ecological dilemmas. More than sixty mining and mineral processing sites bear the dubious distinction of a place on the U.S. Environmental Protection Agency's Superfund list, a status reserved for the nation's most ignoble, uncontrolled hazardous waste sites. Again, two-thirds of these are in the West.

The federal "Superfund" law, passed in 1980, mandates the rehabilitation of the nation's worst uncontrolled hazardous waste sites. Known formally as the Comprehensive Environmental Response, Compensation, and Liability Act, or "CERLCA," the law requires potentially responsible parties, or "PRPS," to either remediate the site under government direction or pay the cleanup costs. Sites not addressed by a PRP are rehabilitated from a fund supported by a tax on the chemical industry. The predicted cost to reclaim these inherited mining and mineral processing eyesores and environmental wounds is virtually imponderable. Reliable estimates to rehabilitate all of the disturbed mined lands and successfully treat contaminated mine waters run into tens of billions of dollars. Unfortunately, aside from those sites being addressed under the federal Superfund cleanup program, very few have been addressed in a meaningful and permanent manner.[14]

In Montana, one study estimated that between 20,000 and 26,000 abandoned hardrock sites collectively cover 150,000 acres and pollute 1,300 miles of rivers and streams. This affected area is roughly one-third of the total in the eleven western states and Alaska. And 1,300 miles approximates the length of the Colorado River. A separate investigation came up with *only* 6,000 abandoned hardrock mines.[15]

Montana's inventory represents mostly abandoned sites, either those without identifiable operators or, more likely, those owned by the descendants of the original operators who are without the financial means to clean them up. There is no money, no concerted program, no comprehensive federal law requiring responsible parties to correct these aberrations.

Where the Mike Horse Mine sits among these statistics is debatable. It is not a national Superfund site, nor is it a benign, dry hole on some remote mountainside. But given that the site finally received attention from Montana regulatory authorities in the early 1990s, it is a fair statement that the Mike Horse is likely among the fifteen thousand worst sites in the West.

2. Discovery

Discovery of a Mine: the bona fide discovery of a commercially valuable deposit of ore or mineral, of a value materially in excess of the cost of discovery, in natural exposure or by drilling or other exploration conducted above or below the ground.—Article 219, *Income and War Excess Profits Tax Regulations no. 45*

There is nothing in the history of the vast majority of the dividend paying mines of to-day from which the most imaginative can weave an exciting tale. No poor prospector has of late years stumbled onto a body of ore containing fabulous wealth. In fact, accidental discoveries are rarely heard of, and the question of luck as a factor in mining is nearly, if not altogether, eliminated.—John Byrne, inspector, *Fourteenth Annual Report of the Inspector of Mines of the State of Montana*

ON A MID-SEPTEMBER MORNING in 1898, a veteran prospector and miner named Joseph Hartmiller rose and began preparing breakfast over an open fire on a ridge above Beartrap Creek.[1] Nearby, a cold spring bubbled to the forest floor. Above him a broad, timbered ridge rose skyward another thousand feet, while below him, the canyon narrowed darkly. Something he cooked, bacon possibly, attracted a bear. Actually, Hartmiller later admitted that he never really saw the bear but inferred its presence from his horse's reaction, which was to bolt.

His horse's abrupt departure left him in a quandary. He could pursue his horse and leave his breakfast to the whims of an unseen bruin, or he could take the time to sack up his food and carry it with him as he chased his nag down the canyon. History ignores whether he lost his breakfast or chased his horse the extra distance. Oral history does record, however, that upon returning to his campsite Hartmiller noticed a quartz-bearing rock that had been turned over in the melee. Glinting in the morning light was the recognizable sheen of silver and lead.

The presence of quartz on that rounded ridge was anomalous,

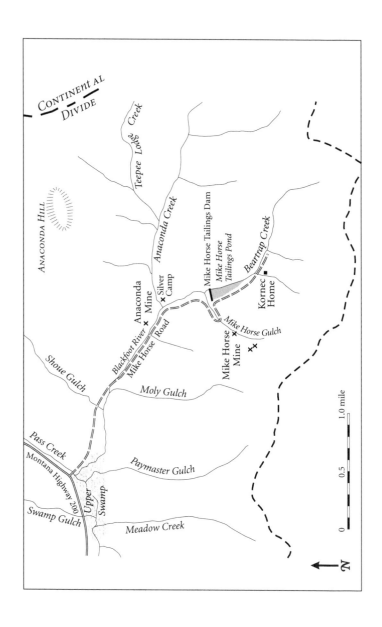

Map 2. Mike Horse Mine and Blackfoot River headwaters.

for the local bedrock was argillite, a maroon to olive green rock without intrinsic value. Argillite is unexceptional in western Montana; entire mountain ranges are composed of it, including those at the headwaters of the Blackfoot River. But quartz was another matter entirely. Prospectors love nothing so much as an anomaly, especially the mineral quartz, the most common of nine crystalline forms of silica oxide. Most beach sand and many sandstones are made of quartz, which occurs both by itself and with many other rock types and minerals. It also occurs with gold and silver.

Finding a chunk of quartz is not nearly the same as discovering the mythical mother lode. Rather, it is only the beginning of possibilities. After retying his horse and gulping his breakfast, Hartmiller likely broke out his pick and shovel. He did not know where the chunk of quartz came from, so what followed must have been prospecting of the most fundamental sort. If the silver- and lead-bearing quartz had crept down the slope from somewhere above, he would have had to dig and poke his way uphill until he found its origin.

Somewhere on the mountainside, Hartmiller found his lode and named it after his horse, Old Mike. Hartmiller's sentiment in this respect was common, if suspicious. A surprising number of animals show up in western mining history by virtue of their performance in accidental mineral discoveries. Hartmiller's story may be fact or fiction.[2]

Nineteenth-century miners had already developed their own vocabulary by 1898, one much different from that of the modern geologist. What today's geologist calls a vein, miners called a lode, which is a bastardization of the verb *lead*. The lode is whatever a miner followed to reach ore. To a mining geologist, a vein is an occurrence of ore, usually disseminated through a gangue. *Gangue* is the geologist's collective term for nonvaluable minerals associated with the ore, while *ore* is a mineral, or aggregate of minerals, from which a miner may economically extract a profit. A vein has a more or less regular length, width, and depth and is confined between rather definite rock boundaries. A lode may be composed of several veins spaced closely enough so that a miner can work them as a single unit.

Today, geologists know that ore in the Heddleston district occurs as veins, or as shoots within veins, and can be from one to five feet wide and up to one hundred feet long. The ore typically contains quartz, plus a variety of sulfide (sulfur-bearing) minerals, including galena (lead sulfide), sphalerite (zinc sulfide), tetrahedrite (a copper-antimony sulfide), bornite (copper-iron sulfide), chalcopyrite (another copper-iron sulfide), arsenopyrite (iron-arsenic sulfide), and the ubiquitous pyrite and its chemical twin, marcasite (iron sulfide).

The Mike Horse Vein, which is what geologists ultimately named Hartmiller's find, is composed of a dark-colored rock termed *diorite*. The diorite vein, enclosed in worthless argillite, contained quartz, one piece of which somehow made its way beneath Old Mike's hooves. In addition to quartz, the vein was composed of copper, zinc, and gold, but especially silver and lead.

In 1898 the surrounding mountains, canyons, and ridges were a mosaic of living lodgepole pine and the remains of charred and burned trees. Forest fires had scorched the region in the 1840s and again in 1888. Some lodgepole stands had escaped both fires and in 1898 were sturdy specimens one or two hundred years old. Other stands had regenerated from the 1840s fire and supported mature timber, while those acres that had burned only ten years earlier sprouted young pines just reaching waist high. Thin organic soils covered with pine needles lay beneath the surviving timber, but layers of charred wood and ash blanketed the earth beneath the burned trees.

Lightning probably started the 1840s fire, but it is likely that men caused the 1888 fire. Prospectors had traipsed through these canyons many times since the 1860s. Campfires got away from them frequently. In fact, prospectors occasionally set fires to clear the slopes of the timber and brush obscuring the bedrock. And once a fire started, no one tried to hustle up a bucket brigade. The land was too vast to bother with several acres of burning trees.[3]

Hartmiller's strike occurred in a mountainous area that, to prospectors and nonminers alike, looked pretty much like anyplace else in western Montana. Miles to the south, mining fortunes had already been made around a major geological anomaly, the Butte Batholith, a unique bubble of igneous rock that had pushed its way through the earth's surface. Compared to the Mike Horse

Vein and the Heddleston district, the Butte and Helena strikes appeared easy. Hartmiller and his successors would have to sweat a bit more to eke out their fortunes.

Rocks that make up the earth's surface are the aged and wrinkled skin of an ancient planet. Modern geologists calculate the earth to be, in round numbers, 4.6 billion, or 4,600 million, years old. This contrasts markedly with England's Archbishop Ussher, who, in the early seventeenth century, reckoned from the Old Testament that God created earth in 4004 B.C.

Modern geochemists hang their number upon known rates of decay of natural, radioactive isotopes found in common minerals. By measuring how much "daughter" isotope remains in crystallized "basement" rocks—rocks composing the earth's crust— it is possible to calculate how long ago the "parent" mineral crystallized. Geologists have found no rocks, anywhere, older than 4.6 billion years. In Montana, the oldest such basement rocks crystallized about 2.7 billion years ago.

The rocks underlying the Heddleston district accumulated as soft mud in seas that did not exist until 1.5 billion years B.P. (geologists commonly say "B.P.," meaning "before present," instead of "ago"), when western Montana was characterized by featureless coastal plains and shallow seas.[4] Once sediments began settling, however, the process continued for 600 million years. Ultimately, the sediments solidified into mudstone, sandstone, limestone, and the ubiquitous argillite. These sediments-becoming-rock were themselves buried in newer shallow seas, while the North American continent drifted thousands of miles across global oceans until its west coast anchored near modern northern Idaho.

A tenet of physical geology states that when sediments like sand, mud, and silt settle in oceans or lakes, individual sediment layers always settle horizontally or very close to it. The process of rock making commonly preserves these horizontal bedding planes. Consequently, when a geologist observes sedimentary rocks with bedding planes other than horizontal, he or she knows that a change in the rock's attitude occurred after the sediments solidified. It is not much different than a baker knowing a bite snitched from a finished wedding cake had to occur after the cake had been baked, frosted, and decorated.

Geologists possess their own way of classifying sedimentary rocks. *Formations* are layers of rock strata useful for mapping in the field. For example, a fifty-foot-thick slab of a peculiarly maroon-colored sandstone that contains unusual ripple marks and can be found throughout several counties or states might be termed a *formation* by geologists attempting to map the area. A collection of related formations is a *group*, and an assemblage of comparable groups is a *supergroup*. Most of western Montana, including the Heddleston district, is composed of and underlain by the Belt Supergroup.

Beginning about 90 million years ago, the earth's crust beneath the Pacific Ocean collided with North America's west coast and began to compress the continent and shove it eastward. These forces thrust the accumulated Belt formations both eastward and upward. Consequently, from Canada's Yukon south to Mexico, the Rocky Mountains rose over a relatively brief geologic span of 20 million years, a mountain-building era geologists subsequently named the Laramide Orogeny. Located in the center of this activity, Montana has not been the same since.

The Heddleston district has not changed much in the past 50 million years, at least when compared to the preceding billion or so. The mountains have not changed states, much less continents, and the Blackfoot River still flows where it did when the mountains finished rising—that is until relatively recently, when glaciers dominated western Montana. This glacial dominance occurred over the past 2.5 million years, the geologist's Pleistocene epoch. Strangely, the Heddleston district escaped the most recent glaciation that affected nearly everything around it. The landscape has evolved. The process continues.

Following the rise of the Rockies and 20 million more years of relative geologic calm, a wave of surface and subsurface igneous activity occurred throughout central and western Montana. Volcanoes swarmed into existence. Solutions of molten rock rose from great depths and intruded fractures in the overlying Belt formations.

It is not hard to picture cracks and fractures in the Belt formations. If you doubt this, take a sledgehammer and pound on the concrete foundation of your home or driveway, or observe the foundations, driveways, and sidewalks in old neighborhoods, the ones that have been around for several decades or more. More than likely you will notice hairline cracks in the older concrete. The owners might admit that these cracks allow water in their basements in the spring, when snow melts and the earth thaws, or in the summer, if they place their lawn sprinkler too close to the house. In a comparable sense, fractures in the Belt formations allowed molten solutions to penetrate just as cracks in tired concrete may allow water to pass.

As these igneous solutions crystallized, *dikes* formed. Radioactive-isotope dating of minerals in these dikes indicate a consistent age of approximately 50 million years. These dikes contain some of the metals that form the cornerstone for mining in the Heddleston district.

Two types of mineral deposits originated from these igneous intrusions: porphyry-type copper and molybdenum deposits and silver-lead-zinc veins. *Porphyry* simply describes large crystals in an otherwise fine-grained rock mass. Copper and molybdenum are metallic elements in this ore. Separate but genetically related silver-lead-zinc ores were emplaced as shoots within quartz veins intruded into the argillite. Quartz veins are fairly common in nature, ore considerably less so.

Thus, in a land of timber-clad mountains that have been banged around, fractured, then randomly shot through several times with molten fluids that may or may not have contained precious metals, how easy could it have been to locate a comparative sliver of lead and silver ore just several feet wide that dipped almost straight down into the mountains? By analogy, locating ore seems a million times more difficult than predicting where, without opening the carton, you might confidently intercept the fudge in a gallon of fudge ripple ice cream.

In retrospect, John Byrne, Montana's first inspector of mines, had it all wrong. Hartmiller's find was nothing less than good luck, a chance incident that he pursued with far less than predictable results. Knowledge of geology was limited and unsophisticated in 1898, especially among untrained prospectors. Hartmiller discovered his lode with Old Mike, a pick, and a shovel.

Hartmiller was from Ohio, and after arriving in Montana in 1882 as a fresh-faced lad of twenty-three, he became an avowed miner.

In the beginning, he claimed little interest in lead or silver.[5] At that moment in American history, however, everyone had uses for gold.

The opening of each new frontier seems always to start with the pursuit of gold, instead of other precious metals. Gold's value-to-weight ratio was, and is, much higher than that of lead or silver and justified the financial risk of extracting it from the earth. In a remote corner of an isolated western territory, where transportation was limited to pack trails and footpaths, the prudent miner more willingly excavated half a mountainside to recover a brick of gold rather than an equal value of lead. A brick of gold could be carried on his back or thrown on his packhorse. An equal value of lead required six horses and a sturdy wagon, plus a road to haul it. Given the absence of infrastructure and transportation in frontier Montana, the preference for gold just made sense.

To Hartmiller, however, there was also national and Montana history. Only five years before Old Mike kicked over a chunk of quartz, an international economic debacle closed virtually every silver mine in the western states. This event came to be known to economic historians as the Silver Panic of 1893.[6]

The roller coaster began in 1890 with congressional passage of the Sherman Silver Purchase Act, which required the Treasury to buy 4.5 million ounces of silver each month for coinage. Conceived by senators from the western mining states as a means of boosting and guaranteeing silver purchases, the act did increase silver production from western mines. But a panic ensued when debtors began paying their bills with silver instead of gold, which they began hoarding. International markets eventually grew to distrust this habit so much that they would accept only gold from American buyers.

The result was disastrous. The value of silver dropped like a boulder down a mine shaft, and silver mines throughout the West began closing. The Sherman Silver Purchase Act was repealed in 1893, but the damage was already done, and a national economic depression caused by the international silver panic continued into 1894 and beyond. Montana's mining and transportation industries began to recover by 1898. Gold was discovered in the Yukon, which had the combined effect of drawing off many of Montana's out-of-work or underutilized miners and boosting the broader national economy. Montana's wheat crops were bountiful, grain prices rose, and the first wave of sodbusters showed up on eastern prairies. The silver panic eventually diminished to little more than a bad memory.

Against this background it seems uncharacteristic for a gold prospector like Hartmiller to care about a discovery of lead and silver ore. But it is not uncommon to find lead and silver in association with gold, so perhaps he proceeded with high expectations that gold might become part of his strike. Both lead and silver could be smelted relatively close to the Mike Horse and the Heddleston, and this may have played into Hartmiller's logic. Fifty-some miles to the south, in 1888, a lead smelter had been constructed in East Helena—known then as Prickly Pear Junction. In addition, there was a silver smelter in Great Falls, sixty miles over Rogers Pass and to the east. (Eventually, both the East Helena and Great Falls smelters formed the core of the modern corporate mining and smelting giant, ASARCO, which organized as the American Smelting and Refining Company in 1899.)[7]

By the end of the century, an improved wagon road stretched between the small mining town of Lincoln, located on the Blackfoot River a dozen miles to the west of Hartmiller's find, eastward over Rogers Pass to Wolf Creek, and on to Great Falls. But no improved thoroughfares linked this wagon road with the mines and prospects within the Heddleston district, which was dissected by deep canyons and for the most part heavily forested.[8] The distances across which equipment and materials had to be transported to the district, after which the ore had to be hauled from the mines for smelting and processing, made development costly. The prohibitive expense of serious mining in the Heddleston would have tempered Hartmiller's optimism.

Almost from its beginning, the district's production was based upon lode mining, as opposed to *placer* mining.[9] The Calliope Lode had been discovered and developed in 1889 by William Heddleston, the district's namesake, and his partner, George Padbury. Several miles north of Hartmiller's eventual discovery, on Pass Creek, they took eleven thousand dollars of gold from a small lode over several years. Heddleston and Padbury were not alone, however. Being so close to Helena, the state capital and a thriving mining city, prospectors and miners would not have bypassed the district.

Within a decade, the Heddleston district looked much like any other in the western states. Prospectors had been over the area time and again for more than forty years. Still, activity increased dramatically following Heddleston and Padbury's gold strike. In fact, most major strikes in the district occurred in the 1890s, even though principal development and mining did not occur until after 1900.

Initial prospecting in the Heddleston district in the 1890s attempted to define lead-silver veins. Later exploration would chase the bounds of the deeper copper and molybdenum ore deposit. Both waves of exploration were hampered by poor surface exposures of veins that inexplicably thinned and disappeared at depth. Both efforts also suffered the loss of time and expense that went into conceptualizing and plotting the ore in three dimensions. Geologists and mining engineers would ultimately spend years in the Heddleston district defining the ore's subsurface network.

Although the district's appearance by 1900 likely raised no eyebrows among its residents, it was pockmarked with both shallow and deep holes dug by prospectors attempting to define the extent of chance ore exposures. The visual scarring from these pits would not begin to heal until left undisturbed for a decade or more.

When Hartmiller discovered the Mike Horse Vein, he unquestionably knew the strength of the controlling 1872 federal mining law. It was, in effect, the miner's bill of rights. Even though his discovery automatically triggered legitimate property rights, he had to demarcate the borders of his lode claims and promptly file notice of their location with the county recorder. Hartmiller's vehicle for filing his two claim locations was the Mike Horse Mining Company, which was already in existence by 1898—at least in his mind—though it did not incorporate until 1902.[10] He filed notice of the Mike Horse Lode claim on 15 September 1898 and followed this with notice of the Hog All claim six days later.[11] The Mike Horse Vein extended roughly northwest-southeast. Hartmiller's Mike Horse and Hog All claims butted end-to-end for three thousand feet along this exposure. The forty-plus acres that made up these claims would prove enough to keep Hartmiller and his initial partners comfortable for more than a decade.

The Mike Horse Mining Company never patented these claims. Outright ownership was not necessary. Under the General Mining Law of 1872, Hartmiller's company legally controlled the surface, its mineral deposits, and all mining thereon. But it never *owned* the land or the minerals as such. The simple discovery and creation of mining claims were enough to establish a conclusive and legal "right to mine."

In an industry and era when speculators, crooks, and fools abounded in equal measure, county records suggest that Hartmiller possessed at least average business acumen. An 1899 mining deed records Hartmiller's sale to William Rothermel, for one hundred dollars, of an undivided one-twelfth interest in the Mike Horse and Hog All lode claims. Hartmiller's signature is confident and orderly. In fact, the document reflects the same penmanship throughout; one person wrote everything. Related mining deeds involving Hartmiller and different buyers at other times likewise exhibit the same handwriting. The common denominator is the witness signature of George Padbury, William Heddleston's partner in the district's initial Calliope Lode and by then a Helena notary public. Could it be that Hartmiller and his first partners were unable to sign their own names? Apparently, literacy was not a prerequisite to functioning in Montana's mining industry at the beginning of the twentieth century.

By 1902 Hartmiller sold an additional undivided one-third interest in the same two claims, for $400, to Frank Rothermel, possibly William's brother, as well as separate one-eighth interests to Michael Dobler and Henry Gruhle for $325 each. Gruhle later sold his interest to Dobler for $555. Thus, within three years of his strike, Hartmiller sold off two-thirds of all interests in these two claims.

Hartmiller's organizational talents were as significant as his salesmanship, and in June of 1902 the Mike Horse Mining Company was incorporated in Helena. One hundred thousand shares of capital stock were authorized, each claiming a par value of one dollar. Seventy-five thousand shares were distributed to its four original incorporators: Hartmiller, Dobler, and both Rothermels. True to the interests Hartmiller had sold, Hartmiller and Frank Rothermel each took one-third of the shares, Dobler a quarter, and William Rothermel one-twelfth. If only to themselves, they somehow justified inflating the value of their initial investments by several thousand percent. Modern bankers and accountants tell of similar opinions held by many of today's independent hard-rock miners, although unguarded optimism might be a better description of their behavior than duplicity.

Five more contiguous lode claims were involved in the mine's birth: the Pine Hill, Black Ore, Little Nell (named for Hartmiller's wife, Nell, whom he married in 1908), Detroit, and Sterling Lode claims. Conrad Fuchs sold the first three to the Mike Horse Mining Company in 1913, although no one knows how he came to own them. Perhaps he exercised the time-tested strategy of many prospectors and simply filed claims next to the Mike Horse and Hog All and waited for his price. In the same year, S. L. Boyer sold the Detroit and Sterling claims to Robert Koontz, who quickly transferred them to the company. The company added two more claims to its collection in 1915.[12]

Finding a promising lode is not the same as being rich. Following his discovery, Hartmiller had decisions to make. Considerable thought, planning, and backbreaking work remained before the smelter paid its first fees. Hartmiller's initial test was deciding how and where—in that canyon or on its overlying timbered slopes—to actually open his mine. To reach into the heart of the mountain and extract his ore, he had two options. He could begin driving an *adit*, or he could sink a *shaft*. An adit is a horizontal underground passage by which a mine is entered or dewatered from the surface, whereas a shaft is a vertical or near-vertical entryway. The appropriate entry considers the lode's geometry and how it fits into the local topography.

Fortunately for Hartmiller, the lode's geometric inclination was straightforward and consistent. Hartmiller likely had traced the vein on the surface over at least the length of his first two claims, or three thousand feet (decades later, the vein would be followed for four miles across the surface of the district), but it dipped southward into the earth at an angle of seventy degrees. Hartmiller had to choose between sinking a shaft directly on the vein or driving an adit from lower on the mountain slope with the hope of intercepting the vein inside the mountain. Standard mining practice then, and now, held that the preferred method was to follow the lead from the surface—in Hartmiller's case, sinking a vertical shaft on the vein—to allow ore recovery from the very beginning and thereby cover some or all of the development costs. Another cogent reason for following the vein is stated in a popular twentieth-century miners' handbook: "An ore body can do some erratic things in a very short distance, and the sooner an operator can learn its behavior and peculiarities the better off he will be. Disregarding this rule has caused much needless work. Many hillsides in mining areas have large dumps that show that a long crosscut adit was driven to intersect an ore vein at depth . . . but [it] was not found at depth, or it was too low grade to mine, or funds ran out before the project was completed."[13]

Sinking a shaft costs more than driving an adit because every bit of waste rock and ore must be hauled up and out of the shaft before it can be discarded or processed. If the mine begins to fill with water, like a giant well, pumps must be installed and operated to keep the mine workable. Alternatively, driving an adit, even if off the lead, has several advantages. By mining horizontally, gravity works with, not against, the miner who advances into the mountain like a badger burrowing into a hillside. And if the miner advances the adit with even a slight upward gradient, mine groundwater will drain naturally without incurring pumping costs.

At the Mike Horse, Hartmiller seems to have disregarded the cardinal rule of staying with his lode and began driving an adit from the canyon floor. Perhaps he realized that getting supplies higher on the mountain would prove difficult. Or maybe he knew from other experiences in the district that he would encounter groundwater and that sinking a shaft would be costly. He had to know that transporting ore to the smelter in Prickly Pear Junction was expensive and that he might not see smelter returns for months.

Driving an adit began with pick-and-shovel work. Miners scraped away loose soil until reaching solid bedrock, while shoring up their incipient adit portal with timbers. From that point on, advancing an adit and an underground mine involved drilling, breaking, and removing rock. The breaking was accomplished with the proficient use of drills and explosives. Once drilled and blasted, *mucking*, or removing the broken rock, became the dominant activity. Underground mining at the end of the nineteenth century demanded long hours of intense physical exertion in a dark and uncertain environment.

No one knows whether the first drilling in the Mike Horse Mine was done by hand or by pneumatic drill. The latter method had been in use in western mines since the mid-1880s. Pneumatic drilling used compressed air to generate the drilling energy, as well as to blow the rock dust out the hole. Given the difficult access to the Heddleston district and its marginal financial backing, it is doubtful that steam boilers and compressors had made their way to district mines. Conversely, pneumatic drills had so thoroughly revolutionized western underground mining by that time that their efficiency may have been what made the Heddleston's mines worth developing in the first place.

But in remote 1898 Montana, it seems more likely that Hartmiller and his cronies drilled by "hand steel," which is the process of hand-drilling the holes used for explosives.[14] In "single jacking," a lone miner held a one- or two-foot length of drill steel in one hand and hammered on it with a four-pound hammer. "Double-jacking" required two or three miners taking turns holding the drill steel and swinging an eight-pound hammer overhead. Double-jacking was faster but more perilous. The hammering miner had to focus on his task; a missed blow could easily break the hand or arm of his partner holding the drill steel. Holes drilled by single- or double-jacking were rarely deeper than two or three feet. More commonly they were from four to twelve inches deep.

There was a method to advancing an adit. Adits in the first days of the Mike Horse customarily were five feet wide by seven feet tall. The adit's size and direction of advance were determined by the placement and spacing of the drill holes. The tougher and harder rock necessitated more holes and more explosives. Although hole terminology varied from district to district, the principles controlling the planned detonation of the explosives did not. The idea was to set off the dynamite in the center holes first to create a free rock face against which successive and surrounding detonations would break.

Holes typically were loaded with dynamite and primed with detonating caps and fuses, then detonated as the miners were going off shift. This allowed time for dust to settle before the next shift arrived at the adit's working face. Broken rock, or *muck*, was removed from the mine by human- or mule-powered ore carts.

This steady rotation of drilling, blasting, and mucking was, and remains, the time-tested means of advancing underground.[15]

By whatever means he used, Hartmiller made considerable progress. Within three years, the Mike Horse Mine was, "developed by a main tunnel [adit] 1,100 feet in length, besides two other tunnels higher on the lead. The vein shows from three to four feet of ore, which carries high values of lead and silver. There are also large bodies of concentrating ore."[16]

Hartmiller could not avoid the need for constant mine development, the process of gaining access to and opening up ore reserves to actual ore extraction. Development is critical to any mine's future but especially to an underground operation, where a miner can infer, but not actually see, the ore and how far and in which direction it extends.

To many optimistic yet hapless nineteenth-century prospectors, the lode always widened and grew richer with depth. By contrast, twentieth-century geologists reason in terms of quantitative trends and statistically significant increases in the metal content of the ore. A modern, hard-nosed mine manager, who must justify costs to directors and investors, thinks and plans in terms of proven reserves and how to open them up for future extraction. As Montana's Inspector of Mines John Byrne summed up nearly a century ago, "the most productive mine, however extensively it may be developed, is always in a prospective stage of development."[17]

Conditions and inferences, rather than solid evidence, suggest that limited ore shipments may have made it to the smelter at Great Falls prior to 1898. In this respect, as a term used colloquially as both noun and verb, *high grade*, is relevant. When used as a noun, as in, "The high grade contained gold," it is a convenient way to abbreviate conversation. In mining country, no one is confused. *High grade* and *high-grade ore* are synonymous. But miners also use *high grade* as a verb, as in, "He high graded the deposit," meaning he extracted only the richest ore and ignored anything of more modest value. Likewise, the verb may apply to miners who steal ore by slipping chunks of the high-grade stuff into their clothing during work.

High-grading is what Hartmiller and his fledgling company likely undertook at the Mike Horse, the reason being more practical than sinister and reflecting the era's laxness toward efficiency, economy, and conservation. Mining blindly into a mountainside required faith, a quality Hartmiller and his partners obviously possessed.[18] By the time Inspector of Mines Byrne visited the Mike Horse Mine in 1902, the miners had intercepted their objective.

Most ore initially uncovered in the Heddleston district was not rich enough to justify its transportation to the smelter. Consequently, any ore hauled by mules to rail points and on to the ASARCO smelters at Great Falls or Prickly Pear Junction must have been very high grade to justify the expense. Without better access to a railroad or a way to concentrate lower-grade ore, only the richest rock left the district.[19]

Concentrating ore, as the term implies, was ore rich enough to justify smelting only after it had gone through a mechanical concentration process that separated metal-bearing minerals from waste, yielding an enriched product called, appropriately enough, *concentrate*. Lacking the means to concentrate the ore at or near the mine, the Mike Horse owners continued development in hopes of finding truly rich ore or in expectation that a concentrating mill would be constructed nearby.

In that era of little record keeping and no tax reports, Hartmiller probably did extract and ship some high-grade ore. Decades later, a geologist would report rumors that in 1894, four years *before* Hartmiller filed on his first two claims, thirty thousand dollars of high-grade lead-silver ore was shipped from his mine to the smelters. The report also refers to "various other considerable sums between that year and 1899 of which record was not kept." [20] Hartmiller may have thus profited from his strike years before staking legal claims and incorporating his mining company.

An uncharacteristically thorough 1915 engineering analysis of the Mike Horse Mine paints a much different picture, one of a mine and district struggling to exist. J. Alden Grimes, one of Montana's leading mining engineers of the era, described the district's primary population center as a simple tent-and-cabin community called Silver Camp, located near the mouth of Anaconda Creek. A crude road linked Silver Camp with Silver City and Helena by way of Flesher Pass. Another road meandered between the district and the small community of Wolf Creek on the Great Northern Railway by way of Rogers Pass. Both routes culminated at railway loadouts and both necessitated climbing and crossing the Continental Divide.

Grimes also identified a proposed rail line that would extend westward from Lincoln, move up the Blackfoot River, and then leave the river to cross the Divide at Cadotte Pass. The rail line, planned before World War I by the Chicago, Milwaukee, and St. Paul Railway, was intended to link Great Falls and Missoula. So certain was this line that grade stakes had been surveyed along its proposed path. In spite of this promise of improved transportation links, Grimes lacked enthusiasm for the mine: "The Mike Horse Mine has always been a small mine. The smelter returns have not paid for the present development work and no quantity of ore of commercial grade is left in the mine. The dump contains a couple of thousand tons of vein matter that could be milled but would not yield enough to warrant investment in a mill. In my opinion future development is a very hazardous enterprise financially." On his final page he wrote, "At this time the district as a whole offers some opportunity for small scale mining, but none for operations of any magnitude." Then, in careful script, Grimes signed his name in black ink.[21]

Perhaps Hartmiller and his partners solicited Grimes's report and lost heart; Grimes did not identify his client. Maybe the Mike Horse Mining Company finally exhausted its capital. At that time Hartmiller was in his late fifties, and he must have been tiring of the rigors of his profession. For whatever reasons, in 1916 the company sold its nine lode claims and on-site assets to O & M Mines Company for one hundred thousand dollars.

O & M Mines realized that a concentrating mill was necessary to make the Mike Horse pay. It spent another sixty to seventy thousand dollars to erect and equip a log mill building several hundred yards down-canyon from the portal of the no. 3 adit, which had by then become the primary passageway into the mine. A steam-driven sawmill was assembled on-site to cut lumber for the mill building, mine office, and bunkhouse and to use as fuel for the mill's steam boilers. O & M Mines also installed narrow gauge tracks from the mill into the mine to where the no. 3 adit intercepted the Mike Horse Vein. A lone horse or mule pulled one-ton ore cars from the mine interior to the mill and back and carried waste rock to the mine entry, where it was dumped to create a benchlike pad in front of the portal.

In 1917, without ever putting the mill into operation, O & M Mines produced a small quantity of ore. Perhaps the company high-graded in order to make payments against the purchase price and to finish putting the mill into operation. But it was not enough. The property reverted to Hartmiller's company, and O & M Mines seems to have lost its entire investment.[22]

The Mike Horse Mining Company turned the property around the next year and sold it to Liberty Mining Company for $150,000. Liberty was more colorful than its predecessor, although a later account described its unidentified owner as one who, "was unsuccessful in his operations so far as production of metal was concerned . . . this failure [being] due to inefficient management and a desire rather to sell stock than to produce metal."[23] Again, the mine reverted to the men that had opened it nearly twenty years before.

3. Hard Times and Early Signs

In the thirties, it was kind of tough to get a job or make any [money]. Min-ing was the big thing. Everybody mined, you know. That's all there was, placer mining, underground mining. —John J. Thompson Jr.

Life is tough. I hope you make it. —Anonymous

IN 1919 SEVERAL DOZEN FARMERS from Wenatchee, Washing-ton, formed the Sterling Mining and Milling Company and se-cured the mine from the Mike Horse Mining Company for $155,000.[1] From this point forward, Joseph Hartmiller and his partners seem to have had no connection with the mine or its operation.

Montana's mining community appears to have been insulted by the prospect of farmers dabbling in their industry, especially when the farmers managed the mine themselves. Nonetheless, the new owners reopened the mine and initiated an aggressive underground development program. They restarted the mine's sawmill and manned it with twenty "Finlanders," who cut cord-wood to fuel the mine's steam-powered concentrating mill. Be-fore long, concentrate shipments were headed to the smelter at Prickly Pear Junction—now called East Helena.[2]

In its first year of operation, Sterling shipped six thousand dol-lars of lead-silver concentrate. Conflicting records characterize the farmers' success over the next four years. One report indicates that Sterling produced seventy-five thousand dollars of concen-trate during this period—three-fourths in lead concentrate and the balance in silver. Apparently, its best years were 1923 and 1924, when it milled and shipped 1,120 tons of concentrate. For this, Sterling received, after smelting allowances, about forty-six dol-lars per ton. Inexplicably, Sterling's own reports to Montana's sec-retary of state claim the company did more than three hundred thousand dollars in business between 1920 and 1923 and that no business at all was conducted in 1924. The truth of it may never been known.

Sterling idled the mine in 1925. The following year, a new firm, Cook & West, leased the property and took its turn. Cook & West looks to have risen and fallen in a single year, shipping just enough ore and concentrate to make slightly more than fourteen hundred dollars in royalty payments to the Wenatchee farmers.[3] In spite of its spotty business success, Sterling did manage to achieve something of considerable significance. In November of 1925, the federal government granted Sterling patents on seven of the key lode claims composing the Mike Horse Mine.[4] From that day forward, the land was private property. The American taxpayer likely received less than a thousand dollars for the 120 acres and its underlying mineral wealth.

In 1926 Chester T. Kennan, a consulting geologist and mining engineer from Helena hyped the mine in an apparent effort to sell it.[5] His report exudes the jargon and optimism of someone seeking a commission and, in effect, served as a prospectus for potential buyers. Kennan derided the Washington farmers for taking turns in managing the mine and mill and implied that Sterling was not making a go of it. Kennan clearly considered the farmers rubes.

Kennan reiterated the claim J. Alden Grimes made ten years earlier that the Chicago, Milwaukee, and St. Paul Railway would soon connect Missoula and Great Falls and pass within a mile of the Heddleston district. He waxed eloquent about the future prospects for lead prices and noted that since the Heddleston district was the geological twin of the famously profitable Coeur d'Alene district of northern Idaho, it was obviously on the verge of a remarkable ascent. The quick-minded buyer could procure the mine for a song. In spite of Kennan's optimism, however, no one bit. Sterling filed its last report with Montana's secretary of state early in 1927.[6]

For the next dozen years or so, there seems to have been no organized mining activity at the Mike Horse. Full-scale mining operations apparently ceased in the district. However, hearsay suggests that the Mike Horse operated covertly and intermittently during this period. The heart of the Great Depression, the 1930s, was exceptionally tough on the American West. Many men pushed into the mountains, where small-scale mining operations provided one of the few moneymaking opportunities available to them.[7]

I did not know it at the time, but my initial encounter with the Kornec brothers occurred during my first visit to the headwaters of the Blackfoot River. The January day had been uncommonly gray and wet, and the unplowed gravel roads were as slick as a greased hockey rink. My knuckles whitened on the steering wheel when I encountered an oncoming truck.

In Montana, as in much of the sparsely populated rural West, custom requires drivers to wave when they meet. Likely derived from equal parts genuine friendliness and long intervals between one person's glimpse of another, it is regional protocol. Under such adverse driving conditions, I deemed stopping to exchange a verbal greeting the proper thing to do. It probably mattered that I had not seen anyone else since before dawn.

Our trucks slid to uneasy stops and we rolled down our windows. Inside the other vehicle, two weathered male faces grinned broadly at me. Sleet poured onto our laps as we complained about the weather and road conditions. When they mentioned that they lived at the end of the road, beyond the Mike Horse Mine, I mentioned my interest in its history. They invited me to their house for coffee, but I deferred and said I would come by another time.

Eight months later I took them up on their offer. In the interim, I was asked frequently if I had talked to "the brothers at the end of the road," as the Kornecs were referred to, and I heard so many pronunciations and spellings of their name that I ceased taking notes. If I wanted to know more about the Mike Horse, and especially its historical environment, I needed to talk to the brothers.

Autumn had rolled around by then and the days were cool enough to warrant a jacket. My truck's heater fan hummed cheerily as I drove up the Blackfoot River. Cottonwoods and aspen blazed yellow and gold, and clouds draped over the ridges and perched like cotton atop individual trees.

A solid gate marked the end of Mike Horse Road. Four-inch iron posts, buried in concrete, stood on both sides of the gravel track. Earthen berms on both ends prevented adventurous drivers from bypassing the posts. A swinging arm fabricated from welded pipe hung from one post and barred access. In the center of the cross-arm, where an approaching driver could not miss it, a black-and-white sign bluntly stated the obvious: road closed. In the West, as elsewhere, good fences make good neighbors.

A two-story building sat in a clearing eighty yards beyond the gate. Clad in corrugated metal, it was painted neatly in gray with contrasting white doors and window frames. Smoke rose from a chimney that stood next to a rooftop TV antenna. A Dodge pickup, an old sedan, and two more pickups were parked alongside the house. Squatting in front, insisting that this was not some city dweller's vacation cabin, several tons of purposeful iron took the form of a veteran D-8 Caterpillar bulldozer. Behind the building, Beartrap Creek tumbled from the Continental Divide.

I approached on foot, stepping over mounds of birdseed and bread crusts scattered between the house and the parked Dodge. A sign hung above the door: White Hope Mine Inc. I walked to the screen door, paused, and knocked. Two male voices promptly responded in sunny unison, "Come on in!"

I entered a cavernous kitchen, clearly the nerve center of the house. A long wood table governed the center of the room, surrounded by an eclectic collection of straight-backed chairs. A sink sat against one wall beneath a pair of windows from which hung stiff yellow, green, and orange print curtains. The walls were painted the color of aspen. Outside another window, a dial thermometer registered forty-four degrees. In a corner, a wood-burning stove radiated enough heat to explain the open screen door. The stove had been cut and welded from a fifty-gallon drum. Over its muffled crackling a radio churned out the Helena news. It was a tidy room but one boasting a degree of bare simplicity found only among men living without women.

I was unexpected, but the Kornecs seemed pleased to have company. Maybe they were pleased precisely because I was unexpected. They are not listed in the Blackfoot Valley telephone cooperative directory, and they do not own a telephone. When necessary, they communicate with the outside world by CB radio.

When I reminded them of where and how we met, their heads bobbed in recollection as they recounted to each other how treacherous the road had been. My eight-month procrastination in accepting their invitation to coffee was not mentioned.

The younger brother poured coffee into a mug from a thermos sitting on the table and handed it to me. A tall, spare man, George Kornec moved about in a forest-green work shirt and matching trousers. His sleeves were rolled partway up his forearms, as if I had interrupted him from wrenching on the bulldozer parked outside. When I asked his age, he answered softly, "sixty-three." He accentuated the "three," as if to ensure many more birthdays were a given.

Dan was nine years older, shorter, but just as wiry, and similarly work-tempered. When speaking, he cocked his head and stuck his chin forward. When excited—the propensity for which depended upon the topic under discussion—the volume of his voice doubled. He had already survived a heart attack, and although he complied with his doctor's directives by using a salt substitute brought now and then by a visiting niece from Seattle, he was still a passionate man.

George volunteered some family history by recounting that as a boy Dan's cheeks reddened easily in the wind and cold. He suggested I address his older brother by his family nickname—Rosie.

"He prefers it," George added.

Both men smiled readily. Each exuded mental and physical vigor. They were confident and open and seemed to consider candid opinions the only ones worth expressing. When I asked about the Kornec family and the Mike Horse Mine, Rosie launched an account without taking a breath.

"Mining family. Our whole life has been mining and heavy equipment."

The brothers told me that the Kornec name came to North America with their father, Samuel, when he escaped the chaos of the Russian Revolution. Following brief stints in northern Michigan and Alaska, Samuel landed in Wallace, Idaho, where he toiled underground as a miner in the Coeur d'Alene district. Samuel Kornec had loftier goals than to labor underground forever—at least for wages—and soon found an experienced partner in Walt O'Connor. O'Connor had been superintendent of the Mike Horse Mine for the Wenatchee farmers. O'Connor warrants additional mention in the Kornec family history because his sister, Margaret, married Samuel Kornec. George and Rosie still refer to him as Uncle Walt.

1. Kornec boys and the Kornec family's second home in upper Beartrap Gulch, circa 1939. Kornec family members lived in this cabin continuously for approximately thirty years. Courtesy Daniel and George L. Kornec.

O'Connor interested Kornec in the relatively unknown Heddleston district. They spent summers prospecting there through the 1920s, returning to northern Idaho's mines over the long winters. In 1928 O'Connor and Kornec filed on a cluster of lode claims east of and adjacent to the Mike Horse Mine. Sometime in the mid-1930s—Rosie no longer remembers the exact year but believes it was 1936—Samuel relocated his family to western Montana and his mining claims. It was the midst of the Great Depression.

Kornec moved his family into a clapboard cabin O'Connor had built several years earlier. Later, he constructed an eighteen- by twenty-four log cabin for his family one-half mile up Beartrap Creek, at an elevation of fifty-six hundred feet, where Montana winters arrive early and stay late. The Kornecs called the cabin home until after World War II.

It was a challenging environment in which to live. After each winter's first good snowfall, Rosie led his younger brothers in banking snow against the cabin's outside walls to help insulate the family against the bone-aching cold.

While the elder Kornec and O'Connor developed their mining property, Rosie and his brothers explored the Divide and surrounding canyons, fished, and hunted. They frequently fished the upper Blackfoot River, even though they had to walk three miles to find a stretch of river that would support trout, a hike that took them below Pass Creek. Fish could not survive immediately downstream from the Mike Horse Mine.[8]

It is mid-June, and along the upper Blackfoot River drenching spring rains have been replaced by occasional afternoon thunderstorms that pound the earth for twenty minutes before drifting over the Divide. Along the river, meadows are finally drying out. They are overwhelmed by phlox and shooting stars, minute blossoms barely visible among the tangled willow and bunchgrass. On the slopes above the valley floor, larkspur and lupine flash from openings in the timber. And in the shade of ridge-bound pines, glacier lilies burst from beneath rotting snowbanks. In unison with hundreds of burnished, cobalt forget-me-nots, they ripple in the wind.

On foot, I follow an abandoned-mine road that angles down into Moly Gulch. Deserted mine roads crisscross the district, although thickets of head-high lodgepole pine limit their use. In the absence of regular traffic, the forest reclaims its own. Above the road, the slope has at some point been gouged out by heavy equipment. Almost buried by slumps of organic soil and jackstrawed piles of toppled lodgepole pine, unfamiliar gray rock reflects the afternoon light. I stop and stare. These mountains are composed of red and green argillite. Gray is sorely out of place.

On a hunch, I climb over the ridge crest and into Mike Horse Gulch and confirm that the gray rock is immediately opposite an adit of the Mike Horse Mine. The anomalous three-foot band of gray rock is one of the veins whose ore justified the mine's existence. I am not surprised. Geologists mapping the Mike Horse Mine have traced its supporting vein system for three or four miles across the Heddleston district.[9]

From above the collapsed adit, I gaze over most of upper Mike Horse and Beartrap Gulches. The landscape has changed a great deal in the past sixty years. The mountainsides facing me are lush with a thirty-foot regrowth of lodgepole pine and Douglas fir. Prior to World War II, they were largely bare, having been cut or burned over during the district's first half-century. By 1940 the slope opposite the mine sprouted little more than sun-bleached stumps. North of the mine, the fifteen-hundred-foot rise to the Divide had more stumps than standing timber. After dropping and limbing standing trees on the ridges, loggers slid the green cordwood down wood chutes to the canyon floors, where it was collected and delivered to the mine's boilers to generate steam power.[10]

A thorough environmental characterization of the district from before World War II does not exist. But simple calculations suggest that miners had by then removed at least seven thousand cubic yards of rock and ore just from the Mike Horse Mine, dumping the waste rock and low-grade ore onto the slopes and gulch bottom below the mine portals.[11] In its new environment, the ubiquitous pyrite in this waste inexorably began to alter its surroundings.

Symptoms of problems with mine water quality were evident as early as the mid-1920s, when geologists of the U.S. Geological Survey, after visiting the Mike Horse Mine, observed that, "owing to the free downward movement of water permitted by the mine workings, oxidation is in progress in the lower levels. In the east drift on level 2 conspicuous soft flocculent coatings of black manganese oxides, white carbonate of lead, reddish-brown oxides of iron, and blue-green brochantite, a sulphate of copper, are being deposited by the mine waters." [12] Similar signs were also apparent elsewhere in the district. The same government geologists examined the nearby Anaconda Mine and reported that, "In tunnel 2, beyond the oxidized zone, blue copper sulphate is being deposited by the mine waters. Tunnel 1 was not entered by the writers. Acid mine water issuing from it has almost completely dissolved the rails of the car track. The combined dump of the tunnel and shaft shows much pyrite." [13]

In short, chemical reactions involving mine water and exposed pyrite were beginning to create acid strong enough to eat iron.

In spite of these occurrences, the Mike Horse was nothing more than a typical mining operation of the times. Its practices were sadly consistent with records and commentary about mines from throughout the West.[14] Without federal or state laws mandating environmental protection, most of the environmental consequences of hardrock mining were ignored. After all, the West, particularly Montana, was expansive and undeveloped.

Nothing was so offensive or noxious as to alter the attitudes or practices of the miners or the mine owners. It was business as usual. They worried about profits, not water quality, timber, fish and wildlife, or scarred landscapes. Company stockholders invested for dividends, not a clean environment, and they did not want company proceeds diverted from their pockets.

As a consequence, decades later biologists would find the three-mile run of water below the Mike Horse Mine nearly void of life. But the Mike Horse was neither mined out nor abandoned for good. Its best years were ahead, as were more serious consequences for the upper Blackfoot River.

4. Rebirth

From a geological standpoint the veins in the Heddleston district have distinct merit. We consider the Mike Horse mine and the area in general as having promising prospective possibilities. —C. P. Pollock and Keith Whiting, ASARCO, September 1944

[D]isposal of waste, refuse and mine water from the mine or mines on the demised premises . . . shall not be a nuisance nor injure the property of the Lessor, or to others, nor obstruct or contaminate any stream, or obstruct any right of way or other means of transportation or travel on the lands of the Lessor or others. —Lease agreement between ASARCO and Norman Rogers, 1 April 1958

All the money went back East. . . . People back there didn't give a goddam if the creeks were running red or green or blue here. —David Newman

SOMETIME IN 1940—no one today recalls for sure—the Mike Horse stirred.[1] Within a year, the mine began to produce again, until it closed once more in 1952. This twelve-year period saw more ore mined, more concentrate milled, and more jobs created and wages paid than all mining and milling at the Mike Horse before and since. It was the Mike Horse's heyday. This period also set the scene for continuing and future environmental impact, even though nature would not make its wrath evident for another three decades. For a while longer, the Blackfoot river would suffer silently.

Precisely which factors justified the mine's reopening remain as unknown as the precise date of its rebirth. The first shots of World War II, in September of 1939, certainly nudged metal prices upward worldwide, especially for those metals needed by twentieth-century industrial war machines: lead, zinc, and copper. Wars are generally profitable for the mining industry.

Another impetus for the Mike Horse may have been America's emergence from the Great Depression, from which western Montana had suffered miserably. The mine's rebirth may have also been due to the entrepreneurial instincts of like-minded miners who recognized that the Mike Horse was too good a property to leave idle. Regardless, boards and timbers were pulled off the portals, and mice and spiders were chased from the mill. Unemployed miners throughout the Northern Rockies began hearing rumors of a startup at an obscure lead-silver mine located along Montana's Continental Divide.

The mine's rebirth was also caused by conditions established much earlier, when the Sterling Mining and Milling Company failed in the mid-1920s. When Sterling defaulted on its bonds, the bondholders sued in Lewis and Clark County district court. In August of 1927, they won a judgment forcing the Mike Horse Mine, its mill, and twenty-one mining claims to be sold at public auction to satisfy their claims.

The amount of the winning bid, $230,432.29, seems of less consequence than the identity of the winning bidder: Sam Stampfly, trustee for the original bondholders. The bondholders forced the sale of the Mike Horse, then purchased the mine at the sheriff's auction.[2] In effect, they paid for the mine with money from their right pocket, put it back in their left pocket, *and* gained control of the mine and the company's assets. They must have believed the mine could be resold for a profit, but the Wall Street crash of October 1929, and the ensuing depression obliterated their chances of attracting a buyer for the once-fallen silver mine. The Mike Horse remained inactive for another decade before dedicated and experienced miners finally pounced.

A key personality in the Mike Horse's 1940 rebirth was Charles C. Goddard Jr., a mining engineer for the powerful, Butte-based Anaconda Copper Mining Company. So important was Anaconda to Montana's economy that Montanans simply referred to Anaconda as "the company," an identifier still heard on Butte's streets more than a half-century later.

In October of 1940, Goddard informed his Anaconda superiors that the Mike Horse Mine presented an attractive business opportunity.[3] Sam Stampfly, still trustee for Sterling's former bondholders, had leased the Mike Horse and its claims to four investors who, in turn, wished to offer the property to Anaconda.[4] Goddard identified the lead investor as A. E. Wilkinson, also a senior Anaconda employee.

In addition to spelling out the mine's status, geology, and potential, plus the availability of nearby water and timber, Goddard indicated that the "current lessees are planning to reopen and develop the mine." In his report, he wrote that "car load lots of unsorted ore were shipped during the summer of 1940 to the American Smelting and Refining Co. [ASARCO], at East Helena and resulted in a profit of $3.00 to $4.00 per ton after hauling, royalty and smelting charges were paid. Payments on this material was on lead, silver, copper and gold; the zinc content was not paid for, but brought a penalty on treatment charges." [5]

What Goddard failed to relate to his Anaconda superiors, at least in his report, was that he was one of the four investors who leased the mine from Stampfly. The other two were "Boo" MacGilvara and the foursome's leader, Edgar Estill.[6] Actually, Estill had acted months earlier, in March, when he leased the Mike Horse's ore dumps and shipped them to a smelter to determine the prudence of reopening the mine.[7] (This was the same ore referred to in Goddard's October report to Anaconda's executives.) In fact, the foursome had leased the Mike Horse from Stampfly in the same month that Goddard recommended the mine to Anaconda.

I doubt Goddard and Wilkinson attempted to hoodwink their Anaconda bosses. Given Montana's small, close-knit mining industry, it is unlikely that their involvement with the Mike Horse was unknown within Anaconda's hierarchy. Anaconda's bosses may have disregarded Goddard's apparent moonlighting simply because the Mike Horse was a lead-silver play and hence not competitive with Anaconda's copper operations.

The absence of a documented Anaconda reply suggests that Goddard and his cronies quickly realized they were on their own. Subsequently, on 19 December 1940, following the addition of John Dwyer to their small group, they incorporated as the Mike Horse Mining and Milling Company.[8] On the final day of 1940, they collectively transferred their lease on the Mike Horse Mine to the new company and committed to its reopening.[9]

The original lease with Stampfly and the bondholders provided for royalty payments based upon the quantity and grade of ore mined, shipped, and smelted. The agreement also granted the lessees, for a period of eight years, the option to purchase the Mike Horse for $160,000. Royalties amounted to between 10 and 15 per-

2. Mike Horse Mining and Milling Company, looking south toward the portal, circa late 1930s. Montana Historical Society, Helena.

cent of the "net mill or smelter returns of the ore mined," which were defined as the amount received after deducting the costs of milling, smelting, and haulage from the mine to the mill or smelter.[10]

Significantly, the royalty schedule failed to allow for the cost of mining. Thus, Mike Horse Mining and Milling paid all costs of mining and still expected to profit, after royalties, from 85 to 90 percent of what the concentrate brought at the smelter. Although they were clearly optimistic, this arrangement ultimately proved untenable. An amendment to the lease decreased royalty payments by about one-third.[11]

The new owners of the Mike Horse recognized that major capital improvements were necessary, not the least of which were modifying the mill and bringing electric power to the mine. Whereas the original mill relied on wood-fired steam boilers for power, the young Mike Horse Mining and Milling Company wanted to string electric power lines through the Blackfoot Valley from Lincoln so they could run their mill using the more efficient flotation technology. In addition, they wanted to impound mill tailings behind a dam to be constructed in the mouth of Beartrap Creek.

Concentrating mills separate valuable minerals from the value-

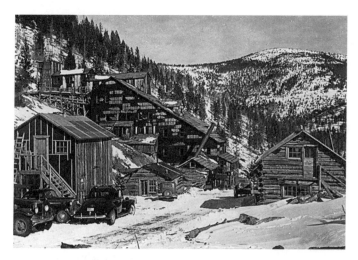

3. Mike Horse Mining and Milling Company, old campsite and mill, circa early 1940s. Montana Historical Society, Helena.

less gangue in a three-step process. The first step, crushing and grinding the ore to the size considered most amenable to concentration, is called *comminution* by mineral processing engineers. The second step concentrates the metal values into a smaller volume. The final step actually recovers the metal.[12]

At the Mike Horse, cars loaded with two or three tons of ore exited the mine and ran north along the west side of Mike Horse Gulch to the mill, where the ore was dumped into a single, nine-by fifteen-inch *jaw crusher*. In milling terminology, the jaw crusher represented *primary* crushing, or the first of three stages in the comminution process.

From the jaw crusher, ore was fed through two *roll crushers*, which constituted *secondary* crushing. In contrast to the jaw crusher, which crushed the ore between two mechanical arms, each roll crusher was composed of two horizontal cylinders that revolved toward each other, similar to the action of hand-operated wringers on early tub-style washing machines.

The last stage to comminution was grinding, also called *tertiary* crushing. Grinding is used where the metal values can only be separated from the gangue by grinding the ore finer than, say, three-quarters of an inch in diameter. Both the 1916 gravity mill and the improvements added in 1941 completed the comminution process utilizing a *ball mill*. Ore that passed through the primary and secondary comminution circuits was fed into the cylinder and tumbled with three-inch cast-iron balls that crushed and ground the ore to about one-quarter inch in diameter.

The next step in the mineral dressing process is the separation of the ground ore into two products: *concentrate* and *tailings*. The former is enriched, metal-bearing material, whereas the latter is presumed to be waste. Thus tailings are little more than ground ore from which the valuable minerals have been extracted.

The original 1916 gravity mill separated concentrate from crushed ore by taking advantage of the difference in specific gravity between valuable minerals and the gangue. The separating mechanism was called a *shaking table*. Ten such tables, measuring more than five feet wide and up to fifteen feet long, complemented the Mike Horse mill. A dense slurry of ground ore and water was fed onto the table's upper end. Continuous, side-to-side vibrating actions caused the lighter, barren waste to vibrate off the side of the table, while the heavier, metallic component—the concentrate—ran the full length of the table before it was collected. The tailings were flushed into Mike Horse Gulch below the mill.

The gravity separation process worked reasonably well in the mining districts of the early West. Successful variations on the principle predate the Mike Horse by decades and remain in use today. But in the years immediately following World War I, milling at the Mike Horse did not meet expectations. Oral history insists that assays of the gravity-separated concentrate were little different from the quarter-inch tailings flushed into Mike Horse Gulch.[13] In effect, Sterling wasted half the metal content of its ore. The mill's inefficiency would seem at least partially responsible for the company's eventual failure.

Goddard and his cronies probably knew all of this when they pursued their Mike Horse venture, but when they inspected the mine in late 1939 or early 1940, their spirits must have dropped. The log mill building lay idle and broken, its original equipment long since fallen into disrepair or stripped by parts scavengers. Its few unbroken windows faced a barren, rock-strewn gulch. Ocher-stained waste rock and rusting machinery were scattered about. Unpainted buildings not constructed of logs were fabricated from rough-milled lumber protected from the elements by tar paper. The camp's only two-story frame building was held upright by logs propped against its outside walls.

Looking at that scene, Goddard and his partners would have known, or soon determined, that more than paint was required to make the mine productive. A more efficient milling process, though expensive, was imperative if their venture was to have a chance. Subsequently, they began expanding and refitting the mill with new flotation equipment even as they put the mine back into limited production. At first, ore was trucked to several other mills in the county, but by 1941—for the first time in sixteen years— both the Mike Horse Mine and mill were producing again.[14]

The corporation quickly added Robert Porter to its board of directors and made him mine manager.[15] Porter's mining expertise derived from his operation of a sizeable placer gold operation in the Helena Valley. Although placer mining, which is similar to a complex sand and gravel operation, differs markedly from lode mining, Porter was a respected mining man.

Also joining the Mike Horse's roster of miners was Samuel Kornec. His eldest son, Samuel Jr., likewise found work at the mine, although as a truck driver.[16]

During those first months of renewed activity, water for mining and the mill was provided from Mike Horse Creek upstream from the mine's no. 3 portal. To avoid winter freeze-ups, waterlines had to be buried five or six feet. Hand-digging those waterlines proved to be the least popular job at the mine. Installing waterlines during the summer months was gut-wrenching enough, because there was more bedrock than soil. But thawing frozen waterlines in winter proved brutal. Men assigned this task built fires on the surface above the frozen pipes then picked and shoveled away the thawed soil until the fire could be rebuilt deeper in the hole. Eventually, the waterlines thawed.[17]

Electricity came to the Heddleston district in the spring of 1941. The Mike Horse Mining and Milling Company strung it through the Blackfoot Valley from Lincoln under an agreement with Montana Power Company. At the Mike Horse, the primary consumer of electricity was the updated mill. Stung too many times by mining companies demanding electricity but unable to stay in business long enough to pay for the capital cost of stringing power,

Montana Power Company worked out a plan whereby Mike Horse Mining and Milling built the line and deducted the construction cost from its monthly bills.[18]

In contrast to the 1916 mill, which used gravity to separate metallic minerals from gangue, the new mill utilized the more efficient selective flotation process. The mill was larger, too; it functioned on six or seven working levels. The building was eighty feet wide and rose approximately seventy-five feet from the floor of its concentrate bins to the peak of its shed roof above the ore car dump.[19] Mills utilize gravity as much as possible to move ore through the mineral dressing process. For this reason, and because mining frequently occurs in mountainous country, mills are commonly built vertically. Ore is fed into the mill at the top and cascades downward through each process until the concentrate is delivered to trucks waiting at the bottom for transport to the smelter.

One of the most significant differences between the gravity and flotation milling processes is the concentrate *size*, or how fine the ore is crushed and ground in the comminution step. Whereas gravity mills typically crushed and ground the ore to about one-quarter to three-quarters inch in diameter, the more efficient flotation mill probably reduced the ore to "forty-eight mesh," finer than one-hundredth of an inch in diameter, or the texture of fine sand.[20] This makes for more efficient flotation and metal separation, but it simultaneously exposes hundreds of times more pyrite mineral surface area to oxygen and water, which inevitably accelerates undesirable chemical reactions such as acid formation.

Flotation works by separating minerals according to differences in their surface properties. In practice, the ore is reduced to the *size of liberation*, generally the mineral grain size. Water is added to create a *pulp*, along with chemicals to regulate the pulp pH and to modify the surfaces of individual mineral grains. Frequently, acids are used in this step to etch and clean the metallic mineral faces. The pulp is then agitated to a froth by air forced into the system. The desired minerals attach themselves to the froth and are recovered as concentrate: the end product. By design, the gangue neither floats nor froths. Instead, it sinks to the bottom of the flotation chambers to be discharged as tailings.[21]

In addition to increasing mill efficiency, the Mike Horse's new manager was charged with locating new ore reserves. Workings on all three levels were extended along the Mike Horse Vein, and a *winze*, a vertical or near-vertical shaft connecting two mine levels, was sunk to begin development of a new no. 4 level, 125 feet below the no. 3 level.

Mine production more than doubled between 1941 and 1943 to 57,809 tons. Increased production did not automatically lead to profits, however, and by mid-1944 the company was struggling financially, even with the benefit of war-time *premiums*, government subsidies paid for strategic metals. In fact, without the premiums, the Mike Horse lost an average of nearly a dollar per ton of mined ore. Over this three and one-half year period, only the receipt of premiums allowed the Mike Horse to show an operating profit.

During this time, labor shortages and other increased operating expenses caused per-ton mining costs to almost double. It cost close to four dollars to truck a ton of lead concentrate to ASARCO's East Helena smelter. Zinc concentrates were trucked to the railroad siding at Silver City then freighted by rail to the zinc smelter in Great Falls for about the same cost. Other problems also emerged, such as cave-ins in the upper two levels, which resulted in the loss of ore reserves. And nearly four thousand feet of mining on the new no. 4 level proved disappointing.

In response to decreasing certainties about the mine's future, Mike Horse Mining and Milling did what any modern troubled American company might do: it sought a "white knight." It found one in ASARCO, which took interest in the property in late 1943. As Mike Horse Mining and Milling looked around for a savior, ownership changes also occurred. Two of the original five investors, Estill and Dwyer, sold their stock to latecomer Robert Porter, who now owned more than 60 percent of the company and effectively controlled the mine.

ASARCO's initial in-house assessment of the Mike Horse Mine and mill was less than optimistic. ASARCO employed some of the most capable and experienced mining engineers and geologists in North America, and problems faced by the Mike Horse owners did not go undiscovered. ASARCO concluded that records were poorly kept and the mine poorly managed. In September 1944, ASARCO investigators opined that, "the outlook for the continu-

ance of production at the Mike Horse is uncertain, and not especially promising beyond the period of premium payments." Still,
the Heddleston district had the advantage of being geologically
similar to ASARCO properties in northern Idaho's Coeur d'Alene
district, and ASARCO's geologists believed that the Mike Horse, Intermediate, and Little Nell Veins all offered promise. Ultimately,
in spite of all their financial, geological, and engineering reser-
vations, ASARCO's investigators determined that the Heddleston
district had "distinct merit." [22]

ASARCO, through a wholly owned subsidiary, Federal Mines, acquired all the stock of Mike Horse Mining and Milling Company
in mid-1945 for a rumored one million dollars.[23] The original Sterling bondholders also sold to ASARCO the Mike Horse Mine and
supporting patented and unpatented lode claims.[24] ASARCO executives quickly named themselves the board of directors and managing officers of the Mike Horse Mining and Milling Company.[25]
Nearly fifty years after its discovery, the Mike Horse Mine was
finally owned and operated by an experienced, knowledgeable,
well-capitalized, and fully functioning integrated metals mining
and smelting corporation.

ASARCO promptly adopted the company town of Mike Horse,
Montana, as its own, a town whose sole purpose was to support
the mine. By the end of World War II, the mine employed up to
250 miners, mechanics, truck drivers, cooks, engineers, geologists, and other support staff, most of whom lived in the town.
The town had its own company store, post office, and two-room
school. The company maintained local roads, and daily company
buses shuttled nonresident miners between Mike Horse and Lincoln and ferried in groceries and other supplies from Helena. In
addition to constructing a large bunkhouse for single employees,
ASARCO brought in forty prefabricated houses for miners who had
both families and seniority. The separate housing district was located about one-half mile below the mill. Houses came with free
electricity and were heated with fuel oil sold by ASARCO at a subsidized price.

Anaconda Creek now provided the water supply for both the
mine and the town, which were also serviced by a central sewer
system. But in 1945 there was no wastewater treatment comparable to 1990s practices. Instead, sewage was piped from the hous-

4. Mike Horse Mining and Milling Company, main camp: bunkhouse (C), mill (D), office (E), cookhouse (F). Photograph taken following ASARCO's purchase of the property in 1945. Montana Historical Society, Helena.

ing district to a central disposal system located down Mike Horse Gulch then drained directly into the stream.[26]

ASARCO's geologists and engineers developed plans to expand the mine, believing that the Mike Horse Vein, but particularly the Little Nell and Intermediate Veins, would improve with depth. Prior to 1945, neither of these two thinner veins had been seriously developed, although the no. 3 tunnel intercepted both en route to the Mike Horse Vein.

The Mike Horse Mine, never large by industry standards, became a giant anthill. Its workings extended over five hundred vertical feet and reached horizontally for more than a thousand feet along two vein systems and more than two thousand feet on the Mike Horse Vein. To access anticipated reserves, ASARCO added two new levels, no. 6 and no. 8, two hundred and four hundred feet, respectively, below the no. 4 level, even though the latter had proven unprofitable. Levels no. 6 and 8 were also serviced by the inclined shaft, or winze, sunk at the end of the no. 3 tunnel. The mine was a three-dimensional maze, with each level connected to the others by *winzes* and *raises*. In effect, a raise is similar to a winze, differing only by virtue of its construction upward from one mine level to the next. Adjacent vein systems were linked by short *crosscuts*. On the no. 2 level, so much ore and waste was pulled from a *stope* that two sets of ore car–tracks were laid abreast. Battery-powered *trammers* pulled ore out of the mine and returned empty cars to the working faces.[27]

ASARCO controlled the Mike Horse for just several months and had little opportunity to turn the mine around before World War II ended. With the war's end also came the cessation of federal premiums. About this time, the company also realized that its three vein systems were not growing richer with depth as its geologists had predicted. Nonetheless, ASARCO continued mining.

In July of 1949, the mine's management expressed doubt to ASARCO's corporate office in Idaho that significant ore would be located on the no. 8 level of the Mike Horse Vein.[28] Five months later, declining lead and zinc prices compelled the company to suspend mining in the Mike Horse. For 1949, nearly 58,000 tons of ore had been mined, from which 100 ounces of gold, 121,382 ounces of silver, 5,076,000 pounds of lead, and 4,649,200 pounds of zinc were recovered. The concentrate also produced 394,800 pounds of copper.[29] As a result of deeper mining, a new metal now contributed to the mix.

The onset of the Korean War in June of 1950 once again caused world metal prices to surge, and the mine reopened in July. Accompanying this renewed activity was the construction of twenty-one hundred feet of new drifts and crosscuts, mostly on the mine's two lowest levels.[30] The Mike Horse had sputtered, yet once again produced metal for the nation's industrial machine.

By the beginning of 1952, levels no. 4, 6, and 8 were nearly mirror images of level no. 3, which had been mined for more than fifty years. But in August, the mine manager again informed his Idaho bosses that most of the richest ore had already been mined and that if the reserves they knew about were of comparable grade it might not be worth developing.

The mine had reached its greatest underground extent. ASARCO had initiated no new levels since the end of World War II. Instead, mining had proceeded horizontally from along the inclined shaft. Workings reached more than twenty-five hundred feet along levels no. 1 and 2, and upward of forty-three hundred feet along no. 4. Even levels no. 6 and 8 had been mined for over six-tenths of a mile. In all, the Mike Horse possessed more than four miles of underground development. The mountain was a honeycomb.[31]

Groundwater pumping costs in the Mike Horse increased incessantly with the mine's expansion. Miners wore rubber boots against water that ran along the floors of the drifts and crosscuts. Surface water increasingly infiltrated the mine. This was especially problematic on the east end of the no. 2 level, which extended beneath Mike Horse Gulch within thirty vertical feet of Mike Horse Creek. Natural fractures and cracks in the bedrock, augmented by decades of repeated mining-related blasting, provided a ready avenue for creek water to enter the mine. Mine water was collected in a sump on the no. 8 level and pumped to the no. 3 level so it could drain to the ground surface. An estimated two hundred gallons per minute drained from the mine through a partially buried six-inch pipe.[32]

The armistice in Korea had the customary impact of the end of all wars: metal prices began to slide. On 10 November 1952, ASARCO announced the closure of the Mike Horse, naming as its reasons low lead and zinc prices and declining reserves. The company disclosed intentions to remove all equipment from what had been expanded to a three hundred-ton-per-day flotation mill.[33] The water pump below the no. 8 level was switched off and the mine's workings began to flood. Eventually, when water levels rose to the no. 3 level, the mine would begin draining to Mike Horse Gulch and the upper Blackfoot River.

The brief era of big-time mining in the Heddleston district was over. For its investment, ASARCO had produced nearly seven million dollars of concentrate in slightly more than eight years, a time during which operating costs per ton had nearly doubled. The mine showed an operating profit, before accounting for corporate overhead, in six of those eight years. Almost 385,000 tons of ore had been mined, milled, and concentrated.[34] If this ore was consolidated into a single rock cube, it would measure just 165 feet on one side.

In hardrock mining, it is axiomatic that when a once-profitable mine has been worked out by a company, someone else will attempt to prove that the property is still capable of earning a buck. Industry geologists and engineers, as well as most lesser-trained prospectors, cannot seem to help themselves. It is commonly assumed that bad luck or management incompetence, or both, conspired to close down a mine; high-grade ore is always deeper. For this reason, reconnaissance exploration reports throughout the mining industry, both past and present, hardly ever write off an area completely. No one wishes to be thought the fool if a later operator hits it big after they have recommended against it. This axiom proved true with the Mike Horse Mine. Less than eight months after ASARCO closed it, Norman Rogers leased the property from ASARCO and reopened the mine.

From Helena, Norman Rogers was an experienced small miner. He had reputedly been Montana's first independent copper miner, until Anaconda Copper Mining Company refused to buy any more copper ore from him. But Rogers saw opportunity in the idle Mike Horse, and in 1953 he negotiated a lease with ASARCO.[35]

Almost fifty years after Rogers's initial lease, few small mining concerns of Rogers's kind remain. Modern federal and state mine safety and environmental laws and regulations make most small-scale operations substantially more difficult to run profitably. Moreover, few individuals possess the skills necessary to survive economically in small-scale mining operations. The practices of today's capital-intensive, heavily mechanized hardrock mining in the West are vastly different from industry practices five decades ago. Modern hardrock miners are apt to feel more comfortable maneuvering a D-10 Caterpillar in the open-pit gold mines of Nevada than selectively mining a three-foot quartz vein inside a Montana mountain.

By any measure, the Norman Rogers Mining Company was a modest business venture. It employed fewer than ten men—usually half that many—and mined the highest grade ore from the most accessible workings utilizing the simplest and least expensive methods. In contrast to ASARCO, which mined an annual average of forty-eight thousand tons of ore during its tenure, Rogers barely mined a thousand tons in all of 1954. Yet his selective methods were profitable, probably because he engaged in minimal development, shipped bulk ore, and did not operate the mill. Rogers primarily bulldozed the surface above the mine until he exposed a fairly wide zone of mineralization then extracted ore using a crane and a "clamshell" bucket, a method that was simple, relatively inexpensive, and profitable.

By the end of 1956, Rogers had exhausted most of the known

and accessible ore. Still wishing to mine from the surface if possible, he trenched and bulldozed the ground surface east of Mike Horse Creek, near the portal of an abandoned adit to the long-known but unexploited Hog All Vein. The Hog All Lode claim was one of the first two Joseph Hartmiller filed in 1898, even though Hartmiller never mined it. Nor had anyone else.

Rogers thought he was onto something. By this point, he had cumulatively mined and shipped just under five thousand tons of ore. He suspected mineralization in the Hog All Vein east of Mike Horse Creek but halted further work in the area until he could renegotiate his lease with ASARCO.

In response to Rogers's August 1957 request, ASARCO dispatched two experienced engineers to the Mike Horse. They were impressed with what they saw and heard. Rogers had done a pretty fair job of mining the best ore left near the surface. In fact, they calculated that Rogers's selective surface methods had produced ore of higher grade than any of his predecessors, including ASARCO. ASARCO's engineers nonetheless doubted whether any new ore bodies discovered and developed by Rogers would be any better than what the company had already taken from the mine. But after comparing ASARCO's mining costs and profits for the period 1945 through 1952, with royalty payments paid to ASARCO by Rogers under the existing lease, they concluded that leasing the mine to Rogers was 60 percent more profitable, on a per-ton basis, than if ASARCO operated the mine. Ultimately, Rogers received his new ten-year lease and mined the Mike Horse area through 1964, although little ever came of his Hog All aspirations. For its part, ASARCO continued receiving royalties from Rogers on low tonnages of comparatively high grade ore of lead, silver, zinc, and copper.[36]

Because Rogers mined principally on the mountainside above the mine, and not in the gulch bottom, it is unlikely that he made existing environmental conditions worse. Qualitatively, Rogers was neither better nor worse than ASARCO or its predecessors. Just smaller.

America's World War II needs, as well as those for the years immediately following, made environmental sacrifices on a national scale expedient. Hardrock mining had for decades successfully justified the need for such sacrifices, so nothing altered the industry's approach. Available Mike Horse Mine records for the era fail to mention any environmental problems related to the mine and mill's operations, including the effects of mine dewatering on the upper Blackfoot River. This is not surprising, really. But the absence of documentation of significant environmental damages during the 1940s and 1950s is not evidence that the river was recovering from past mining or that mining practices or conditions in the district were improving. Rather, it is an indication that no one cared enough to document change or force the collection of useful scientific information. Few national voices of the time, and no one at the mine or in the Heddleston district, took notice of or attempted to address the river's ongoing degradation. So what if there were no fish? Callous disregard was not criminal. It was business as usual. The consequences of the hardrock mining business included putting up with contaminated public waters.

In spite of this state of affairs, the 1940 lease between Stampfly and Goddard and his partners contained an intriguing clause: "DISPOSAL OF WASTE, REFUSE AND MINE WATER: The Lessees shall make such provision for the disposal of waste, refuse and mine water from the mine or mines on the demised premises that the same shall not be a nuisance nor injure the property of the Lessor, or of others, nor obstruct or contaminate any stream, or obstruct any right of way or other means of transportation or travel on the lands of the Lessor or others."[37]

Rogers's 1958 lease agreement with ASARCO also prohibited him from disposing of mine waste or waters in any manner that would prove a nuisance to others or "contaminate any stream."[38]

To the nonlawyer, these lease clauses seem to have been designed to protect water quality from the effects of mining, and one might logically wonder why somebody did not do something at the time. Actually, though, the language was intended to shield the lessors (that is, the owner) in the unlikely event of civil litigation resulting from environmental damages. Misleading contract language such as this was standard boilerplate. Including such a clause gave the lessor a plausible excuse that the lessee had violated the contractual agreement and was solely responsible for any damages. Indeed, lessors could claim that they were as much a victim as anyone.

In retrospect, clauses like these were not credible. Enforcing such contractual language would have necessitated civil, not criminal, complaints, and no one in remote mining districts like the Heddleston bothered with such trivial matters. Further, no toothsome federal or state statutes of the era protected water quality, and no federal or state agency prevented mines from contaminating streams and rivers adjacent to their operations. No crimes were committed. Such clauses were, in effect, empty promises, and both parties agreed to them with the proverbial "wink and a nod." Anyone who truly objected to the harsh realities of hardrock mining could battle the mining company in court.

Fifty years later, long after the Mike Horse had its best days, we know that the exploits of the 1940s formed the basis for future monumental environmental consequences. The cause-and-effect link was not obvious at the time, but nature was patient. Big changes were coming.

5. The Dam

The disposal of mill tailings is a major environmental problem. Apart from the visual effect on the landscape, the major ecological effect is usually water pollution, arising from the discharge of mill water carrying fine particles, dissolved metals, mill reagents or sulfur or cyanide compounds. . . . The most widely used method is to contain the tailings within a man-made dam. —Gordon L. Zucker and Hassan E. El-Shall, *A Guide to Mineral Processing*

The [Mike Horse] dam was breached during the storm of June 17 through June 20, 1975. The breach on the east abutment of the dam is about 150 feet across and cut to bedrock. . . . The dam is not functioning as a holding structure. Runoff is washing toxic sediments downstream into the Blackfoot River. —Helena National Forest, August 1975

CLIMBING INTO UPPER BEARTRAP GULCH, the human eye picks out a curious straight line nearly hidden in the trees. At first, the eye is drawn to the linearity, even if the brain does not know why. Natural scientists are trained to distrust straight lines in nature, so the eye focuses on the form until its identity is clear. It is the five-hundred-foot-long crest of the Mike Horse tailings dam hunkered squarely in the center of Beartrap Gulch.

Beneath a warm September sun I clamber down and across Mike Horse Creek and walk to the toe of the dam. The ankle-high grass is lush and wet, the underlying earth soft and spongy. The moisture feeding this turf rises from beneath the dam's east end, where seeps coalesce in a small channel to flow several hundred feet before joining Mike Horse Creek. The seepage is clear and cold; nowhere is the stream more than a foot deep and several across. Prior to 1975, this minuscule flow supported a small population of cutthroat trout. There are no fish today.

Where this clear-running seepage meets Mike Horse Creek, a peculiar chemical reaction takes place. Above this junction, Mike Horse Creek runs rusty and thick as cream over broken rock smeared with iron hydroxide. Nothing lives in this reach of the creek, nor has it for decades. Below the confluence, the pH of the combined flows rises, and dissolved metals precipitate and settle to the stream bottom. As these metal hydroxides gag the streambed, the water grows crystalline yet remains lethal to most aquatic life.

Downstream, Beartrap Creek flattens, and the canyon floor widens to something like a hundred feet. Shattered rock covers the canyon floor, much of it angular and rough edged, unlike the rounded cobbles that normally form a mountain valley bottom. Over centuries, streams roll boulders downstream, where they become sand and rounded cobbles after being banged together and their corners knocked off. The angular fragments in Beartrap Creek tell a different history. These were blasted from the heart of the Mike Horse Mine. Most are green or maroon argillite, but occasionally larger chunks of diorite are visible.

There is little streamside vegetation. The only plant life is random lodgepole saplings. The only evidence of former sizable trees is a single charred and rotting stump. It is more than a foot in diameter where it protrudes through the mine waste.

A quarter-mile downstream, I am drawn to an adit penetrating the mountain from near stream level. Like most district adits, it is not on local maps. Its roof has collapsed and the depression that was once the portal is obscured by Douglas fir and lodgepole pine springing from the canyon side.

A quarter-mile farther, the valley widens again where Anaconda Creek approaches from the right. Two weathered board-and-tar-paper shacks stand in a sunny meadow, all that remains of Silver Camp, the so-called demographic heart of the Heddleston district in its first years. The vigorous pine and fir standing in this meadow have escaped the effects of Mike Horse Creek.

As I retrace my steps upstream, I notice a sliver of previously unseen water entering Beartrap Creek from the canyon's east slope. In the sun, the trickle shines like a new penny. I track it to its source, a narrow patch of mill tailings stranded near the foot of the slope, above and away from Beartrap Creek. Stained gray, brown, and red, the sandy material is saturated by seepage from another adit hidden behind ten-foot fir and ground-covering juniper. The adit discharges less water than a garden hose—barely two gallons per minute—but after penetrating the tailings it continues down-canyon bright as a child's ribbon.

Much later, atop the east end of the dam, I gaze south over perhaps ten acres of impounded water. Its surface ripples in the afternoon breeze. Its color mimics a pale sky. Above the dam, upper Beartrap Creek is so crowded by aspen, willow, knee-high grasses, and wet-loving forbs that one can find the stream only by following the lowest line on the canyon floor and thrashing about until one's boots are soaked. Upper Beartrap Creek feeds and nourishes this artificial lake, which, according to the Kornec brothers, supports a healthy population of fair-sized cutthroat trout. "Two-pounders," they say.

Modern floods of upper Beartrap Creek are routed through this man-made lake by a carefully engineered bypass structure. But in June of 1975, following an ugly sequence of meteorological events, Beartrap Creek flooded and breached an emergency spillway on the dam's east end. Because the dam was constructed of little more than tailings—fine sand, really—nothing kept the running water from cutting to its core. Coursing water ate through the heart of the dam like hot steel through ice, entraining mill tailings that had been stored for decades. The Blackfoot River was assaulted once again.

When the Mike Horse Mining and Milling Company reopened the mine in 1940, more than a decade had passed since its closure. Yet during this brief interval, public attitudes toward mining and long-standing industry practices had begun to change. From the Appalachian coalfields to the hardrock mining districts of the West, the industry had been pilloried by the press, the public, and the courts for discharging mining and milling waste directly into streams, rivers, and lakes. Federal and state laws had not outlawed such practices; rather, it was the rising tide of public opinion that precipitated these changes. In the West, discharging raw mill tailings into streams and rivers was no longer acceptable.[1]

In Mike Horse Gulch, it was too late for new mill tailings disposal practices to have beneficial effects. Mike Horse Creek, lower Beartrap Creek, and the upper Blackfoot River were already barren of fish and other aquatic life at least as far downstream as Pass Creek and the upper swamp, a distance of three miles. Even so, the new owners chose to permanently store all future mill waste behind a dam rather than flush it into Mike Horse Creek.

Although the new owners did not leave a record of their reasons, their approach may have been brought about more by enlightened self-interest than faddish public opinion. In their upgrade of the Mike Horse Mill, they were implementing the most modern milling technology available. Significant changes were probably necessary. Developed and refined in Australia at the end of the nineteenth century, the new flotation technology had only been in use in Montana since 1911.[2] Flotation was more complex than gravity separation but had already proven capable of treating complex ores more profitably than gravity separation. To achieve this greater concentration efficiency, flotation required that the ore be ground to the uniform texture of fine sand. The owners further anticipated increased mineral dressing rates, which would result in the generation of more tailings. The combination of finer texture and greater volumes made tailings management more difficult, a problem the company addressed by building a dam and impounding the tailings behind it.

The dam site was obvious. There was little room to store the predicted quantities in Mike Horse Gulch above the mine and mill. Economics and common sense likewise dictated that the tailings be moved by gravity, which eliminated any disposal site above the mill. Practical operational constraints also ruled out a dam across Mike Horse Gulch below the mill, because there was no telling whether the company might wish to expand its surface facilities in the future.

The company sited the dam just above Beartrap Creek's confluence with Mike Horse Gulch, where the mountains crowded the canyon floor to form a natural notch. The mill was above the dam site, so tailings could be gravity-fed to the impoundment in elevated wooden flumes without incurring unwanted power costs.

A laborer known to the Kornec boys only as Mr. Watt directed the tailings slurry at the dam. By periodically building additional, higher flumes and guiding the tailings discharge back and forth across the mouth of Beartrap Gulch, Watt steadily raised the dam height and increased storage capacity behind it. The heaviest and coarsest tailings particles settled from the slurry first, followed by finer sands, called *slimes*. The dam crest rose as the coarser solids

5. Mike Horse tailings dam and impoundment at the mouth of Beartrap Gulch, circa late 1940s. Courtesy John J. Thompson Jr.

settled adjacent to the dam, while the slimes and water ponded upstream and behind it. This *perimeter discharge* method allowed Watt to successively raise the dam's crest while preventing ponded water and slimes from flowing downstream to the river.[3]

An inherent limitation to the use of uniform, fine-grained tailings to construct a dam is its lack of engineering strength. A detailed explanation of the engineering principles at work are beyond the scope of this text, but a primitive experiment can demonstrate the problem. Take a bucket of sand from a child's sandbox, dump it upside down on the ground, then lift the bucket. If the sand is damp, it may stand upright in the cast of the bucket. More likely, especially if dry, the contents will slump to a shapeless pile. Wet or dry, the sand cast will not support any appreciable weight without collapsing. It is largely for this reason that early dams constructed from tailings are prone to failure. Fortunately, the vast majority of modern earthen embankments are painstakingly designed and constructed with carefully selected and managed materials, few or none analogous to tailings.

An associated problem triggered by the new tailings disposal facility was that Beartrap Creek flowed into the impoundment behind the dam. Above the dam, Beartrap Gulch drains a mere one and one-half square miles and during much of the year generates little natural stream flow. But intense thunderstorms or abrupt spring snowmelt could unleash torrents capable of destroying the tailings storage facility and breaching the dam. Thus, Beartrap Creek had to be diverted around the impoundment, and emergency means of releasing water from the impoundment had to be devised in case it unexpectedly filled to capacity.

The company responded to these challenges with several standard engineering fixes. To handle the normal flow of Beartrap Creek, the company excavated a ditch along the impoundment's west side. Stream flow was diverted into the ditch, around the impoundment and dam, and released to Mike Horse Creek below the mill. Water impounded behind the dam was decanted from the pond by a twenty-four-inch diameter concrete pipe. When water in the impoundment rose high enough, it entered the vertical decant pipe and flowed through it until "daylighting" below the dam. The inlet elevation for the decant pipe was lower than the dam crest. As long as the combined flows into and bypassing the tailings impoundment did not exceed the capacity of the diversion and decant system, the dam was theoretically in no danger of being overtopped and breached.[4]

As the dam and Beartrap Creek diversion became a reality, friction developed between the company and Samuel Kornec. No one questioned that the company owned the patented mining claims composing the mine and blanketing the nearby area. And there is little doubt, today, that the dam and diversion lie off these same claims. But in the early 1940s just who controlled the surface beneath the dam and stream diversion was less clear.

At the time, Heddleston district residents implicitly assumed that all surface within and surrounding "their" district could be fairly lumped into one of two classes: patented claims, which were and remain private property, and unpatented claims, which were treated like private property even if they were not, regardless of whether formal title had been transferred from the federal government. Unpatented claims were those that had been filed on with the Lewis and Clark County recorder but had not been developed to the point where title could be awarded to the miner. Because of this uncertainty, a dispute developed between Kornec and the company. More than fifty years later, we do not know the origin of the dispute, only that it occurred and that hearsay and knowledge of the times suggest that the dispute centered on surface control.

Samuel Kornec and his family had prospected and mined in and around Beartrap Gulch since the 1920s. He had filed on lode claims there in 1928. (At one time, the Kornec family had ninety claims "under ribbon," meaning they had identified and marked the claims on the ground but had not completed formal surveying and filing with the county recorder, the next legal step required to perfect their rights under the 1872 mining law. Years later, the Kornecs reduced the number to thirty-six and filed on them. Later still, they reduced their core holding to the ten unpatented claims the family controls today.[5])

Regardless of their legal status and whether individual claims were under ribbon or unpatented, miners and mining companies of the era treated the land as if it was theirs, a practice essentially unchanged since the Civil War. In mining country, claims, whatever their actual legal status, are treated as private property. Claimants expected the same treatment accorded proven property owners. These attitudes persisted even though their claims fell within the federally owned Helena National Forest.

Exactly when the dispute erupted is unknown, although evidence and memories suggest it sparked in 1944. The dispute pitted Kornec against a man named Lee Marty, a carpenter for the mining company. The company had directed Marty to construct a new stream diversion on Beartrap Creek about one-quarter mile above the tailings dam. Since its beginning in 1941, the dam had been raised several times and the tailings pond had continued to back up Beartrap Gulch until the original diversion became inoperable. (The practice of diverting and rerouting streams around tailings impoundments is prevalent throughout the mining industry. The practice protects downstream aquatic environments more than if streams and tailings are mingled and left uncontrolled.)

Kornec apparently claimed the surface where Marty began building the diversion. Perhaps Marty was told by the mine superintendent where to build the diversion; perhaps he took it upon himself to fix the spot. Rosie Kornec insists that his father had an agreement with the mine superintendent on what was and was not Kornec's unpatented surface. The company's patented and unpatented claims would likely have been marked and well known. Presumably, the company was free to place the diversion on its own property or on unclaimed forest service land.

Precisely where the contested diversion was constructed in 1944 is not clear. What is known is that Samuel Kornec and Lee Marty argued several times over as many days, and that at some point Marty ended the debate by planting the blade of a shovel against the side of Kornec's head.

Margaret Kornec had her first clue that something was wrong when her husband failed to appear for supper. She eventually found him wandering in the dark through the brush near the diversion site, bleeding and confused. He was never the same. In the following months he became increasingly confused. His mind wandered and his speech stopped in midthought. At some point he was unable to work. Two years later he died. The Kornec family received no compensation for the loss of its primary breadwinner.

Rosie and George still have their father's death certificate. A half-century after its composition, the neatly typed, well-preserved single-page document states the cause of death as "multiple brain abscesses of one-year duration due to active, bi-lateral pulmonary tuberculosis." Physicians at Sacred Heart Hospital in Spokane, Washington, expressed disbelief that anyone could have lived with such brain damage, much less for several years. The certificate's reference to long-term brain abscesses supports their collective opinion, although mention of "active, bi-lateral pulmonary tuberculosis" makes no medical sense. Queried medical professionals have no reasonable explanation for this bizarre phrase. Possibly it was born between a tired doctor's handwritten notes and a bored administrative clerk's faulty typing.

As for Lee Marty, history and memories are less forgiving. George and Rosie are unaware of any criminal or civil complaints pressed against the company carpenter; Marty retained his job and appears to have never suffered legal consequences for his violence. When asked what became of Marty, Rosie said, "He was around here for years. He finally ended up in California where some guy buried a sledgehammer in his brain. That guy was just plain mean."[6] More than fifty years after their father's death, George and Rosie are reconciled with history and their family's treatment. They tell their story without bitterness or animus. It is how things were.

By November of 1952, when the Mike Horse Mine finally closed and the mill ceased discharging waste to the dam and tailings impoundment, the unsung Mr. Watt and his successors had raised the dam crest between 50 and 60 feet above the creek and extended it 450 feet across the mouth of Beartrap Gulch. The dam was a giant plug stuck in the canyon's craw. Stored in and behind the dam was an estimated *one million cubic yards* of tailings, a portion of which was covered with 50 acre-feet of water.[7] (An acre-foot is the quantity of water necessary to cover an acre to a depth of one foot, equivalent to 43,560 cubic feet, or 325,872 gallons.) Although puny in comparison to the massive concrete and steel structures erected throughout the West by the U.S. Bureau of Reclamation, the Mike Horse tailings dam was a sizable edifice. Less obvious was that the dam's stability depended upon the limited strength of the sandy mill waste from which it was constructed.

Historical hindsight is perfect, and looking back from the 1990s makes for flawless retrospection. It is easy to question the dam's original construction, as well as the decision to abandon it without arranging for its continuing maintenance. At least hypothetically, ASARCO should have been responsible for the dam embankment's integrity and for the twenty-four-inch decant pipe and the Beartrap Creek diversion. But at this juncture in America's mining history, the difference between moral responsibility and practice was vast. When mining companies closed down unprofitable mines and mills, they characteristically salvaged what equipment they could and moved on to their next project. The General Mining Law of 1872 stood unchanged, and federal land management agencies lacked effective rules—some critics would insist the agencies lacked spines—requiring monitoring of abandoned or inactive mine and mill sites. Likewise, the 1950s preceded enactment of effective hardrock mining statutes at the state level. Certainly, this was the case in Montana. Regardless of the causes and failed responsibilities, however, the Mike Horse tailings dam, like hundreds of similar structures throughout the West, was awarded, at best, little thought. At worst, it was ignored and forgotten.

Montana's Rockies experience more than frigid, snowy winters and hot, dry summers. During the spring and early summer months, the mountains are occasionally pounded by rains from frontal systems stalled over the region or by intense, short-lived downpours from afternoon thunderstorms. When combined with warm temperatures, heavy rains can wreak havoc on mountain snowpacks and cause significant floods.

Historians describe the floods of June 1964 as among the most devastating in modern history. Throughout western Montana, raging waters scoured stream- and riverbeds and flooded towns. Many small dams were overtopped and breached. Later that year, Helena National Forest undertook an engineering inspection of the Mike Horse tailings dam and found the structure to be deteriorating. Likewise, it noted that an emergency flood spillway had been added to the dam's east abutment earlier in the year. Who constructed the spillway is unclear, although it may have been Norman Rogers, ASARCO's lessee.[8] In the 1960s, mining companies rarely, if ever, returned to the scene of past operations to improve environmental safeguards.

When the June flood occurred, Beartrap Creek exceeded the combined capacity of the diversion and the pond's decant pipe. The overflowing pond used the emergency spillway. Fortunately, these three structures safely passed the 1964 flood. But the dam did not escape unscathed. As impounded floodwaters flowed over the lip of the spillway, the spillway itself nearly failed. When the dam was inspected again, forest service engineers observed *headcutting* in the face of the dam beneath the spillway.[9] Headcutting refers to the incision made in unconsolidated materials—in this case the sandy tailings—by the erosive force of running water. The spillway had worked as designed, but not without incurring some damage. The Blackfoot River clearly dodged one of nature's most formidable assaults.

Enter the Anaconda Copper Mining Company.

ASARCO had given up on the Mike Horse Mine and the Heddleston district in 1952, but by 1963 Anaconda Copper Mining Company, the Butte-based copper giant, had developed its own exploration program for the district, one focused on suspected deep copper and molybdenum reserves. ASARCO still controlled most patented and unpatented claims in the district, including the

Mike Horse Mine and mill, so Anaconda was forced to lease these properties. By late 1964, Anaconda had either leased the claims or purchased them outright. Included in these transactions was the transfer to Anaconda of Norman Rogers's Mike Horse lease with ASARCO, which Rogers had been working since 1953. For just his lease rights, Anaconda paid Rogers nearly $106,000.[10]

Jerry Stern, the Lincoln district ranger for the Helena National Forest, advised Anaconda in November of 1964 that the forest engineer had inspected the Mike Horse tailings dam since the June floods. In response to concerns subsequently expressed by his engineer, Stern requested that Anaconda "determine a course of action to bring this structure up to safety requirements."[11]

Anaconda representatives met with Stern in the first week of December and somehow convinced him that his concerns were unfounded. An internal Anaconda letter summarized the meeting: "Upon learning about the design and operation of the water bypass facilities and the relatively small volume of water retained by the pond, he [Stern] decided that little or no such danger exists."[12]

In short, Anaconda and the forest service soothed each other into believing that because the tailings dam had survived the disastrous 1964 floods with little more than minor headcutting, nothing more needed be done to maintain its structural integrity.

Anaconda had already hired John Thompson to maintain the diversion ditch and watch the dam.[13] This possibly is what allayed Stern's concerns. Thompson was no stranger to the Mike Horse, having trucked concentrate and other supplies for the mine and mill since 1940. When ASARCO closed the mill in 1952, Thompson had moved to Lincoln and made his living, along with his son, John Jr., as a heavy equipment operator and trucking contractor.[14] Thompson would have kept the diversion free-flowing and clear of debris for Anaconda and cast an occasional watchful eye on the dam. If the dam required repair or professional inspection, Anaconda surely would have insisted on professional engineering assistance.

Eight years passed. In November of 1972, a new Lincoln district ranger, Neil Peterson, again voiced concerns for the Mike Horse dam's safety. In a 2 November memorandum, Peterson recounted that both past (presumably 1964) and recent (September 1972) inspections indicated "deteriorating conditions which could lead to failure problems."

Peterson raised two noteworthy points. First, there was no obvious operating outlet from the impoundment except the "unlined, earth emergency spillway which will not stand any prolonged flow due to prior (1964) un-repaired damage"; and second, Anaconda's construction of a new regulating structure at the head of the impoundment earlier in the year had revealed the bypass ditch to be weak.[15] Almost nothing had been done since 1964 to improve or stabilize either the dam or the flood-control facilities.

Anaconda again refuted the district's concerns and insisted that the dam was safe and well-maintained. An internal company memorandum from 6 December followed by a single day a meeting between forest service and Anaconda officials, during which all reportedly agreed that Anaconda had assumed responsibility from ASARCO for operating and maintaining the Mike Horse dam and that the dam's condition was largely the same as had been observed in the 1964 forest service engineering report. No reference was made to Anaconda's reported reconstruction of the Beartrap Creek diversion structure above the tailings impoundment earlier that year.[16]

Anaconda had forced the forest service to blink at least twice when the dam's reliability was questioned. By the 1970s, the forest service was only beginning to assemble the technical expertise capable of evaluating inactive and abandoned mining facilities on forest land. The agency's lack of confidence and assertiveness is understandable. Yet nature is ambivalent to human compromise, and while Anaconda and the forest service engaged in eight years of self-delusion, nature's clock kept ticking.

In retrospect, it is fair to note that Anaconda had other pressing concerns. During the early and mid-1970s, Anaconda was waging a battle for its very corporate life, having had the bulk of its mineral assets nationalized by Chile and its North American operations paralyzed by labor unrest and low copper prices. After substantial downsizing and implementation of minimal operating budgets, Anaconda had neither the means nor the corporate resolve to oversee and maintain its far-flung mineral empire, especially a marginally stable tailings dam in an inactive mining district.

June of 1975 began much like any other June in the Northern Rockies. April and May had been cool and cloudy, which allowed the mountain snowpack to linger. But in a region prone to meteorological extremes, averages do not apply; weather fluctuations are as dependable as weather itself.

On 17 June 1975, a Tuesday, a warm, moist air mass from the Gulf of Mexico drifted north and collided with colder air over western Montana, resulting in three days of statistically ordinary rainfall. Three days of steady rain might normally fill mountain streams and cause minor flooding. As long as heavy rains do not pound the earth and flatten young plants, farmers and ranchers on the plains smile at the always-needed moisture. But so much rain falling on the Divide's residual snowpack had nowhere to go but into streams already swollen from melting snow.

Warm nights aggravated the situation. Cool nights allow a gradually melting snowpack to refreeze, or at least slow the rate of melt, but warm nights permit the melting to continue. Covered by melting or frozen snow, the earth was unable to absorb or retard the runoff. Beartrap Creek began to rise.[17]

By the next day, Wednesday, John Thompson and his son were concerned about the Mike Horse tailings impoundment, and they snagged a ride on a Montana National Guard helicopter to inspect upper Beartrap Creek and the dam. Most streams in the upper Blackfoot River drainage were already out of their banks. Mike Horse Creek, normally little more than a trickle, raged through the mining camp, gouging out a new channel four to six feet deep and twice as wide. Several abandoned-mine buildings had collapsed into the torrent and were torn apart as they rolled and floated down the gulch.

Beartrap Creek roared past the Kornec house and into the tailings impoundment. From the air, the Thompsons observed that the twenty-four-inch decant pipe, normally expected to direct floods safely past the dam, was not up to the task. Thompson later redirected Beartrap Creek into the diversion along the impoundment's west side leading to Mike Horse Creek below the dam. The Thompsons recognized the dam's tenuous situation, but with flooding already making access difficult they believed there was little they could do other than warn Margaret Kornec, George and Rosie's aging mother, who still lived alongside Beartrap Creek.[18]

6. Mike Horse tailings dam following the 19 June 1975 flood that breached its east end (left side of the photograph). Beartrap Creek flows unimpeded through the breach into Mike Horse Creek. Montana Department of Fish, Wildlife and Parks.

The Kornec residence had no phone, so the Thompsons called Rosie Kornec in Butte. Rosie recalls the warning: "They got all excited and called me in Butte and said they'd been over here with a helicopter and she's marooned in there. And I told them, 'what the hell do you mean, she's marooned. She's got more food stockpiled in there than all Lincoln's got." [19]

Characteristically, Margaret Kornec could take care of herself. And her son knew it.

George Kornec was working in Lincoln at the time and living with his mother. His memory of the morning of Thursday, 19 June, is solemn: "When we got up, we could see where the water was up high enough to wash on that right hand [east] side of the dam over on the hillside. So we . . . called John Thompson and Charlie Potter [an Anaconda employee known to the Kornecs], and told them you'd better get up here and look at this tailings dam, that it's washing out on one side. Told them, if you want, we can take our bulldozer and open up that diversion ditch over on the other [west] side to keep it from washing the dam out. They said, 'Oh, don't even worry about it. We'll check it tomorrow.' Well, we told

7. Close-up of breached Mike Horse tailings dam following the 19 June 1975 flood. Exposed mud is actually mill tailings. Montana Department of Fish, Wildlife and Parks.

them the way this stuff [runoff] is coming off [from the Divide], it might not be here tomorrow." [20]

For a while, the diversion performed adequately. But on Thursday evening, two related failures sealed the dam's fate. The hill slope beneath a portion of the Beartrap Creek diversion slumped into the pond and forced the creek into the impoundment. The same small landslide also plugged the twenty-four-inch-decant pipe, which had until then been running full. Later, the diversion structure at the head of the impoundment failed, allowing Beartrap Creek's entire flow to enter the impoundment. The water level in the small reservoir continued rising. At this point, the dam's sole remaining flood-control structure was the damaged emergency flood spillway. When the floodwaters reached the spillway elevation, the impoundment began spilling.

The emergency flood spillway had not been repaired since the 1964 flood. Escaping waters quickly exploited the existing headcuts and sliced through the unconsolidated mill tailings. As the torrent enlarged the incision, the discharge increased, widening the breach to 150 feet. Floodwaters did not stop their downward excavation until reaching bedrock.

For the next several days, even after the rainfall ended, Beartrap Creek continued its free-flowing surge through the breached tailings dam. Tailings that had been stored behind the dam for three decades were flushed into lower Beartrap Creek and on to the Blackfoot River.[21]

The flood and the breach of the tailings dam effectively isolated George and his mother from the outside world. Beartrap Creek rose until it surrounded their house and eroded channels on both sides. When the floodwaters finally receded, their house perched on a muddy island, intact but teetering. Miles downriver, the flooding Blackfoot River backed up behind the embankment where Flesher Pass Road crossed the river. Logs floated behind the embankment. Muddy, gray water shot through the culvert beneath the highway.

Response to the failure of the Mike Horse tailings dam was slow in coming, although little could have been done immediately following the flood. Surface access to the dam and upper Beartrap Creek was impeded by the now-declining floodwaters. Pass Creek had washed out much of Mike Horse Road near its junction with the river. Four-wheel-drive vehicles could not navigate the three-feet-deep floodwaters near the mouth of Shoue Gulch.[22]

John Thompson alerted Anaconda, and company officials flew over the site within forty-eighty hours.[23] The first state of Montana regulatory official did not arrive on the scene until six days after the dam's failure. By the time the official arrived, Anaconda was repairing the diversion structure and ditch. He estimated that twenty thousand cubic yards of tailings had been washed downstream for at least a mile. His one-page report notes that until this event his agency had hardly been aware of the dam's existence.[24]

Two months later, forest service officials reported that *two hundred thousand* cubic yards of pyritic, metal-bearing tailings had escaped the impoundment and been transported at least ten miles downriver.[25] A month following the publication of this report, Anaconda's consultant asserted that, "About 100,000 tons of tailings were released into the lower reaches of Beartrap Creek and the upper Blackfoot River drainage." [26]

Most of Montana first became aware of the dam failure on Sunday, 29 June, ten days after the event. Helena's *Independent Record* reported that state regulatory authorities had both flown over and visited the site on the ground and quoted a spokesman for the state's Department of Health and Environmental Sciences as saying "there is substantial stream damage due to the ruptured dam. We're hoping the effects won't be as bad as it looks now." Anaconda spokesmen assured the public that the company was already working on repairs.[27]

The next day, 30 June, the *Independent Record* provided more information concerning the failure's significance. An ecologist for Montana's Department of Fish and Game reported that cutthroat trout had been spawning at the time and would be affected: "When you see how bad it looks, it's hard to imagine it won't have detrimental effects on the river." Ominously, he compared tailings impoundments to "time bombs that are scattered wherever there has been mining, and which are just sitting there waiting for circumstances to cause something like this."[28]

While Anaconda hurried to repair the dam and return Beartrap Creek to the diversion, evidence mounted concerning the significance of the release of mill tailings to the river. Immediately following the dam failure, observers who flew over the area noted that they could, on the basis of color alone, distinguish floodwaters affected by tailings from those influenced by logging. For several days following the dam failure, ash-colored, tailings-laden waters were observed as far downriver as the Blackfoot River's confluence with Landers Fork, nearly fifteen miles below the dam. Only below Landers Fork did dun-colored waters from Landers Fork and other tributaries mask the influence of the tailings.[29]

Anaconda temporarily repaired the stream diversion within nine days, but the breached dam continued to allow tailings into the river system for at least three weeks. The river transported tailings down river for several months after the disaster. As floodwaters slackened, the fine-grained mill waste was deposited into the river and streambeds and on adjacent floodplains.[30]

Even if no one walked the riverbank to count dead fish, fishery biologists were able to partially document the consequences to the river's fishery and supporting aquatic ecosystem. Cutthroat trout in the tailings pond had vanished, and the flood markedly worsened the already poor aquatic habitat in the upper river by smothering it with fine-grained sediment. Over the following weeks, biologists undertook limited water quality, aquatic bottom fauna, and fish survival studies and compared the results with comparable data from several years earlier. Not surprisingly, the fishery and supporting ecosystem evidenced severe impacts as far downstream as where Highway 279 crossed the river, a distance of roughly ten miles. Brook and cutthroat trout populations had been reduced by approximately 80 percent. Either cutthroat had been unable to spawn, or there had been a frightful mortality of eggs or young-of-the-year after spawning had taken place. Moreover, the number of bottom fauna had declined by from 65 to 85 percent. The diversity of those genera—which represents a well-established means of characterizing overall ecosystem health—showed similar reductions.[31]

Detailed toxicological examinations of dead trout to ascertain what killed them were never completed, but one state biologist satisfied his own curiosity by placing live trout in a screened box immersed in the tailings-laden river water. The fish died.[32]

Bob Dent is a spare, serious man, fiftyish, with graying hair. He knows the Blackfoot River well, having spent boyhood summers fishing it from a family cabin in Lincoln. Educated in the 1960s at the University of Montana, he became the state's first fishery pathologist and then the first trained aquatic biologist employed by a mining company in the United States.

More than twenty years after the dam's collapse, he is engaging but cautious. A career spent responding to hostile environmentalists and regulatory officials makes one that way. Over coffee in a café near his Colorado home, he was polite and patient. He still seems to believe in Anaconda.

In 1964 Anaconda began exploring a deep copper and molybdenum ore body in the Heddleston district with an eye to opening a large open-pit mine. Anaconda recognized, with encouragement from Montana's Department of Fish and Game and in spite of a growing awareness of chronic problems with the Mike Horse Mine, that the Blackfoot River was a valuable fishery. Over the next decade, Anaconda intermittently supported and participated in biological and water quality studies on the river. When Dent joined Anaconda in 1971, he was assigned to the company's Heddleston project, even though he was, as he put it, "a kid wet behind the ears, fresh out of school, picking bugs along the Clark Fork River."

On the day after the dam failed, 20 June, Dent was one of the first to fly over Beartrap Creek and the breached dam. The company had already decided to act, and Dent had been assigned to manage the problem's resolution. Anaconda also retained an engineering firm to evaluate the failed dam, make recommendations, and design and oversee its rehabilitation. Dent coordinated the consultant's activities.

Anaconda felt the pressure of some of Montana's first environmental bad press. According to Dent, the company responded admirably: "Anaconda didn't cut any corners. I tell you, it was balls to the walls from the get-go to get that thing closed in so we didn't experience another environmental problem the following spring. Remember our window of opportunity. The thing washed out in June. Snowfall drives you out of there in November."

Indeed, in the aftermath of the dam failure and release of so many thousands of cubic yards of stored tailings into the river and its aquatic ecosystem, Anaconda was under considerable pressure to make things right. Dent acknowledged that the company was "so sensitive to environmental bad press that we really didn't ask a lot of questions or try to determine who really was responsible."[33]

Helena National Forest officials also did not waste time quibbling over accountability for the dam's failure. The agency must have known that there were reasons to suggest its own miscarried responsibility. In addition to being faced down twice by Anaconda—in 1964 and again in 1972—the Beartrap Creek diversion structure above the pond was located on forest service ground. Should the agency have been involved in controlling flows into the impoundment? Might not the forest service be subject to some of the blame?

By August Helena National Forest completed and released an environmental analysis of various alternatives for the dam's reconstruction. The analysis was required by the National Environmental Policy Act, signed into law by President Nixon just six years earlier. The environmental analysis specifically stated that "Restoration of the tailings holding capacity is imperative before the spring runoff of 1976."

Chief among the alternatives analyzed and compared by Helena National Forest was Anaconda's proposal to reconstruct the dam, emergency flood spillway, and Beartrap Creek diversion and to manage the dam under a special-use permit from the forest. Anaconda already bore responsibility for the dam under its lease agreement with ASARCO, but its relationship with the forest service was less clear and required clarification. Not surprisingly, the forest service's environmental analysis concluded that "restoring the dam has less environmental impacts than not restoring it." The federal agency authorized Anaconda to proceed.[34]

Within weeks, Anaconda's Salt Lake City-based engineering consultant, Dames & Moore, submitted its design recommendations for the repair of the tailings dam and stream flow conveyance structures.[35] As Dent proclaimed, it had been "balls to the wall." Rarely are significant earth-moving projects designed, evaluated, and approved so quickly, especially when glacially paced federal agencies and corporations are involved. But winter was approaching, and the following spring could prove even more disastrous for the Blackfoot River without the dam's rehabilitation. It did not hurt that every party to the decision, public included, eagerly sought such repairs.

Dames & Moore proposed to fix the breach in the remaining embankment with an engineered earthfill "plug." Additional fixes would protect the repaired embankment against future floods. Notably, Dames & Moore concluded that at least a portion of the tailings embankment had been marginally stable even before the 19 June breach, likely because of the dam's steep downstream face.[36] Following reconstruction, the downstream face would have a gentler slope, and the dam would be markedly more stable.

In contrast to the sandy, noncohesive tailings from which the original dam had been constructed, Dames & Moore utilized several types of soil to reconstruct the tailings dam according to modern engineering standards that would make it capable of withstanding a sizable earthquake. In the public eye, and in fact, Anaconda was ensuring that this particular dam would not become a future nuisance.

Dames & Moore proposed to replace the original emergency flood spillway with a reinforced concrete culvert fifty-four inches in diameter to be buried within natural soil on the impoundment's west side. The advantage of a larger culvert was its capacity to transmit much greater volumes of water through the impoundment than its twenty-four-inch predecessor. Prior to 1975, the combined capacity of the stream diversion and the pond's twenty-four-inch decant pipe had been approximately thirty to fifty cubic feet per second (cfs). The larger, fifty-four-inch culvert was designed to safely pass 418 cfs, more than eight times as much. Dames & Moore predicted that this new flood conveyance structure would safely pass a "200-year return period flood"—scientific jargon that expresses the maximum stream flow expected during a flood that might occur, on statistical average, once every two hundred years. Stated differently, the probability of such a flood occurring in any one year was about one in two hundred, or half of 1 percent. Anaconda's consultant also proposed to repair the original diversion and the twenty-four-inch decant pipe. The proposed repairs and improvements to the flood conveyance capability around and through the Mike Horse tailings dam were indeed significant.[37]

Once the final reconstruction plans were approved by Anaconda and Helena National Forest, Dames & Moore swung into action. In fact, site work began on 9 September, nine days *before* Dames & Moore completed its final design report. Site work was completed within ten weeks of mostly twenty-four-hour days. By mid-November, on schedule and ahead of winter snows, it was done. The reconstructed dam crest was five hundred feet long and fifty feet high.[38]

In addition to rebuilding the dam and flood conveyance structures to higher engineering standards, Anaconda attempted to rehabilitate fish habitat between Anaconda and Pass Creeks.[39] The reasoning for this attempt is undocumented, and in light of known fishery conditions then and now, it is surprising anyone tried. The reach had been largely void of trout or other significant aquatic life for decades. According to Dent, it was a "biological desert."[40] Nonetheless, four fish ponds were excavated along this reach of upper river. In retrospect, it is irrelevant whether the ponds improved trout habitat. Water quality alone ensured there would be no trout.

More than twenty years after the dam's failure and Anaconda's commendable repairs, it remains a peculiar footnote to the era that no criminal or civil penalties were sought by the state of Montana or any agency of the federal government for damage to the river.[41] Anaconda spent considerable sums to correct the problem, and government appears to have written off the tragic event as an "act of God." Never mind that the failure was avoidable, hadn't Anaconda reacted promptly?

In light of modern litigious behavior, such generosity and lenience is barely conceivable. If these sorry circumstances were repeated today, both private and government attorneys would be all over Anaconda, ASARCO, and perhaps even the forest service before the last cutthroat finished flopping on the banks of the Blackfoot River. Yet precedents for issuing fines for environmental misdeeds were largely lacking in 1975, especially in Montana, where the company still possessed a strong grip on state culture and political life.

Anaconda's influence was waning rapidly by 1975, but Montanans needed no reminder that the copper giant had and still played a major role in the state. Long the state's largest industrial employer, Anaconda had also for many years been connected to Montana's primary utility: Montana Power Company. (John D. Ryan served simultaneously as president of *both* companies until 1933.) In addition to its Butte mines, Anaconda owned and operated metal smelters, refineries, and reduction works in the cities of Anaconda, East Helena, and Great Falls, lumber mills near Missoula, and hundreds of thousands of acres of western Montana timberland. To help protect these assets against public and political rabble-rousers, until 1959 Anaconda owned eight major daily newspapers across the state, which controlled 55 to 60 percent of the state's daily press circulation. The papers reportedly had little autonomy and were directed by Anaconda's executive offices. Most of these various entities had been sold, closed, or liquidated by 1975; the company was much weaker, both politically and economically, than it had been even twenty years earlier. Nonetheless, Anaconda's image remained a potent force in everyday Montana life. No one knowingly trifled with even the ghost of the company that had once considered the state of Montana "little more than a corporate asset."[42]

Within Montana's regulatory agencies, publicly chastising or fining Anaconda for such an "accident" would have been very risky politically and professionally and controversial within the public body politic. More regrettable, however, is that no effort was undertaken to determine just how many other inactive or abandoned tailings impoundments existed in Montana and whether they were in a comparable and tenuous state.[43]

Ultimately, the damage was done and Anaconda responded appropriately. The public all but forgot about it within months. To do more was not possible. Another major weakness in the General Mining Law of 1872 had been exposed.

6. An Open Portal

Metals from historic mining activities in the Blackfoot River headwaters were clearly the most acute water quality problem in the watershed. — Montana Department of Health and Environmental Sciences, "Water Quality Investigations in the Blackfoot River Drainage, Montana"

[N]atural contamination of water in contact with undisturbed mineral deposits should be expected. Concentrations of metals in water may be orders of magnitude higher in mineralized regions than in nonmineralized areas, even in the absence of mining. —Donald D. Runnells, Thomas A. Shepherd, and Ernest E. Angino, "Metals in Water: Determining Natural Background Concentrations in Mineralized Areas"

THE RAIN HAD PLUMMETED onto the January snowpack all night and in the soggy gray light of mid-morning it was a balmy forty degrees. I shook my head in disbelief. Winter in the northern Rockies sees rain only rarely. The common denominators are snow and cold.

Dry and warm in my truck, I turned off Highway 200 onto Mike Horse Road and continued up the Blackfoot River. The gravel road was armored with old snow hard-packed to glare ice. The rain made the road as slick as oiled glass. I berated myself for not having studded tires. Hoping four-wheel drive *might* keep me from sliding into the four-foot roadside snow berms, I fishtailed my truck to a stop and twisted in the front hubs.

A half-mile off the highway, an abandoned log cabin squatted on the left side of the road. Its corner logs were distinctively notched. Someone knowledgeable about early Montana architecture could tell me which ethnic group had constructed it—maybe Norwegians, Welsh, or Finns. Its weathered logs were marbled slate gray and chocolate brown, and chinking still gripped some logs. Cracked and twisted window frames remained but held no

87

glass. Tattered green asphalt roofing paper sagged through holes in the roof.

As I drove higher into the drainage, snowflakes the size of half-dollars merged with the rain and muffled the drumming on the truck. I was in vertical limbo between snow and rain, where neither dominated but both soaked the landscape. Lumpy gray clouds that had been scudding overhead lifted slightly to reveal fresh snow draping the pine forest on both sides of the valley.

Another mile up-valley, the Blackfoot River, here barely ten feet wide, pinched a thick-bodied Douglas fir against the road. The trunk had been splintered by lightning twenty-five feet above the ground. Below the splinter, thick limbs circled the trunk. It looked as if the tree had dropped its needled crown to its knees and then been whacked off at the waist. A black and yellow forest service property boundary sign rattled against the trunk.

As I drove on, the Anaconda Mine stared at me from across the river. Above the mine, Anaconda Creek and Beartrap Creek meet to form the Blackfoot River. After I spun and slithered up Beartrap Creek another half-mile, before the road crossed a stream and doubled back on itself, I stopped to look at where the stream entered a culvert poking beneath the road.

A red orange milk flowed where ice water should have. A sludge of the same hue smothered the streambed, which zigzagged up-canyon several hundred feet before disappearing around the nose of a timbered ridge. On my right, a narrow road traversed the canyon's steep west slope, switchbacked, and traversed again, gaining elevation quickly and efficiently. I was close.

I pulled up the hood on my anorak and began hiking alongside the colored stream. Soon, I reached the toe of a waste-rock dump leaning against the mountainside. The slope was mostly ice, and I clambered up on all fours, frequently slipping and losing ground before I stepped onto a flat surface roughly measuring one hundred by two hundred feet. In its center was an ice-covered depression. Above, fir and pine faded into the hovering clouds.

Two men in insulated coveralls stood in the center of the ice-covered pond. They had drilled a small hole through the ice and were in the process of taking measurements and collecting water samples. Their snowmobiles were parked nearby. We waved to each other as if we met here every morning.

A sheet-metal roof protruded from the snow-covered mountainside and I headed toward it. A blue plastic tarp hung from the roof over what appeared to be an opening. Before I had taken a dozen steps, one of the pond-samplers shouted to me, "Are you with one of the agencies?" He clearly meant one of the state or federal regulatory agencies interested in this mining district. Both men owned thick, dark beards.

"Nope. Just curious." I continued toward the blue tarp.

They looked at each other and reached an unspoken decision. The speaker turned to me again. He was friendly but confident. "Guess I'll have to ask you to leave."

Driving up-valley that morning, I had seen no signs blaring "No Trespassing" or the more threatening but less common "Go Away—Survivors Will Be Prosecuted." I knew the Mike Horse portal was beneath the blue tarp. The crimson stream led me here. Still, a portion of the canyon was blanketed by patented mining claims and was, in fact, private property. The two bearded faces looked as if they belonged here. They stared at me, obviously believing I did not.

Wanting to be neither a nuisance nor an ass nor attract attention to my trespass, I began retracing my steps. "No problem. I'm easy to live with," I said, as I stepped over the edge of the berm and boot-skied and stumbled back to my truck.

Another time, I reasoned.

I returned early the following summer. Winter snow was long gone in the canyons, and no workers were visible as I nosed my truck up the narrow access road to the top of the waste-rock dump. The pond was free of ice, and the water shimmered from suspended metals and sediment. Around its perimeter, orange and amber sediment glistened just beneath the surface. Without snow cover, the sheet-metal roof of January had become a complete shed, the blue tarp had vanished, and the portal was visible. A small, rusty stream dribbled from the portal toward the pond.

The shed was ten or twelve feet wide and perhaps thirty feet long. Where it entered the mountain, reinforced concrete walls framed a rectangle of pitch black. Through that blackness was the mine. Corrugated metal was wired, bolted, and welded onto a frame of two-inch iron pipe reinforced by several six- and eight-inch iron I beams. Only time and rust would pull down this shed.

I stepped beneath the roof and placed my hand against the shed's inside wall. It came away the same brilliant red orange as the water flowing past my feet.

As my eyes adjusted to the dim light within the shed, I remembered one of my older and more careless habits: no one knew I was there. I had left Helena without telling anyone where I was going or when I planned to return, a practice my mother had failed to break me of decades ago. I had also forgotten my headlamp. Standing water extended two feet up the concrete and sheet-metal walls, at least several inches deeper than my boots were tall. I chose not to go farther. Entering an unknown mine is a precarious activity in the West and wading makes it more difficult. Beneath an innocent surface may lurk a shaft or winze. One step too many can lead to a wet and icy tomb.

The main portal opened to a single adit, or tunnel, reaching into the mountain. Although I could see no more than ten or fifteen feet into the darkness, this no. 3 level extended more than eleven hundred feet before intersecting the Mike Horse Vein, following a compass bearing of 225 degrees, or due southwest. Geologists restate 225 degrees on a compass as 45 degrees west of due south and write it as "S 45° W." The directions are the same, just written differently. The Mike Horse Vein trends along a compass bearing of 300 degrees. A bit of mental geometry indicates that the no. 3 tunnel meets the Mike Horse Vein at nearly a right angle. Most likely, the tunnel was constructed with an eye to future production efficiency.

Until 1945, all mining occurred in the mine's three highest levels. Miners removed ore and waste rock by advancing both horizontally and upward. In some cases, they stoped upward practically to the ground surface; in mining jargon, they "mined to the roots." When ASARCO gained control of the mine in 1945, it believed future prosperity lay deeper and devised a plan to follow the Mike Horse Vein downward. After 1945, mine production occurred primarily from below the 300 level.

Access to deeper ore could have been obtained by driving another adit from the surface into the mountain below the 300 level. Yet accessing deeper ore reserves by means of a new tunnel several times longer than no. 3 would have entailed considerable cost. Consequently, the new owners did about the only thing they could and sank a winze, or decline, on the Mike Horse Vein at the end of the no. 3 Tunnel and followed the vein downward. By the time the mine closed in late 1952, most ore production came from the 800 level, five hundred feet below the mine's primary access. The 400 and 600 levels were also developed during this era.[1] In one sense, the mine can be thought of as an underground hotel with large rooms and connecting vertical and horizontal passageways.

As the mine deepened, groundwater became more of a nuisance and operational problem because the mine no longer self-drained. A conviction common to those unfamiliar with groundwater science is that groundwater resides in underground lakes and migrates via subterranean streams and rivers. Some geologic conditions are conducive to these beliefs, such as the limestone country of southern Indiana and Kentucky. But in the metamorphic and igneous rock of the Heddleston district, as in nearly all western mining districts, groundwater migrates primarily through fractures in the rock. When mine workings intercept these fractures, water drips or squirts into the mine. The first groundwater intercepted has usually resided in the rock for hundreds or thousands of years, although a mine's subsequent drip-drip-drip may derive from surface water percolating slowly through overlying soils and rock. The amount of water entering a mine through these fractures is proportional to the size of the fractures, the degree to which they are interconnected, and how well they are, in turn, connected to the ground surface. Groundwater typically moves only several tens of feet per year, but a direct connection between underground mine workings and the ground surface is all that is required to provide a constant supply of water infiltrating a mine.

Much of the water exiting the Mike Horse Mine originates with Mike Horse Creek itself. Hartmiller initially followed the vein system both northwestward and southeastward. The latter course took him beneath Mike Horse Gulch, where his workings eventually came within fifty feet of Mike Horse Creek. Groundwater scientists believe fractures in the rock beneath the creek directly connect it with the underlying workings.

The air was both clammy and cool in the shade of the portal shed, but the temperature around my knees and thighs was cooler. The mountain was exhaling dense, cold air, as if ridding itself of

8. Mike Horse Mine main portal shed, 2 September 1987. By this date, the shed was likely all that remained of the mine, mill, and town site. Acidic mine waters flow from the mine across the surface in the foreground. Montana Department of Environmental Quality.

something undesirable. I detected two odors: sulfur and wet rock. There is nothing unusual about the smell of wet rock; it is a generic aroma of the mountains. But my nose also filled with the pungency of sulfur. I was prepared for this clear-cut and definable smell of weathering sulfide minerals. The source of most significant and troublesome water-quality problems associated with mining is acid, and the acid begins with sulfide minerals. Known widely by the technical acronym AMD (acid mine drainage), the phenomenon is characterized by mine drainage with low pH, abnormal and elevated metal concentrations, and iron-rich precipitates.[2] Unfortunately, the process is the result of natural chemical reactions that may occur with or without mining.

Acid formation in mines is reasonably well-understood, especially by geochemists, that subspecies of geological scientists intrigued by the chemistry of rocks and minerals. One of nature's least charitable chemical reactions occurs simply because the necessary ingredients are everywhere. Iron, sulfur, and oxygen are ubiquitous; they are among the five most common natural elements on Earth. If keenly appreciated, however, the process is neither simple nor short term.

The process begins with pyrite, the mineral form of iron sulfide, nature's most common chemical union of iron and sulfur. Pyrite's less common but chemical twin, marcasite, also participates when present. (A mineral is a crystalline phase of two or more combined elements. Chemically reduced mineral forms of sulfur, combined with metals, are called metal sulfides. Valuable metals such as gold, copper, zinc, and lead frequently form sulfiides, which explains why sulfides are as common to mining country as soil is to farming.) Almost worthless in its own right, pyrite occurs commonly with valuable minerals, usually as a gangue mineral. Its shiny yellow appearance confuses many first-time gold-panners, a deception that provides the basis for its other name, "fool's gold."

Pyrite's ubiquity explains why acids form in such diverse and unrelated mining regions as Appalachia's coalfields and the precious-metal districts of Montana and Colorado. Pyrite is not inert, however. In the presence of water and oxygen, it chemically reacts—*oxidizes*, in the chemist's lingo—ultimately creating two new and very different compounds: the seemingly stable but troublesome ferric hydroxide and the problematic sulfuric acid.

Sulfuric acid triggers the first of many of mining's distinctive water-quality problems. It dissolves and mobilizes metals in adjacent minerals, releasing constituents that cascade through the environment with profoundly lethal consequences. These metals, including aluminum, lead, zinc, copper, and iron, and not the acidity, are what is most toxic to aquatic life.

Acidity produced by the initial oxidation of pyrite is limited. It is chemically finite and the resulting pH does not drop below 4.0, which is acidic but not terribly out of bounds in nature. (The pH scale is logarithmic. A pH of 4.0 is ten times more acidic than a pH of 5.0. The pH of most natural water ranges between 5.5 and 8.0. A neutral pH, neither acidic nor alkaline, is 7.0.) If the initial oxidation of pyrite was the only chemical reaction driving the AMD process, water-pollution control engineers and fishery biologists could worry less, because many natural waters possess enough balancing alkalinity to neutralize acid formed in this initial step. But once begun, AMD is not readily self-limiting. A second and more treacherous phase of AMD, just as natural as its predecessor, often overwhelms native alkalinity in groundwater or nearby rock. More acid is created and more metals are mobilized and released to the environment.

The true culprit is iron, which is why the pyritic combination of iron and sulfur is so significant (otherwise, all metal sulfides might be as troublesome). When initially freed from its mineral union with sulfur, the iron is in a soluble and reduced state. But this ferrous iron is chemically unstable; in the presence of oxygen and at an acid pH, it oxidizes to its more stable form, ferric iron. When this ferric iron *hydrolyzes* (what chemists call the process of a *salt*, the ferric iron, combining with water to create a *base*, the ferric hydroxide, and an *acid*), more acid is created, more than that generated by the initial oxidation of pyrite.

Stated more succinctly, the continuing oxidation of iron creates a pH-lowering acid that allows more pyritic iron to oxidize and become ferrous, then ferric iron; more acid is then created when the ferric iron hydrolyzes. In mining country, profuse ferric hydroxide deposits are termed *yellowboy*. Yellowboy imparts a reddish earth color to affected streambeds and is the single most obvious indicator of AMD.

There is more bad news. Acid generation often accelerates in the presence of certain bacteria, namely *Ferrobacillus ferrooxidans*, *Ferrobacillus sulfooxidans*, and *Thiobacillus Thiooxidans*. The rate of iron oxidation in conjunction with these bacteria actually increases as the pH declines. Thus, these bacteria indirectly increase acid production. This in turn accelerates their role in oxidizing iron, a process that further increases acid production. Perhaps equally as ominous, acid production may occur or be facilitated by these bacteria without oxygen. Some research scientists suggest that bacteria may account for as much as 75 percent of the total acid produced by AMD.

When iron oxidizes in the presence of these bacteria, the pH may decline to 3.0 or less, low enough to mobilize metals normally insoluble at a pH of 4.0. For example, the iron in pyrite is relatively insoluble at the near-neutral pH of natural water and remains insoluble until the pH lowers to a critical value. Sulfuric acid, iron, and bacteria accomplish this and allow these minerals to dissolve, mobilizing their metals and releasing them to surrounding ecosystems.

The process comes full circle. Dissolved metals mobilized by acid do not remain in solution indefinitely. Acid water draining from a mine or seeping from the toe of a forgotten waste-rock dump naturally and gradually grows more alkaline, which is to say its pH now increases. Under such conditions, metals are less soluble. They precipitate, transforming from material in solution to a solid. All metals do not precipitate at the same time and rate; each precipitates to its own drumbeat of tumbling water, oxygen, and solubility at a given pH.

Iron is the least soluble of the common metals. Its abundance and relative insolubility lead to its appearance as yellowboy. Downstream from where yellowboy smothers a streambed, lustrous and chalky precipitates of aluminum might drape the streambed as effectively as the initial ferric hydroxide. In theory, one could continue downstream past a succession of metal precipitates, each metal having altered from its dissolved form to its solid specie in accordance with its native solubility at a given pH. Typically, only iron and aluminum are plentiful enough to be visible.

An obvious question arises: if the active ingredients and environmental conditions are ubiquitous, why doesn't the natural creation of acid spin out of control and render all water unsafe? After all, there is plenty of iron, sulfur, and oxygen around.

One answer is that nature provides its own neutralizers. AMD can be limited by other natural processes even if the initial AMD process is not self-limiting. For example, limestone and its component mineral, calcite, neutralize sulfuric acid created by pyrite oxidation. Although metals precipitating under rising pH conditions help solve the metals toxicity problem, yellowboy and streambed-smothering still occur. Thus, calcite might only influence *where* metals precipitate. Neutralizing agents like limestone can be effective in treating impacted waters, but they do little to halt pyrite and iron oxidation and acid generation.

Another reason why acid generation, once begun, does not continue unabated is that nature's processes generally require millennia to play themselves out. What is pollution to modern people is an irrelevant tick on Earth's absolute clock. AMD occurs at its own pace independent of human desires and civilization. The competing and opposing chemistries are comfortable with one another and have been for eons. Most pyrite exposed to water and oxygen by native forces either has already been thoroughly oxidized and has unleashed its limit of acid or is so tightly bound in its rock host that its acid production is paced by nature's neutralizers. Over centuries, undisturbed pyrite attains a harmless status quo with its environment. Either way, acid production rarely creates runaway conditions toxic to entire ecosystems. The cycle is tight, the process slow. There is a balance, until mining disturbs it. Drilling, blasting, and dumping uncover minerals which have never seen sunlight or been exposed to the atmosphere. Pyrite is routinely involved. It makes no difference whether pyrite is part of the waste rock or the ore.

Mining compresses the natural geochemical reactions of tens of thousands of years into hours. Imagine a six-sided rock measuring one hundred feet on a side. The six sides of this cube have ten thousand square feet of exposed surface. As a whole, the boulder has sixty thousand square feet of exposed surface. Now, let us shatter this boulder and pound it into a pile of equal-sized miniboulders measuring just one foot on a side. Thus disassembled, the original boulder now constitutes one million cubes, each measuring one foot by one foot by one foot. Each of these cubes has six square feet of exposed surface. The original boulder has become six million square feet of exposed surface, an increase in the exposed surface area by 9,900 percent. Assuming that these freshly exposed surfaces possess pyrite in the same proportion as the original boulder, our hypothetical mining has clearly exposed more pyrite to the elements than was the case before we pounded apart the original boulder. It is less the total amount of pyrite-bearing rock, less the premining exposure of this pyrite to the atmosphere and water than the gargantuan increase in pyrite exposure brought about by mining's actual physical fracturing and crushing.

Modern minerals processing requires finely ground ore for efficient and effective metals recovery. It is not uncommon to grind ore to sand-sized particles measuring just three hundredths of an inch in diameter. Together, mining and milling create an almost unlimited amount of surface area from previously undisturbed rocks. The pace of acid production increases proportionally and all too frequently overwhelms the innate neutralizing characteristics of the surrounding soils, rocks and water. The amount of acids and metals released by past mining and minerals processing is hundreds of times greater than that which would have been produced by the same rocks had they been left undisturbed.

Limiting AMD by avoiding the disturbance of pyrite is an unimaginable task. In most cases it is near impossible to segregate one set of metal sulfides from another prior to milling. Selectively mining particular zones to avoid pyrite is rarely possible, practical, or effective, and to further complicate the matter, distinguishing ore from waste rock is often a matter of gradation and fluctuates with metal market prices. Today's waste may be tomorrow's ore.

Historically, miners could not see where they were headed as they blasted their way into the mountain. They simply followed their lead. Anyone suggesting they forego mineralization in an effort to minimize AMD would have been laughed out of the district—that is, if they cared, which they did not, or if they knew what caused AMD, which they likewise did not.

Given sufficient time and distance, an impacted stream or river might cleanse itself. Metals attempt to settle from the moving water as minute crystalline precipitates, or more likely, adsorb onto suspended sediments, including other suspended precipitates. Combine this natural diminution with inflows from uncontaminated tributaries and you have the basis for the grizzled polluter's adage, "Dilution is the solution to pollution." Nonetheless, AMD is amenable to some control. Pyrite-bearing materials can be moved, and engineered solutions can be implemented to isolate them from water and oxygen. This is possible both with waste rock and mill tailings. Until the past decade or two, such practices were not part of a mine's normal functioning and minerals processing operations. But times are changing. Under the watchful and encouraging eye of modern state regulatory agencies, industry frequently incorporates methods of isolating the most pyritic materials and sealing them against water or oxygen. AMD is as tough an opponent as any industry has battled.

A mile and a half northwest of the Mike Horse Mine, Paymaster Creek slides almost unnoticed toward the Blackfoot River. Not quite making it, the creek sinks into the floor of Paymaster Gulch short of the river after emptying a watershed of little more than a square mile. Only strong rains or heavy snowmelt contribute a full channel to the river.

Paymaster Gulch is difficult to find and the Paymaster Mine is little known or recorded. In 1927 government geologists found the mine's several adits already partly caved in.[3] They had apparently not been entered in years, and the geologists were not eager to be the first. In the early 1980s, the Montana Bureau of Mines and Geology concluded that, based on the size of its waste dumps, the mine's underground development had been extensive.[4] There have been vague allegations that the dumps resulted from little-known activities in the fall of 1944 or from those of an equally unknown New York–based operator in the early 1960s.[5]

When I finally located the Paymaster Mine, little had changed. Waste dumps that winked at me through scruffy stands of lodge-pole pine had been described in 1927 as having abundant pyrite that had "broken down to a claylike mass streaked with iron oxides."[6] I assumed a connection between these words and my observation that the pines bore reddened needles and were dead or dying.

Compared to the Mike Horse and Anaconda Mines, the Paymaster seemed insignificant. Paymaster Creek is a narrow, rusty stream, but its flow contrasts sharply with the pale green, brown, and red pines and jade spruce. There was an odd quality to the stream, however. No barren floodplain straddled its sickly flow. AMD normally kills streamside vegetation or smothers the floodplain with yellowboy, or both. In this case the stream's iron-staining and lifeless character were confined to a small channel just several feet across.

I stepped across the stream and scrambled up the waste dump toward the mine's primary adit. The portal was little more than an overgrown depression. Several healthy-looking spruce soaked their roots in water seeping from the depression. The seepage was clear; there was no telltale yellowboy. On the hillside above the portal, lodgepole pine had matured since the mine's abandonment and grew thick and tall.

Seventy years ago, geologists described the juncture of the mine's waste dump and Paymaster Creek: "The mine waters issuing from the dump are depositing considerable amounts of iron oxides, which, when dry, form a fine, reddish-brown to yellowish-brown powderlike ocher."[7]

I reconciled this dated description with what lay before me. Most of the portal's drainage likely percolated into the dump before resurfacing at its toe. Good or foul when leaving the mine, the water reacted with pyritic waste along its labyrinthine course. By the time it reappeared at the dump toe, its quality would be similar to AMD from elsewhere in the district.

I followed Paymaster Creek upstream along a persistent trail of yellowboy. A quarter mile up the gulch I encountered a second collapsed portal and dump. Smaller than the first, its size and location corresponded with the historic record. Paymaster Creek still evidenced AMD above this point, which I presumed derived from the third adit farther up the drainage. But the amount of yellowboy draping the streambed looked out of proportion to the bare thread of water trickling from the toe of the second dump. The third dump would be smaller yet, so a question formed in my mind: How could I reconcile the steady flow of rusty water from upstream from what should be an even smaller mining development?

Rather than continue on to the third adit, I checked my watch. I was late for a meeting with the Kornec brothers. Perhaps they would know the answer.

Of course, George and Rosie knew the Paymaster Mine and its namesake creek. When it came to reciting the locations and histories of the district's natural and man-made features, there was little they could not recall. If one brother appeared stumped and gazed thoughtfully at the ceiling, the other offered the information.

According to the Kornecs, the yellowboy deposits of Paymaster Creek are natural, and the stream is acid for a considerable distance upstream of the three Paymaster adits. This explained why the stream exhibited yellowboy out of proportion to the size and location of the mine and its waste dumps. Water flows downhill, so how could AMD originating with the Paymaster Mine be responsible for yellowboy *above* the mine?

Neither brother knew of an unrecorded mine or even minimal disturbance from mineral exploration farther up Paymaster

Gulch. Paymaster Creek had likely been iron-tainted prior to any mining in the district. That is, Paymaster Creek was acid and iron-encrusted except near its drainage divide, where for reasons unknown to either man, Paymaster Creek was as pure and clear as any other mountain-fed stream tumbling off the Continental Divide.

Rosie claimed that if I hiked to the untainted reach of stream at the head of Paymaster Gulch, I would find several abandoned miners' cabins. To Rosie, it was obvious that miners seeking a decent cabin site would not place it next to a poor water supply. Rather, they would follow the contaminated stream higher into the drainage and construct their shelters where they found the water fit for drinking. It made sense. Miners of a century ago, like miners today, would not have intentionally settled for inconvenient living conditions. They would have constructed their cabins as close to the Paymaster Mine as possible. That they had not was sound reason to believe that they had been forced to build where they could, not where it was closest.

As further evidence of the existence of naturally acid streams, George described a location on Sandbar Creek, opposite its common drainage divide with Paymaster Gulch. There, a spring rises from the hillside with a sulfurous stench, as does another spring in the headwaters of Willow Creek at the base of Flesher Pass. In both cases, he insisted, acid water was associated with exposures of good lead-zinc ore but not with mining.[8]

This supposed existence of a *naturally* acidic, metal-laden stream is not entirely surprising. AMD and its metallic progeny are universally recognized as by-products of mining, but there is no explanation for why *all* acidic streams have to be caused by mining. In some natural cases, where oxidation by-products are not removed quickly enough from the mineral surface, protective *gossans* form, superficial coatings of hydrated iron that isolate the pyrite from further oxidation. Surely, there must be instances where pyrite oxidizes at an intermediate rate, without benefit of mining or the creation of gossans. Nature is rarely black and white.

My curiosity about the geology and mineralogy of natural acidic streams led me to George Furniss, a graduate student in geology at the University of Montana in Missoula.[9] We talked first by telephone, where he unfolded as an affable yet serious researcher with more worldly experience than someone fresh from undergraduate training. Seemingly as an extension of his previous career as a mining geologist, Furniss's proposed doctoral dissertation was an explanation of natural occurrences of acid rock drainage, or what the broader scientific community sometimes refers to as ARD.

Months later, we met in Lincoln. It was a frosty, late October morning under a dazzling sun. As we approached one another to shake hands, I realized that he walked guardedly with the aid of two canes. Months earlier, he explained, he had shattered his left leg in a fall from a roof. His accident had slowed his field research for the year, but not his enthusiasm for his project. After coffee, we drove up the Blackfoot River toward the Heddleston district. Cody, his energetic yellow labrador, rode in the back of his truck.

Furniss's determination to show me his findings along Paymaster Creek overwhelmed any misgivings he might have had about scrambling one-legged over snow-covered deadfalls and along ice-margined streams. He wanted to point out what he believed to be critical relationships in the field, especially when he learned of my interest in the environmental history of the district and the Mike Horse Mine.

Striking similarities exist between water-quality characteristics of Paymaster Creek and drainage from the district's two largest mines, the Mike Horse and Anaconda. Iron concentrations in all three waters range between one and eighty-eight parts per million, at least twenty times higher than any imputed regional "average." Other metals representative of acidic influences, like zinc and lead, exhibited comparable similarities.

Likewise, ferric hydroxide deposits occur along all three watercourses. Yellowboy lines Paymaster Creek and the trickles emanating from the three Paymaster Mine waste dumps. The Anaconda Mine, just below the confluence of Anaconda and Beartrap Creeks, has a small drainage area relative to the Mike Horse Mine, but the incipient channel between the portal and the river is lined with yellowboy. And, of course, yellowboy lies thick and slick from the Mike Horse Mine's no. 3 portal for several hundred yards down Mike Horse and Beartrap Creeks.

The only aberration distinguishing the two mine discharges and Paymaster Creek is water pH. The flows of Paymaster Creek and the Anaconda Mine each log pH readings of between 3.0 and 3.5, squarely within the expected range of AMD or ARD. The pH of Mike Horse Mine effluent varies between 5.2 and 6.5, within the natural variation of unaffected waters. The reason for this exception is unclear, although it may reflect a natural pH shift associated with buffering imparted by surrounding rocks and soils.

Furniss does not insist all ARD is natural. Acid mine drainage is a frequent legacy of mining; this cannot be disputed. But Furniss believes that ARD and AMD are distinguishable by their origins, even if the mineralogical underpinnings and chemical reactions are the same. Only the modes of pyrite exposure and subsequent transport of oxidation by-products differ. His research suggested that ARD is a natural consequence of shallow groundwater coming into contact with pyrite-bearing dikes or veins.

Like me, Furniss had observed Paymaster Creek gliding strangely through the fir and pine forest bordering its banks. His critical observation was that leaves and twigs dropping into the stream were being buried by incremental layers of ferric hydroxide. The hardness and durability of accumulated ferricrete deposits gave him a unique idea. (Furniss emulates academicians in his preference for scientific lingo, in this case for ferricrete, a formal term for soil zones hardened and cemented by oxidized iron. The roots of the term are *ferric*, after the Latin for iron, and *crete*, or cementlike concretion.)

Furniss excavated a ferricrete deposit along Paymaster Creek, and exposed twigs, leaves, and pinecones. Subsequent radiocarbon dating of this plant matter provided ages of more than four thousand years, which indicated, in concert with geologic convention, that the same processes forming ferricrete today were operating thousands of years ago, long before miners showed up on the Blackfoot River. Furniss's preliminary conclusions are provocative because some environmentalists prefer to believe there is no such thing as natural ARD and that all acid waters and yellowboy spring from mining.

Furniss suggests that it is not that simple. Acid mine drainage and acid rock drainage may be the same process, but only the former is anthropogenic. For now, some state and federal regulatory officials remain suspicious, hesitant to embrace the existence of natural ARD for fear that mining companies will argue that AMD presumably under their control is really ARD and that they should not have to deal with or limit nature's bad jokes.

7. Planting Fish

These [fish] are furnished with long teeth on the pallet and tongue and have generally a small dash of red on each side behind the front ventral fins; the flesh is of a pale yellowish red, and when in good order, of a rose red.—Meriwether Lewis, *Journals of the Lewis and Clark Expedition,* 13 June 1805

Productivity and decomposition in terrestrial biotic communities ensure a substantial and continuous supply of organic matter in most watersheds. . . . The combination of strong metal binding and sorbing capacities and abundance in surface waters renders the organics an extremely important influence on trace metal chemistry.—John F. Elder, *Metal Biogeochemistry in Surface-Water Systems—A Review of Principles and Concepts*

[I]t is well known that road building activities are major causes of habitat loss in cutthroat country, because the sedimentation they create smothers spawning gravels, fills in holding water, and eliminates the aquatic plants and insects upon which the little fish depend.—Patrick Trotter, *Cutthroat, Native Trout of the West*

If there is magic on this planet, it is contained in water.—Loren Eiseley, *The Immense Journey*

THE FIRST OF APRIL, and winter on the upper Blackfoot River has nearly expired. I feel its passing in the wind, which blows in cold, hard gusts followed by warmer sighs. Driving along the river, I see running water free from its long winter capture by ice. Like me, it is awakening and stretching.

I find the turn I want and pull off the highway. No tire tracks cut the rotting snow. I am the first visitor of the new year down the narrow track to a riverside picnic area without a picnic table. Ice extends several feet out into the river from each bank, providing a runway for local fauna. Old snow is covered with last night's animal tracks.

Fifty-foot lodgepole pine stand between me and the river. Twelve inches in diameter at my chest, they would be harvested anywhere else. From the still-frozen earth to the height of my shoulders, three have had their bark peeled away to raw cambium. The scars have weathered dry and gray like fine sandpaper; it has been a while since they were abused. One trunk is missing a huge wedge just above ground level in which hardened, yellow sap has clotted like dried blood. Someone practiced beginning axmanship here. From the scattering of small wood chips and the serrated nature of the scar, it is easy to tell that he or she was not proficient. I score this one for the tree.

The river tumbles and spins in the sunlight. I can hear neither its movement nor the highway traffic a quarter-mile away over the sound of the wind in the trees. Last year's grass, bleached bone-white by winter's cold and trampled flat by snow, crinkles as I walk to the river's edge. Overhead, April's first rowdy cumulus roil eastward. Across the river, chest-high willows grow near the water. Drab brown where they protrude from the snow, the branches stretch to khaki, then gold. Pale green buds peek from the tips.

I begin walking upriver but manage only several hundred yards before I am crowded to the water's edge by a steep, muddy hillside. Mottled light filters softly through several tall spruce. The willows are brilliant red here, possibly due to the abundant shade and moisture in this narrow cleft. The snow is scalloped by old deer and elk tracks. Yesterday's sun partially melted the snow, but it re-froze last night. This morning, ice fills the tracks like crude teacups.

On the opposite side of the river, a forty-foot band of dark rock rises steeply from the water and the entire river runs wildly through a fissure scoured into it. I look about with wider eyes. A modest canyon has trapped the river. Elsewhere in the valley, the river meanders across a floor up to one-half-mile wide that is underlain by unconsolidated sediments. Here, solid bedrock breaks the pattern. Geologically, it is surprising to find the river's course fixed in this canyon instead of bound loosely between banks of sand and gravel. The anomaly pins the question: Why?

Later in the morning, from a timbered hill, the geologic story becomes apparent. During the Pleistocene epoch, which began one to several million years ago, glaciers crowded the summits of western Montana, gouging their flanks and filling river valleys with streams of ice. One of these glaciers spilled southward down Alice Creek to its confluence with the river. Today, the moraine is a rumpled, timber-covered ridge rising no more than two hundred feet above the river. Nearly indistinguishable from the highway, it is a residual jumble of sand, gravel, and boulders. At its greatest, the glacier crossed the river valley and pinned the river against its own south valley wall.[1] To continue flowing, the river had to cut into the gray andesite bedrock.

Once the glacier retreated (actually, it melted in place—glaciers do not flow in reverse any more than water flows uphill), the river might have carved through the moraine's sand and gravel and regained its original course. But the glacier had accomplished more than temporarily damming the river. Once established in the shallow canyon, the river could not escape. Like all rivers, it has limits.

In the afternoon, I walk upriver. Greening willows line the banks and fresh deer tracks dot the fresh mud along the banks. Instead of being clear, however, the water is turbid; looking through it at the riverbed is like looking through someone's dirty eyeglasses.

An abandoned bridge crosses the river, on either side of which a forgotten track disappears into tangles of scrub lodgepole and willow growing out of a roadbed of broken rock. Abutments of graying logs twelve to eighteen inches in diameter jut several feet into the river from each bank. Each abutment corner is secured by deeply notched, overlapping logs. Boulders fill the space between the riverbank and the abutment. Three massive logs span the river and connect the opposing banks. Spiked atop these logs are three-inch-thick planks twelve to sixteen inches wide.

When I kick the planks and hear the reassuring thud of sound wood, I wonder why they have not been plundered for somebody's garage or flower bed. The bridge was constructed for trucks hauling lead and zinc concentrate to the East Helena smelter or the Silver City railhead. Its deck hangs three feet above the river surface, barely above normal flood level. Despite the occasional spring runoff that batters every part of this structure, the bridge has endured for more than fifty years and looks like it will last another fifty.

Farther upriver, Meadow Creek enters the river from the south through an overgrown slough nearly hidden by head-high willows and overhanging fir. The river channel is smothered by sandy mill tailings and yellowboy, and nearby rocks and logs are stained iron red. The water is opaque. Along this entire reach of river I have seen no evidence of fish.

In the beginning, there were "natives." Local fishermen may refer to them as "cuts," but both terms distinguish the native westslope cutthroat trout, *Oncorhynchus clarki lewisi*, a member of the *Salmonid* family and thereby related to salmon and other trout. To trout enthusiasts, cutthroat embody western fishing. Collectively, the fourteen indigenous cutthroat subspecies are the most widely distributed of all western trout.[2] The cutthroat is as native as the timber wolf or grizzly bear, more western than Gary Cooper.

The cutthroat's name derives from its physical appearance. All subspecies possess bright red or red orange slashes below and on both sides of its jaw, as if it had been dispatched with a knife. The west-slope member is quite colorful: its back is polished olive, its fins orange, its sides and belly yellow. Its other distinguishing characteristic—irregular black spots on its back that give rise to another of its common names, the "Montana blackspot"—make it easy to differentiate the west-slope cutthroat.

West-slope cutthroat prefer the highest, loneliest, and cleanest of western waters, a preference that contributes to their modest size in the upper end of their natural range. Where a large westslope cutthroat might measure sixteen inches elsewhere in its range, the average cutthroat in tributaries to the upper Blackfoot River might be five or six inches long. Water so pure does not carry enough nutrients to support the insects and other aquatic life necessary to grow and sustain large fish. In addition, the highest streams are so small that "anchor ice" freezes to the stream bottom in winter, killing most aquatic life.

The west-slope cutthroat is native to the headwaters of the Columbia and Missouri Rivers. When mining began in the Heddleston district in the 1880s, the subspecie had already inhabited the Blackfoot River and its tributaries for at least a million years. Its longevity did not count for much against human onslaught, however. Never as cagey as other trout, the gullible cutthroat was readily caught and eaten by any miner who bothered to fish.

Two other indigenous "game" fish also inhabited these same waters: the mountain whitefish and the lesser known bull trout. The historic range of both species partially overlapped that of the cutthroat. Fishery experts believe bull trout inhabited the upper Blackfoot River as recently as World War I. Since then, its range has diminished markedly, and its modern distribution is a fraction of what it was a century ago. Bull trout have not been seen much above Landers Fork, fifteen miles below the Mike Horse Mine, for years.[3]

In the 1880s eastern sportsmen did not often travel to Montana for once-in-a-lifetime experiences because excellent trout fishing was still available almost everywhere on the continent. Besides, Montana was remote. Overfishing was not a threat to its fisheries in the nineteenth century. In this sense, the frontier protected the Blackfoot River. Until World War I, access to the upper Blackfoot River was gained only by foot, horseback, or horse-drawn wagons, all traveling over footpaths and crude trails winding through thick timber and bumping along the river. Following the war, trucks rolled and bounced over primitive dirt roads that were not improved until the late 1930s nor paved until the 1950s.

Wild game and fish flourished in Montana, so it was unthinkable that the state's inexperienced government would attempt to control the fishing and hunting practices of far-flung ranchers, trappers, hunters, miners, and prospectors. Montana's Fish and Game Commission was created in 1895, but the professional side of the agency evolved slowly over successive decades. Prior to the 1930s, Montana's fishing laws were largely limited to such edicts as "Thou shalt use a hook" in an effort to discourage the dynamite-and-dip-net approach.

Nonetheless, at least some of Montana's fisheries declined. "Catch and release" fishing was a foreign concept. Miners and early ranchers responded by planting brook trout, native to eastern North America. In the upper Blackfoot, this appears to have occurred sometime early in the twentieth century. "Brookies" ultimately showed up in nearly every high mountain stream in Montana, due in large part to the efforts of the U.S. Bureau of Fisheries. The federal agency reportedly gave away milk cans of brook trout without much regard for their destination.[4] Today, brookies are ubiquitous in the upper Blackfoot drainage and cohabit many of the same streams as cutthroats. This is not a happy coexistence, however. Over time, brookies may outcompete the cutthroats for available food and even replace them.[5] Downriver, the introduction of brookies to bull trout waters may have hastened shrinkage of the latter's range. Bull trout hybridize with the nonnative brook trout, and their offspring are mostly sterile.[6]

As sport fishing grew in popularity and as indigenous fisheries showed increasing signs of stress, two more trout species were invited to Montana. The German brown trout was introduced from the eastern states after arriving from Europe in 1883. But brown trout prefer the more languid and warmer waters downriver and are rarely observed above Lincoln. They seem never to have made it to the headwaters.[7]

The well-known rainbow trout was introduced from its home waters along North America's West Coast, where it was valued for its feisty nature and propensity for rapid growth. Rainbows were likely introduced where they overlapped the cutthroat's natural range. Unfortunately, when rainbows are introduced to a predominantly cutthroat fishery they typically outcompete their more naive cousins. In time, the cutthroat may disappear.[8]

Montana's fishery authorities began stocking rainbows in the upper Blackfoot drainage in 1938 but ended the practice in 1979 when the state adopted a "natural fishery" policy. During this forty-two-year period, authorities planted more than 320,000 rainbows in the upper river, nearly half of them *fry*—less than two inches long.[9] Montana apparently never planted rainbows in the river above Lincoln, possibly because the effects of the Mike Horse Mine were becoming known. The agency might have asked itself, Why bother stocking where water quality will kill the fish almost as quickly as they get wet? Alternatively, some fishery biologists suspect stocking never took place in the headwaters because the water was too cold for rainbows. Either way, the current cutthroat population in the upper Blackfoot drainage remains genetically untainted.[10]

In the first decades of human activity along the upper Blackfoot River, no one collected scientific data on the distribution and size of trout. What is available are pieces of individual memories preserved by families and passed on to modern record keepers. A notable example is a diary kept by Helena's Ed MacHaffie, who spent eight weeks fishing the Blackfoot River above Lincoln during July and August of 1911. Given to Montana's Department of Fish, Wildlife and Parks in 1985 by MacHaffie's daughter, Joyce Young, MacHaffie's diary conceivably is the only hard fishery information available from that era. It records the day, number, and type of fish caught, the length and estimated weight of the largest fish, where he fished and on what kind of water—differentiating among open and shady holes, still water, ripples, and rapids— and what he used to catch them.

During those two months, MacHaffie spent fifteen days on the river above Landers Fork and caught 294 fish, an average of nearly twenty per day. The fish were nearly equally divided between cutthroat and bull trout. The longest cutthroat caught each day averaged over fourteen inches. Bull trout averaged over eighteen inches. MacHaffie did not record where he fished on the river above Landers Fork, which joins the Blackfoot about twelve miles below the upper swamp. He did note, however, that the upper Blackfoot was equal to the lower river and Landers Fork in terms of its fishery. I doubt he bothered to wet his line very often above Flesher Pass Road. The rock-confined canyon upstream from the road would have been a long day's hike from his family cabin, and the swamps upstream of the canyon would not have attracted more than his casual interest. Would beating a path through the swamp to the edge of thickly vegetated riverbanks have appealed to an impatient young man on a hot summer day?

MacHaffie's penchant for detail suggests a young man fascinated by the lure of big fish. Indeed, big water and big fish seem a priority among those who fished the Blackfoot River, both past and present. MacHaffie even teased his successors toward the end of his diary by writing, "The . . . data was set down by myself faithfully every evening in a little note book and altho the notes were not transcribed until this year—1924—I know that they are accurate in all particulars with the possible exception of weight. . . . This was the best years fishing I had ever had and it was not until 1924 that it was surpassed in number or average size."[11] Unfortunately, MacHaffie did not record, nor does his daughter recall, where he fished in 1924 that was so much better than the Blackfoot. Still, his diary portrays a young man's dream summer spent living and fishing along a great river. Most modern fishermen would swap their souls for a single day of fishing like MacHaffie experienced in 1911.

The causes of the decline of the upper Blackfoot fishery are both distinct and complex yet somehow related to mining. Indeed, hardrock mining in the Heddleston district would have exercised a variety of ways to kill a stream. Mine drainage rendered receiving water lethal to aquatic life. Mineral processing by early stamp and gravity mills clogged streams with processing waste and sediment. Logging and uncontrolled forest fires on the surrounding mountainsides created more sediment in the watershed than could be transported downriver. And no one bothered to protect the river from the customary and sloppy practices of individual miners.

The Mike Horse Mine discharged water from its first days, but if early geologists made no specific reference to the mine water being at least mildly acidic, it is as likely due to oversight as lack of occurrence. Water running from a mine portal was as commonplace as water in a stream. Certainly, the volume of water increased as the mine's underground workings expanded. By the 1920s, pyrite exposed in the mine had already begun generating sulfuric acid, dissolving metals and releasing them into the environment by way of groundwater draining from the mine portal.

Mining and milling were not the only harmful agents. Logging also played a role. The Heddleston district required cabins and firewood for the miners, timbers to support underground mine workings, lumber for construction of mine and mill buildings, and cordwood to fuel the first mill's steam boiler. The closest place to obtain timber was the surrounding mountain slopes. By the late 1930s, the hillsides surrounding the Mike Horse Mine had been stripped bare. On his arrival at the mine camp as a nine year old boy, John Thompson Jr. remembers standing at the Mike Horse no. 3 Tunnel portal and looking across to the opposite, west-facing slope, "You could look clear to the top of that hill and never see a tree in wintertime. It had all been cut off. They cut everything off and used it in the boilers when the old mill was running." [12]

In addition to logging, historical footnotes indicate that forest fires occasionally swept through the district. A 1915 report describes the timber surrounding the Mike Horse Mine as second-growth lodgepole pine and spruce less than sixteen or seventeen years old, suggesting that at least one fire scorched the district just prior to 1900.[13] This would be in addition to those fires of the 1840s and 1888. At the time, there were no requirements for screens to prevent fire sparks from spreading. Sparks had numerous sources in the district: chimneys and flues or the mill's wood-fired boiler. Fires probably escaped regularly, but district residents had no incentive to combat them as long as they did not threaten human life or property.

Once logging and fires stripped the mountain slopes of their protective forests, rainfall and snowmelt eroded the exposed soils and resulted in accelerated sedimentation of tributary streams and the river. Mill tailings also served as an added sediment source, as did, to a lesser degree, metallic hydroxides generated by metals precipitating from solution. From the Mike Horse Mine to the upper swamp, eroded soil, mill tailings, and precipitates choked the river and stream channels far beyond their capacity to transport the muck downstream.

Unknowingly, Samuel Kornec's boys assisted in buffering the upper river's fishery against the Mike Horse Mine. According to George Kornec, Beartrap Creek did not have fish above the tailings impoundment when the Kornecs built their cabin. Yet Rosie grins when he recalls how he and his younger brothers, along with Thompson, pulled off their own fish-planting operation. After walking downstream to Anaconda Creek or to the upper swamp, they caught trout then transplanted them by bucket to upper Beartrap Creek. Transplanting "natives" above the dam must have seemed an obvious benefit to these boys during the early years of World War II. Ultimately, their actions saved a long walk to put fresh fish on the dinner table. Rosie cannot help chuckling when he thinks of his contribution to Montana's fishery resource. As he says, "The Beartrap Creek fishery isn't natural."[14]

Portions of the river's upper watershed seemingly maintained their trout fishery reasonably well during this era. Brook and cutthroat trout sustained isolated fisheries in the lower portions of headwater streams, like Pass Creek, Shoue Gulch, and Anaconda Creek. As long as their habitat was not subjected to high metal concentrations or heavy surges of sediment or tailings, the trout held on. But the bull trout may have already begun to retreat downriver. Causes for its range reduction are as unknown as the timing of its movement. It may have been in response to metal concentrations extending, at least sporadically, downstream. The 1957 completion of the "Central Montana Highway," known now as State Highway 200, linked Missoula and Great Falls by way of Rogers Pass and resulted in greater fishing pressures on the upper Blackfoot. These events likely stressed the fishery and encouraged the retreat of the bull trout to bigger water.[15]

The relationship of sediment to trout reproduction is well understood today, even if no one cared about it sixty years ago. The west-slope cutthroat prefers gravel streambeds for spawning. In the upper Blackfoot drainage, after spending the winter nearly immobile in the icy water, cutthroat reproduce during spring runoff, in June and July. A spawning pair begins the ritual in a foot-deep riffle above pea-sized gravel. By lying on her side and wriggling her body and tail against the gravely stream bottom, the female constructs a *redd* in which to lay her eggs. Upon completing her redd, she lays her eggs as the male exudes *milt* over them. The female then excavates her second redd in a manner that buries the fertilized eggs in the first redd, and so on. This process is repeated several times over as many days until the female exhausts her egg supply, which may number a thousand eggs for each pound of body weight.

After hatching six or seven weeks later, young *alevins* linger in the gravel for several weeks, surviving on remaining egg material until they are large enough to "swim up" and leave the gravel to poke about on their own in the open stream. During this particularly vulnerable period, their size—about one inch—allows them to escape predation in the pores of submerged cobbles and boulders.

Too much sediment destroys trout spawning habitat in several ways, all of which would have occurred downstream from the Mike Horse and the district's other mines. Sediment buried and smothered the trout eggs before they hatched or suffocated alevins before they matured and left the redd. Sediment plugged the protective pores normally present in a cobbly streambed, diminishing aquatic insects that trout eat and exposing fry to predation by sculpins and other *Salmonids*. Further, sediment infilling of pools eliminated the habitat necessary for the rearing of young trout.[16]

Heavy metals play multiple roles in aquatic environments, few of which are beneficial to life. Iron and aluminum are among the most common elements in nature. Their detection in natural waters is routine, their toxicity limited. Other metals, like zinc and copper are also common, if not in quantities to make every landowner a mine owner, at least in detectable concentrations. Lead and cadmium generally appear infrequently or in concentrations almost too small to detect. Chemists collectively label these latter two groups "trace metals," because they occur in trace amounts in the environment. In minor concentrations, some are essential to normal animal and plant metabolic functions. In slightly higher concentrations they can be quite toxic. Some metals are more toxic than others, and for those that are toxic, they are not lethal to all organisms at the same concentrations. Trout pathology is not a simple science.

Trout are especially susceptible to dissolved copper, zinc, and cadmium. These metals are at least partially responsible for decimating the fishery below the Mike Horse Mine.[17] Throughout the West, hardrock mines released metals into stream environments. The Mike Horse was not alone in its unconscious assault upon western rivers.

In accordance with the 1972 federal Clean Water Act, water-quality standards for copper, zinc, and cadmium have been established by the U.S. Environmental Protection Agency.[18] The criteria set concentrations that can be tolerated by, among other species, *Salmonids* in freshwater. In stream environments, very little dissolved copper, zinc, or cadmium is needed to kill trout. For copper, the freshwater aquatic criterion is 18 micrograms per liter of water, for zinc, 320 micrograms per liter, for cadmium, 3.9 micrograms per liter. Another way of looking at micrograms per liter is to think parts per *billion*.

These values are "acute" exposure criteria, concentrations that aquatic organisms can survive for one hour or less no more than once every three years. "Chronic" criteria are based upon a four-day average that occurs no more than once every three years. For copper, zinc, and cadmium, chronic standards are 12, 47, and

1.1 micrograms per liter, respectively. Unfortunately, drainage from the Mike Horse was rich in these metals, especially zinc.

Metals dissolved in water are invisible to the human eye. The water may appear as pristine as melted snow and still turn a healthy trout belly-up in hours. Humans tolerate copper and zinc in drinking water much better than trout do where they swim. Drinking-water standards for humans are one thousand and five thousand micrograms per liter for copper and zinc, respectively. The copper standard is based upon odor and taste acceptability, not human toxicity, and the zinc drinking-water standard is based upon taste. Just because we can safely drink it does not mean that a given water supply will support a healthy trout fishery.

An equally complex issue is the manner in which metals occur in water. If metals are dissolved, they are much more lethal than if they are not. Metal ions possess an affinity for suspended solids in streams, especially sediment and organic matter—dirt, if you will—and readily cling to them. Once adsorbed, these same metals are less available for biologic uptake, and hence they are less toxic.

Metals may also be part of the crystal structure of minerals that make up the sediment. Metals locked in mineral structures are less bioavailable and practically nontoxic to trout. Therefore, knowing the *total* concentration of a metal in water tells you little about whether that water is capable of supporting aquatic life. To answer such questions, one must break down the total concentration into those fractions that are bioavailable, typically referred to as either the dissolved or "total recoverable" fractions.[19]

Precisely *how* copper and zinc kill trout is not thoroughly understood. Both metals concentrate in the gills and interfere with respiration, essentially suffocating the fish. Acute metal exposure can cause trout livers to malfunction, and this can lead to diminished fish growth and reproduction. Acute exposures can also affect fish motor and feeding behavior, which can lead to a reduction of swimming and predator-avoidance capabilities.

Some evidence suggests that selected trout can develop a tolerance for specific metals and bioaccumulate some metals in their flesh and organs, even though the energy demands required for bioaccumulation and adaptation may result in reduced growth, physiological malfunctioning, and diminished reproduction. Diminished reproduction, over time, leads to declines in trout populations. Fishery biologists also suspect that prolonged exposure to sublethal metal concentrations can lead to genetic selection for traits favoring survival under marginal conditions. Rainbow trout, for example, seem to possess internal antennae that allow them to detect and avoid metal-rich waters, as if they sense lethal conditions and move away. However, biologists do not see such natural selection as a panacea. Long-term selection for survival in contaminated water could be at the expense of genetic variability and the ability to withstand and survive other environmental stresses.[20]

Liter Spence's hair is the salt-and-pepper gray that reminds me of a professional country club president, which he decidedly is not. He has spent most of his adult life as a fisheries biologist for Montana's Department of Fish, Wildlife and Parks. Spence is quietly good-natured, serious, and a careful listener. When I spoke to him, he looked attentively at me. If he disagreed with my point, he silently respected my right to hold a contrary, if unwise, opinion and waited until I was finished before responding.

Spence knows Montana's trout and trout streams and grasps the complexities of these ice-clear waters, their aquatic insects, algae, and nutrient sources and how they interact to create healthy fisheries. He has looked me in the eye and said that trout cannot live in water laced with copper or zinc. In the early 1970s, Spence worked in the upper Blackfoot watershed collecting environmental information in advance of an open-pit copper and molybdenum mine proposed by the Anaconda Minerals Company for the heart of the Heddleston district. His final report was being printed when the June 1975 flood struck and the Mike Horse tailings dam failed.[21] Spence's study was the first major investigation of the upper watershed's trout fishery and one of the very few of any kind since MacHaffie's 1911 diary.

Spence's 1975 report is the baseline against which subsequent changes in the Blackfoot River's fishery are compared. Hard data and serious analysis preceding the late 1960s do not exist. When anyone claims the river has deteriorated, they must do so against a 1975 benchmark. The upper river's fishery deteriorated between the 1880s and 1975, but there is little or no scientific evidence to substantiate what common sense and history tell us, a situation that repeats itself throughout the West. We can document only the incremental impact of the most recent decades. We know little about what existed before.

To supplement Spence's study, the Anaconda Minerals Company completed water-quality surveys in 1972 and 1973 "to determine the location and extent of acid mine seepage from abandoned mine tunnels in the Heddleston mining district." The company concluded that "high concentrations of metals enter the Blackfoot River from mine tunnels and tailings. Zinc and cadmium were highest from the Mike Horse tunnel." [22]

Spence noticed that the river below the Mike Horse Mine exhibited "a bluish-gray color" that gave the water a "hazy" appearance. He attributed it to suspended precipitates of colloidal hydroxides of heavy metals, common in surface waters affected by abandoned-mine drainage.[23] Four miles below the Mike Horse Mine, he documented average zinc concentrations in the river of 220 micrograms per liter, nearly five times the chronic freshwater criterion.[24] Not surprisingly, Spence found that "There were no fish in Beartrap Creek below its confluence with mine drainage from Mike Horse Creek, or in the main Blackfoot River below Anaconda Creek." However, "Both cutthroat and brook trout were observed in beaver ponds near Pass Creek [near the upper swamp], indicating improved water quality." "Poor quality water from mine seepage is improved by the time it reaches Pass Creek, but there are still chemical problems below this point for several miles." [25]

In the river above Landers Fork and in its higher tributaries, Spence determined cutthroat and brook trout to be the dominant species. He found healthy cutthroat and brook trout populations in Pass Creek, Anaconda Creek, Shoue Gulch, and Beartrap Creek both above, in, and immediately below the Mike Horse tailings pond.[26] In short, Spence found trout just where trout had been found since at least the 1930s. Of course, those in Beartrap Creek immediately below the tailings dam perished with its collapse in 1975.

As far as Spence is concerned, the 1975 Mike Horse tailings dam failure decimated the struggling Blackfoot River trout fishery as far downriver as Flesher Pass Road. He flew over the area in a

small plane shortly after news of the failure reached state authorities in Helena. When asked how flood-borne tailings impacted
the fishery, he methodically explained how some tailings ultimately settled into streambed gravel and either smothered eggs
waiting to hatch or made the habitat unsuitable for future spawning. The "gray water" also killed fish directly, presumably by "par-
ticle suffocation"—metals collecting on the gills and blocking
respiration. Or the fish ingest metal-rich particulates and insects
and bioaccumulated metals in their tissues and organs, thereby
inhibiting future growth and reproduction.[27] Although minor
trout populations survived in isolated tributaries, all may not be
well. Because the entire life cycle of these populations is limited
to a single reach of stream as short as several hundred feet, their
genetic diversity is sharply constrained. Some fish geneticists suspect that isolated populations like these may ultimately die out.[28]

More personal opinions, based upon individual fishing experiences and "creel surveys," offer a different slant on the upper
river's health and history. Shirley Ashby, a longtime fly fisherman
and summer resident on the river, has fished above and below
Lincoln since the 1930s. He remembers only one or two fishing ex-
cursions above Flesher Pass Road and recalls that "it wasn't too
bad." He rarely fished above Landers Fork because there was better fishing downriver, where he regularly caught cutthroats averaging fourteen to sixteen inches long.

Ashby believes that the 1964 flood ruined the upper river's fishery independently of the Mike Horse Mine and 1975 tailings dam
failure. Before 1964, he says, the river below Flesher Pass Road
meandered broadly across the valley floor. Thick willows crowded
the banks and shaded deep holes. It was prime trout habitat. But
the 1964 flood straightened the river, tore out the willows and
left behind shallow riffles and exposed gravel bars, features still
remaining more than thirty years later. Ashby argues that the
best trout habitat disappeared with these floodwaters.[29]

Paul Roos has also fished the Blackfoot River for decades. Roos
grew up near Lincoln and began fishing the river in 1949. "There
was a nice cutthroat fishery above Landers Fork in the early 1970s,"
he says. In the first half of the 1970s, Roos also fished above the
canyon, in the upper and lower swamps, where he readily caught
plenty of brook trout. But after the dam failure in 1975, Roos

stopped fishing the upper river. He tried the canyon above Flesher Pass Road once but caught nothing. Today, he is a professional fishing guide. His livelihood depends upon knowing where to take his clients. He does not fish the Blackfoot much.[30]

Douglas Dollhopf is one of the most successful mined land reclamation scientists in the West. After completing a doctorate in soil physics, Dollhopf applied his training in soil science and agricultural practices to his work as a nationally acclaimed research scientist with Montana State University's Reclamation Research Unit in Bozeman.

In 1987 Dollhopf led an investigation into the effectiveness of the upper swamp—or *wetlands*, in precise academic terminology—in removing metals from acid mine drainage. Wetlands, by definition, exist where the land is at least periodically saturated with or covered by water. In the words of Dollhopf's group, "Saturation with water is the dominant factor in soil development and in determining the types of plants and animals that are in the soil and on its surface."[31]

Although they focused on a single abandoned mine discharging to the upper wetlands from Swamp Gulch, their conclusions are applicable to the Heddleston district's greater impact on the upper Blackfoot River. The wetlands' upper layer, more than one-half-meter-thick, was composed of aerated, undecomposed organic debris underlain by a thicker gray muck of anaerobic, decomposed organic materials, silt, and clay. Metal concentrations were highest in the upper layer and closest to the Swamp Gulch source, suggesting that the wetlands removed metals from the mine drainage. But Dollhopf's team also concluded that the wetlands did not remove all metals to the same degree, removing lead completely and iron quite readily from the effluent, but copper, zinc, manganese, and cadmium far less effectively.[32]

Anaerobic microorganisms were instrumental in decreasing metals in acid mine water. Located in the upper soil layer, they played a role in raising the pH of the effluent and rendering dissolved metals less soluble, which led to their precipitation and increased adsorption. Sulfate-reducing bacteria were likewise present in the wetlands, and along with ample organic matter and free sulfur reversed the oxidation of sulfide minerals and essentially immobilized the metals through the formation of new metal sulfide precipitates in the wetland sediments.[33]

Dollhopf's group found also that some wetland plant species are more metal-tolerant than others. One type of sedge even accumulated metals, as did common willow and birch. Even lowly forms of moss appeared to concentrate and selectively remove metals from the mine's acidic effluent. Indeed, some plants so effectively concentrated metals, especially cadmium in willow shrubs, that the plants "exceeded the maximum tolerable dietary intake levels for domestic animals, suggesting a potential problem for animals that consume these plants." Domestic animals are not grazed at this location, but the researchers concluded that resident wildlife might be slowly poisoned by ingesting cadmium-enriched willows.[34]

I had heard Johnnie Moore's name many times but had never met him. His name and academic reputation are synonymous with metal movement in the Blackfoot River, research that earned him a full professorship at the University of Montana. When I arrived on campus, Moore was bustling in and out of his office and up and down the hall, frantically organizing a tray of slides for a talk to be presented the following week at the annual meeting of the Geological Society of America. Since we had an appointment, he cheerfully broke off his search and returned to his office.

Moore looked to be in his forties. Graying dark hair fell across his forehead and over his ears. In conjunction with a beard, his head appears bushy. He dressed the part of a geologist itching to be outdoors: a dark wool shirt, levis, and hiking boots.

Articulate and opinionated, Moore's physical and intellectual energy were palpable. His feet bounced on the floor as ideas tumbled forth, and as he talked, he looked around his office, then at me, then around his office again. He is an aging, precocious kid, full of ideas. Beginning in 1988, Moore, assisted by Sam Luoma of the U.S. Geological Survey and Don Peters of Montana's Department of Fish, Wildlife and Parks, began investigating and characterizing the long-term impact on the Blackfoot River of nearly a century of mining in the Heddleston district.[35] Their research objective was to "understand the biological fate of metals mobilized by acid mine drainage." [36]

Building upon the previous research of Spence and others, as well as historical descriptions of the 1975 tailings dam failure, Moore and his colleagues investigated the downriver movement of aluminum, cadmium, copper, iron, lead, and zinc, plus arsenic and whether they accumulated in aquatic organisms (a process termed *bioaccumulation*) and eventually moved into the food web of the adjacent floodplain and riparian zone. They also correlated changes in aquatic insects with increases in metals, expecting that the absence or shortage of aquatic insects would result in dwindling fish numbers or decreased fish health and reproduction.

Prior to Moore's research, some biologists assumed that metals originating in the Heddleston district had been retarded in their downriver dispersion by natural, physical, and biochemical processes operating within the two wetlands just below Pass Creek. They thought swamps naturally purified the water and rendered it safe for aquatic life. Native phenomena were believed to cause metals to become less biologically available, as well as less susceptible to continuing downriver transport.

Key to this natural treatment hypothesis was the role of organic carbon. All biological matter contains carbon; it is an essential and characteristic component of life. Chemists have long known that metal ions readily adsorb to organic carbon. Since swamps possess an abundance of organic matter, it was assumed that metal-enriched river water entering the swamps reacted with the carbon, a reaction that removed the metals. Related mechanisms that were presumed to be operating in this natural purification system included physical filtration and other forms of biological sorption by bacteria, algae, fungi, and assorted plant life.

Wetlands were also presumed to act as natural sediment traps. Free-flowing streams and rivers suspend sediment and transport it until the sediment load exceeds the sediment transport capacity of the stream. Typically, this occurs at a widening and slowing of the river, entrance to a lake, the ocean, or the relatively still water of wetlands. As flowing water slows, its sediment transport capacity lessens and sediment settles. In this manner, swamps can remove sediment—or tailings—from streams and rivers in the same manner that man-made reservoirs remove sediment from rivers, just as Utah's Lake Powell removes sediment from the Colorado River.[37]

After assessing these assumptions, Moore's group detected abnormally high concentrations of most metals in the river, as well as a pronounced mobility of others, fifteen miles below the Mike Horse Mine and far beyond the wetlands. Field observations and aerial photos indicated that the Blackfoot River did not, as had been assumed, disappear into the beaver-dammed swamps where it received natural treatment. Rather, the river channel meandered through the wetlands essentially intact. The water underwent relatively little treatment.[38]

Not surprisingly, Moore's group detected declining and depressed trout populations within the wetlands and farther downriver. Between Spence's fieldwork in the early 1970s and that of Moore's group in 1988, both brook and cutthroat trout populations declined as far downstream as Flesher Pass Road, a distance of about nine miles below the Mike Horse Mine. Cutthroats have essentially vanished from affected reaches of the Blackfoot, although in viable reaches of Pass and Anaconda Creeks, meager cutthroat and brook trout populations hang on.[39] Apparently, not all metals were settling out harmlessly. Since publication of Moore's conclusions, wags have suggested that the most effective method of trout fishing in the upper Blackfoot might be to troll with a magnet.

Downriver from the wetlands, Moore's group found that the most pronounced metals were cadmium and zinc. Both are extremely toxic to trout, which may account for at least some of the documented decrease in trout populations. In fact, brown trout and stone flies had bioaccumulated cadmium and zinc as far downriver as forty-six miles below the Mike Horse Mine.[40] The researchers concluded that the wetlands did not remove or significantly retard metals originating in the Heddleston district: "marsh systems may slow the transport of metals, but they do not necessarily completely stop downstream contamination of the food web by the most mobile of the metals. Particulate contaminants generally penetrated the marsh system to a greater extent than did solute contamination, but the marsh system is complex geochemically, possibly acting as both sink and source for different particulate metal contaminants."[41]

Together, Moore's and Dollhopf's studies demonstrate that metals are not a static part of the environment. Rather, metals unleashed by mining and milling alter readily to other forms and continue moving, dispersing and concentrating in accordance with their own chemical habits. Water quality, for example, may appear to improve as dissolved metals adsorb or precipitate, but the metals are simply present in solid forms not typically measured. Metals persist: they dissolve, adsorb, precipitate, and settle, but they always remain metals. Chemically, they do not alter to something else. Zinc never decays to calcium, for instance.

At some point in their migratory path, metal concentrations in streams and rivers, soil, plants, fish, and insects may slide beneath lethal levels and no longer kill or affect the organisms that ingest them. On occasion, however, these same life forms concentrate metals. Moore has observed bottom-dwelling insects in the Blackfoot River coated with iron oxides.[42] It is impossible to conclude that trout feeding on such insects will not ingest these metals along with the meal.

To a largely unknown degree, mill tailings introduced to the Blackfoot River in June of 1975 spread far downriver, where they ultimately settled as a veneer of sand in pools and on the floodplain. Long-term consequences remain uncertain. Potentially, we may be unable to distinguish these consequences from those of other land uses. Conceivably, little or nothing will change; after all, metals are ubiquitous and ecosystems have had millennia to adapt.

In the meantime, as the evidence is collected, sifted, and debated, the fishery below the Mike Horse Mine remains afflicted. Trout struggle in waters most fishermen have learned to ignore. An obvious question cannot be ignored, however: How many other western waters have been similarly depleted of fish and similarly affected by past mining?

8. When Giants Die

[T]he surging vogue of environmental activity with its enacted legal authority required large staff efforts and capital outlay for plant and other alterations, without providing tangible compensation in the form of increased productivity.—Vincent D. Perry, "Anaconda Geology, Its Origins, Achievements, and Philosophy"

I wouldn't believe anything a mining company would tell you.—Shirley Ashby, longtime Blackfoot River fisherman, 1996.

I HAD CRAWLED MY TRUCK two miles up a steep, four-wheel-drive track through dense, stunted Douglas fir. Just below a break in slope, unable to see the next stretch and not wanting to back down anything more twisting and precipitous than what I had just driven, I stopped, jammed a large rock behind a wheel, tightened my boots, and began climbing.

I emerged from the timber onto a south-facing slope. The air was heavy with the perfume of wet sage, and wildflowers blazed around me. Farther up-slope, the track broke sharply to the right, toward the Divide, but I turned left and wandered westward along a ridge. The sun warmed my left arm and cheek, while my right side felt the damp of last winter's snowdrifts still clutching at the shade of whitebark pine. A mile later, atop the highest point on this nameless ridge, I stopped. Red Mountain and its snow-jacketed neighbors crowned the northwestern horizon. Virescent forest and lush meadows nearly surrounded me, but the idyllic scene was imperfect. To the north, miles of narrow roads crisscrossed the timbered mountainsides from the Mike Horse Mine west to State Highway 200. Nearly invisible from the highway, and now mostly overgrown with lodgepole pine, the roads materialized three decades ago.

More than the abandoned waste dumps, more even than the iron-stained stream in Mike Horse Gulch, the roads characterize the district's recent history. I can avoid individual rock dumps and acidic streams but not roads spanning whole mountain valleys. Road networks like this brand hundreds of valleys and mountains in the American West as having been searched for minerals. They are more straight lines where nature would have none.

While I was still in high school, engineers chiseled these roads in a spasm of mineral activity. Hollywood would have us believe that early western prospectors and miners all looked and behaved like Gabby Hayes. But in spite of individuals like Joseph Hartmiller and Norman Rogers, our western legacy is due as much to the actions of multinational mining companies as to the little guy. I sought the district's whole story in all its ragged pieces. What I found was a tale of how a large mining corporation went about its business in the 1960s and 1970s.

By 1964 the Heddleston Mining District had produced an estimated twenty-five million dollars worth of metals, and some experts thought its mines were exhausted.[1] Originally a silver and lead strike, ASARCO turned the Mike Horse Mine into a major lead and zinc producer during and following World War II. Though zinc and lead were the primary metals extracted from the Mike Horse Vein, it was not uncommon for the ore to generate silver and gold as well. But hidden within reports of the time was mention of copper. Nearly sixty years following its discovery and development, the Mike Horse was to become a copper mine. Surely the geology had not changed. What happened?

Copper was profitably mined in the Heddleston district prior to 1930, although not in quantities enough to draw attention.[2] In 1954 the ever-independent Norman Rogers reported that he mined copper-lead ore from the Mike Horse; in 1955 he claimed production of copper ore. During this same period, Montana Bureau of Mines and Geology indicated that Rogers's operation produced gold, silver, copper, lead, and zinc. By 1964 the operator claimed to be developing the mine for silver, copper, lead, and zinc.[3]

A primary force behind this shift to copper was the now-familiar Charles C. Goddard Jr. In 1940 Goddard was one of the original incorporators of the Mike Horse Mining and Milling Company, while he was simultaneously employed by Anaconda Copper Mining Company. Even after severing his relationship with Mike Horse Mining and Milling Company, Goddard retained a personal interest in the Heddleston district. Twenty years later, he was chief geologist of the Montana division for the recently re-named Anaconda Company, a position from which he once again endeavored to interest his Anaconda bosses in his pet area. In a 1979 history of the company, Anaconda's former chief geologist, Vincent D. Perry, recounted that "Charles Goddard made a vigor-ous effort to interest the company in the Mike Horse Mine near Helena."[4] Few geologists knew the Mike Horse Mine and Heddle-ston district as well as Goddard. He knew it so well that a larger picture formed in his mind, a picture focused on Anaconda's pri-mary commodity: copper.

Many major hardrock mining districts experience a recurring theme of exploration, development, and mining, then more ex-ploration and development and more mining, and so on. One ge-ologist's ruling certainties are inevitably tossed aside and funda-mental field truths and bedrock exposures are reinterpreted in light of new thinking by younger minds. Once a district or mine has proven profitable, mining companies return again and again, never seeming to get enough.

The human ego also plays a part. An experienced mining geol-ogist rarely advises his or her superiors to forget about a particu-lar prospect, mine, or district because of insufficient mineraliza-tion. More likely the geologist concludes only that information is too limited to make a definitive judgment, that conditions are not optimal for immediate company action, or that other prospects ap-pear more profitable. Such waffling may occur even when a geolo-gist is certain that further exploration or development would be a waste of time and money. This reluctance to explicitly write off a prospect is founded upon professional self-preservation. What geologist would wish to convince his or her bosses that a claim or mine has absolutely no value, only to see another geologist and some other mining company acquire the property and hit it big?

To prove his hunch, Goddard and his Anaconda colleagues as-sembled every available scrap of geological and mining informa-tion on the Heddleston district and formulated a plan to add needed detail. In 1962 they received approval to complete detailed geological field mapping in the district. More field mapping and some rudimentary geophysical studies were executed the following year.[5] From this new information Goddard's group concluded that the district included a larger and very different ore body than the one ASARCO and its predecessors had mined. It is likely that ASARCO had been aware of this other, deeper ore body, but Anaconda was clearly the first to focus on it.

Until Anaconda reassessed the Heddleston district, the fundamental geological interpretation of the area and its mineral resources had changed little in sixty years. Generally stated, the district was made up of thick beds of weakly metamorphosed argillites that hosted steeply dipping veins bearing silver and lead mineralization. Zinc, always present, had also become an industrial metal worth recovering. With Goddard's substantial expertise and fresh outlook and Norman Rogers's energetic talk of copper mineralization at the Mike Horse, Anaconda took a deeper look.

Where the district's first miners pursued veins that crosscut the district, Goddard's group pinned Anaconda's hopes on a deeper and broader *copper porphyry* deposit, a term referring to a large deposit of uniformly disseminated, low-grade copper. Goddard's group believed that such an ore body, hosted by an intrusive rock mass, lay beneath much of the Heddleston district. Geological evidence suggested that the district's major ore structures, such as the Mike Horse Vein, were genetically related to this deeper, intrusive porphyry body. Geologic maps showed the Mike Horse Vein originating from near or within the porphyry deposit. Eventually, a senior Anaconda geologist affirmed these suspicions, "The Heddleston porphyry intrusions are also the source for hypogene sulfide mineralization in fault- and dike-related veins productive in the early history of the district."[6] In other words, Anaconda believed that ASARCO and the district's first miners had only scratched the surface.

Anaconda already possessed the knowledge and experience necessary to profitably mine a porphyry ore body. The Butte district hosted a similar ore deposit, and the company had exploited it for decades. Also, the new Heddleston ore body was amenable to the same open-pit mining methods that Anaconda had pioneered in Butte's Berkeley Pit. In terms of total ore reserves, Heddleston was certainly not Butte, but an undeveloped copper ore body was just fine with the company. It also did not hurt that molybdenum, a metal with increasing modern industrial uses, was present in minable values. By late 1963, Anaconda believed it had identified in the Heddleston a copper-molybdenum porphyry deposit requiring more attention and commensurately greater expenditures. First among these needs was control of all property even remotely required for a major open-pit mine.

Norman Rogers's lease with ASARCO gave him almost exclusive control of the Mike Horse Mine and ASARCO's claims in the district. Thus, if Anaconda expected to pursue its grander objective, it had to negotiate assignment of the lease with Rogers. Rogers refused to be intimidated by Anaconda. He had a personal score to settle with the copper giant. Rogers had been a successful and independent copper miner in Montana for a long time, but years earlier, while mining another property leased from Anaconda, he experienced a bitter turn of events. Reportedly, he was mining profitably in an open pit and had completed considerable development work in the form of stripping when his lease was summarily revoked by Anaconda without compensation for the stripping.[7] Independent miners are a fiercely stubborn and independent breed; few take such a blow without harboring a grudge.

Individual miners rarely bested Anaconda in a deal, but with eleven patented and fifty-three unpatented claims at stake, covering more than twelve hundred acres, Anaconda needed Rogers more than Rogers needed Anaconda. In July of 1964, with ASARCO's consent, Anaconda finally agreed to pay Rogers $105,806 for assignment of his ASARCO leases.[8] Rogers gained his measure of revenge.

At the same time Anaconda was negotiating with Rogers, it was buying and leasing other property within and surrounding the Heddleston district. Owners like the reclusive Paramount Estates (which owned the Paymaster Mine), Midnight Copper Mining Company (which controlled claims surrounding the Paymaster Mine), Harrison Kleinschmidt (who controlled claims west of the Mike Horse Mine), and others reached agreements with Anaconda. Landowners with property surrounding the district likewise cut deals with the Butte-based giant.[9] Ultimately, Anaconda acquired control of nearly 16,000 acres in the area, or *25 square miles*, including 41 patented and 187 unpatented claims. To achieve this control, the company spent at least $1.2 million.[10]

Confirmation of these negotiations, deals, and Anaconda's planned exploration drilling was big news in western Montana. Helena's *Independent Record* reported in August of 1964 that Anaconda, along with Kennecott Copper Company, had "acquired" thirty thousand acres centered on the Mike Horse Mine area.[11] Tens of would-be miners flooded Anaconda's employment office. But the company's plans, though large, were slow to develop.

No mining company, whether an international conglomerate like Anaconda or an inconsiderable father-and-son outfit, will invest the capital required to develop a mine and make it profitable without having at least some idea what is there. Anaconda was looking to spend millions to fabricate a major open-pit mine, complete with heavy machinery, office buildings, crushing plants and concentrators, water management and transportation facilities, and roads and parking lots. Shareholders would revolt if company directors authorized the expenditure of millions of dollars without some evidence that the investment might garner an economic return. To prove a project's value, then and now, the mining industry drills.

Between 1964 and 1970, Anaconda constructed nearly thirty miles of gravel roads, which are still visible today, and acres of exploration drill sites to facilitate an intensive exploration program.[12] An exploration program begins with detailed field mapping of the local geology and petrologic and geochemical assays of collected rock samples. But these activities can tell only so much; maps reveal only two dimensions. Geologic mapping and rock analyses are followed by a drilling program designed to provide information about a suspected ore deposit's three-dimensional properties.

Surveying locates the surface elevation and horizontal control coordinates of the drill sites. Subsequent exploration drilling commonly extracts "cores" from the underlying bedrock. These cores, one and one-half to two inches in diameter, are examined by a geologist who notes the depth and rock type that has been penetrated and the mineralization encountered. The core samples are also subjected to geochemical and assay work. When this subsurface geological information is plotted against the horizontal and vertical survey coordinates, the geologist obtains his or her three-dimensional "view" of the ore body.

A simple analogy can be envisioned by considering the same carton of fudge ripple ice cream I introduced earlier. If we assume that the fudge swirls represent mineralization and simply open the top of the carton and look for the fudge, we see only the fudge visible on the surface. We do not know where and how the fudge varies beneath the surface. If, however, we push a series of rigid straws into the ice cream, extract them and carefully split the straws lengthwise, we can determine precisely where the fudge lies. We gain a three-dimensional perspective of the contents of the entire carton and learn how to most efficiently spoon out the fudge.

Anaconda's road network extended from near the Mike Horse Mine westward to State Highway 200, straddling the Mike Horse Road and covering roughly two square miles. Eventually, the company drilled 340 holes to define the ore body, a total of nearly a quarter-million feet, or an average of about 730 feet per hole. Anaconda also drove two horizontal adits from next to the Blackfoot River into the mountainsides. The first adit advanced southward from near the mouth of Moly Gulch. Anaconda drove the second adit northward into the base of Midnight Hill.[13]

Meanwhile, in 1964, the Anaconda Minerals Company realized its greatest revenues and earnings since 1959. Metal prices had been strong, but net income would have been even greater if not for "extended strikes, higher wages and fringe benefits under new labor contracts, and general increases in the cost of services, operating supplies and equipment."[14] In 1965 Anaconda's business boomed ahead. Revenue and net earnings were up again. Copper prices remained strong, even though the U.S. government had rolled back price supports late in the year. Domestic labor strife was minimal and capital improvements were finally paying their way. The only dark cloud on Anaconda's economic horizon was in South America, where the company had invested millions in Chile to develop new world-class copper deposits. There, the company experienced both labor unrest and government instability.[15]

Against these larger issues, the company's Heddleston exploration program began to provide results. By August of 1965, a senior research metallurgist described the company's optimism to a colleague: "This is an ore deposit approximately 8,000 feet by 4,000 feet which surrounded the old Mike Horse Mine which was a lead-zinc operation. This is a true moly halo with the inner circle showing molybdenum and the outer circle showing copper. This is a very interesting prospect, geologically, and will be watched very closely."[16] Anaconda's excitement over possibilities in the Heddleston district was strong enough to warrant first-time mention in the company's 1965 annual report: "Drilling in the old Heddleston mining district north of Helena, MONTANA, has shown encouraging sections of low-grade copper and molybdenum mineralization."[17]

With such goings-on in the neighborhood, the Kornecs could not be faulted for thinking a piece of the pie might be available. In the summer of 1966, several optimistic family members approached Anaconda with an offer to sell the family's twenty-one unpatented claims in upper Beartrap Gulch, which lay south and east of Anaconda's holdings. They asked for thirty-five thousand dollars per claim. Anaconda's operatives did not consider control of the Kornecs's claims necessary to put its mine into operation and responded that, collectively, the claims were not worth more than fifty thousand dollars and that they were "nuisance claims" at that. Insisting "they would never consider such a low offer," the Kornecs departed, thus ending negotiations with Anaconda.[18]

At about the same time the Kornecs approached Anaconda, the company was appraising the utility and value of the remaining Mike Horse Mine buildings, still standing after ASARCO's 1953 shutdown. The main office structure was deemed in good condition and fit for salvage, as was the mill building. But twelve small cabins opposite the tailings dam, almost all that remained of the community of Mike Horse, were considered of no value and were given to anyone willing to haul them away. The Kornecs purchased ASARCO's office building and dragged it to its current location on their claims above the Mike Horse tailings impoundment. Seeking a change as well as opportunity, George Kornec returned to Beartrap Gulch from where he had been working in Butte. Over the next several years, he worked periodically with Anaconda's exploration drilling crews, while also converting the office building into a home for his mother and himself. He has not lived elsewhere since.[19]

Anaconda's mining engineering department took the information developed by Goddard's staff and generated a preliminary plan on how to most efficiently and profitably mine the ore body. Their efforts incorporated much more than the ore body's geology, however. Topography and surface drainage, existing roads and State Highway 200, power requirements, expected mine life, needed buildings, transportation corridors both for incoming labor and supplies and outgoing concentrate had to fit into a coherent plan of operation. As an integral part of this process, engineers estimated the costs to construct all facilities as well as the financial return based upon assumed metal prices and known ore reserves.

The time and effort required to produce this plan was considerable, even for a mining giant like Anaconda. The process was both laborious and dynamic, especially during a time without computers. Today, mining companies make extensive use of computer-assisted mine-planning programs. Complex calculations that used to require hours of effort by hunched-over engineers now take only minutes. In the 1960s, if an Anaconda executive wanted an estimate of the associated costs and expected returns of the Heddleston project, someone first had to make informed decisions about assumed metal prices and known reserves of a given grade. Tedious, complex calculations followed. If a single factor changed, the mining engineers had to revise their figures. If assumed metal prices were increased, and more tonnage of a lower grade ore could be mined, the whole planning operation had to be redone. Today, desktop computers allow calculation of multiple scenarios in a fraction of the time required in 1965.

A critical component of any mine-planning exercise is the *ore reserve*. Every mining company places its own twist on the term. Anaconda defined ore reserves as the "[T]onnage and grade of metal-bearing material that can be mined *at a profit*. Ore reserves increase and decrease constantly depending on mining and metallurgical costs, metal prices, and other economic factors."[20] With new information becoming available each month, company engineers generated a preliminary mine plan by July of 1966.

They envisioned a massive open pit extending from near the confluence of Anaconda and Beartrap Creeks westward to the drainage divide between Paymaster and Meadow Creeks, a distance of about one and one-half miles. The pit's north-south extent reached from the drainage divide south of the Mike Horse

Mine north to the opposite side of State Highway 200 as it climbed Rogers Pass, roughly an equal distance. An ore-crushing plant and mill complex would be built immediately west of the pit, near the highway. The waste-rock dump would occupy an expanse south of the highway from near the upper swamp to below First Gulch. Miles from the center of the pit, a mill tailings impoundment and freshwater supply ponds were planned for lower Alice Creek, opposite the junction of the highway and Flesher Pass Road. Mill tailings would have to be slurried in a pipe for more than a mile. The Blackfoot River would be diverted from near the upper swamp to the mouth of Third Gulch, a distance of nearly two miles. Anaconda's first plan was considerable, indeed.[21]

News of this plan, enhanced by rumor and possibly by corporate leaks, eventually found its way to the public. In northern Idaho, the 4 May 1967 *Wallace Miner* reported Anaconda's Heddleston plans and implied that initial construction was only months away. To house a workforce of between five hundred and eight hundred persons, two hundred to three hundred prefabricated homes were being constructed for delivery to Lincoln, which would grow from four hundred to more than four thousand. Further, the paper reported, a horizontal tunnel was being drilled beneath the Continental Divide from the Heddleston mine site to Silver City, twenty-five miles distant, so that a conveyor or pipeline could move mill concentrates to the nearest railroad load-out.[22] In reality, most of these reported "facts" were little more than internal company guesswork and ideas. Anaconda's board of directors had approved nothing more than continuing exploration and planning.

The year 1966 was again extremely profitable for the company, largely because Chile's government agreed to honor contracts with Anaconda's Chilean subsidiaries.[23] The following year also began in rewarding fashion, but a major domestic labor strike stifled operations during the latter half of the year and ended the period on a sour note. Anaconda's 1967 annual report to shareholders observed, "The last six months of 1967 and the early months of 1968 were particularly difficult times for the company as the longest strike in the history of the domestic non-ferrous industry developed progressively until it closed down almost all domestic copper mining and refining operations, lead and zinc mines."[24]

Industrywide work stoppages cut drastically into Anaconda's operating income. By the end of 1967, all nonessential costs and programs had been cut or terminated, including exploration activities at Heddleston.[25] Nonetheless, the company's mine-planning group had already calculated ore reserves for the Heddleston project at 233,812,000 tons, averaging 0.40 percent copper, 0.021 percent molybdenum sulfide, and 0.18 ounces of silver per ton.[26]

A revised mine plan was completed only months later, in January of 1968. This new plan called for feeding twenty-five thousand tons of ore *per day* to a mill that would concentrate copper, molybdenum, and silver from "all material in excess of 0.3% copper and/or 0.091% molybdenum." Metal prices assumed for the plan were $0.38 per pound for copper, $1.55 per pound for molybdenum sulfide concentrate, and $1.80 per ounce for silver. Most telling, perhaps, was the plan's new assumption that *287,000,000 tons* of ore were available for mining. In effect, the mine's potential was growing even as the engineers planned it. Based on these new assumptions and calculations, the engineers anticipated an after-tax profit to the company of ninety-five million dollars over the anticipated mine life of thirty-three years.[27]

Possibly as a consequence of changing numbers, and certainly as a result of financial hardships endured during 1967 and early 1968, Anaconda's 1968 annual report declared only that "The company's property at Heddleston, Montana, was maintained in readiness for future development." The labor strike ended early in 1968, but the company undertook no exploration at Heddleston that year.[28] With some temerity, Anaconda restarted its Heddleston exploration program the following year, 1969. The company also began committing financial resources to a small but promising platinum and palladium project located in the headwaters of southwestern Montana's Stillwater River. Vacillation of this kind is not uncommon for a large mining company. In this respect, it is no different than any other corporation that has multiple investment opportunities and that makes decisions and capital commitments on the basis of expected financial returns. A defining characteristic of hardrock mining is that actual returns may vary chaotically from predicted returns due to uncontrollable fluctuations in world metal prices and varying results of ongoing exploration and active mining. Costs are also notably difficult to predict and control.

Still, the company's 1969 profits were up another 10 percent—the third highest in company history. Total North American copper production achieved record highs. Yet, south of the equator, the Chilean government had informed Anaconda in May that the company had two choices concerning the future of its Chilean holdings: assent to "nationalization by agreement" or endure outright expropriation.

Anaconda attempted to negotiate, with less than satisfactory results. Chile and the company agreed to a new structural relationship whereby the company placed its Chilean assets with two new companies, then sold 51 percent of the stock in these companies to Codelco, Chile's government-owned, copper-mining giant, in exchange for promissory notes. Anaconda also agreed to sell the remaining 49 percent of these two new companies after 1972.[29] Anaconda was being squeezed out of Chile and forced to surrender tens of millions of dollars in known copper reserves to the Chilean government for cents on the dollar.

As Anaconda continued its Heddleston exploration and development program through the late 1960s, it simultaneously battled increasing domestic pressures that, on the whole, worked against its plans in western Montana. Several of these factors were beyond the company's control, such as the objective nature of the Heddleston ore body and the kind and size of mine it would support as well as the impact of America's rising, politically charged environmental movement. Persistent labor strife also complicated internal workings.

In 1967, when Anaconda first calculated Heddleston's total ore reserve, company engineers concluded that 233,812,000 tons were available for mining. Within months, calculated reserves swelled 23 percent to 287,000,000 tons. Anaconda did not create this increase; rather, it resulted from a more painstaking review of what nature had provided, plus changing metal markets. When the company publicly announced its intentions to mine its Heddleston ore body in 1969, the scale of Anaconda's mining plan stunned the public, but no one familiar with what the company had accomplished in Butte was surprised. The announced plan differed little in concept from the rudimentary plan that had shuttled through the company in 1966. In the publicly announced plan, the Blackfoot River would be diverted through and around key mine facilities in a four-thousand-foot-long ditch. Waste dumps were slated to fill the drainages of Paymaster Gulch and Meadow Creek. Mill tailings would be stored behind a dam in the Alice Creek-Hardscrabble Creek area.[30]

Notably, the plan included a water-supply impoundment in lower Alice Creek. Essential to the dam's construction, however, was gaining control of 680 acres of land owned by the state of Montana—property dedicated by the state constitution to the financial support of public schools. Thus, as designed and proposed by Anaconda, the Heddleston project hinged upon the company gaining control of relatively few acres of state land. In 1970 Anaconda proposed to purchase an easement on the Alice Creek property from the state.[31]

Knowledgeable Montanans insist that the fight against Anaconda's Heddleston plans spawned the state's environmental movement. Robert Woodahl, Montana's attorney general at the time of the company's announcement, said as much. A differing opinion was voiced by Ted Schwinden, who was the appointed commissioner of state lands during this period, and later a two-term governor. Schwinden believes that Anaconda's plan only "crystallized" a movement already in existence and provided a focus for the young crusade to influence state law and policy. To Schwinden, Anaconda's proposal was like "throwing gasoline on a fire."[32] Those fomenting the first environmental challenge to the company in decades did so by pouncing on Anaconda's proposed easement. In their eyes, Alice Creek was the project's Achilles heel.

Throughout the West, federal law from the 1780s stipulates how land is surveyed and subdivided into *sections*, commonly a one-mile square containing 640 acres. At statehood, western states surrendered their claims to most lands within their boundaries to the federal government and in return received a considerable number of sections, the income from which was constitutionally mandated to support public education. Montana's constitution in 1970 required a Board of Land Commissioners to decide policy issues pertaining to the use of the state's "school trust lands." Composed of Montana's four highest-ranking elected officials, including the governor, attorney general, secretary of state, and superintendent of public instruction, the Board of Land Commissioners managed the trust lands on behalf of Montana's public schools. Montana subsequently adopted a new state constitution in 1972, which added a fifth elected official, the state auditor, to the board.

Montana's Board of Land Commissioners held the authority to decide whether to grant easements on school trust lands to mining companies. Although the board did not have the authority to approve or deny a permit for the Heddleston mine—no Montana agency had such authority in 1970—the board's decision on the easement would, in effect, accomplish the same thing. And because Anaconda never indicated it would remove the dam when mining ended, granting the easement largely decided the land's future use.[33]

Given widespread public interest in Anaconda's easement request, the board considered the issue over a period of several months. The first public meeting at which the Alice Creek easement was addressed was held in March of 1970. The meeting was considered so newsworthy that CBS covered it for national television.[34]

Anaconda made its case by offering the testimony of an impressive list of professionals, consultants, and various state and federal agencies, including the U.S. Forest Service, U.S. Geological Survey, and Montana's own Water Resources Board. All favored the project.[35] In fact, the Montana Water Resources Board had already granted Anaconda permission to discharge future mill wastewater directly into the Blackfoot River (which would have finished off the river for good).[36] Lincoln residents supported the project overwhelmingly, although not unanimously. Anaconda had promised the town a new school, sewer system, and hospital when the mine opened.[37]

Montana's homegrown environmentalists responded with their own experts, including a vocal cadre of Lincoln residents, who testified on probable impacts on the Blackfoot River's remaining fishery and the Blackfoot headwaters' abundant elk herds. They insisted that the social structure of Lincoln and the upper Blackfoot River Valley would be changed forever, in their view for the worse.[38]

The historical record concerning the board's action at this initial meeting is contradictory. Surviving minutes make no mention of a formal decision on the easement. Some individuals recall, however, that the board deadlocked 2–2 on granting the easement and could only agree on deferring action to a later date and following further study.[39] In April and again in early May, the board deferred action. Finally, on 20 May, the board voted 3–0 to approve the easement, *with stipulations*. The stipulations had been developed, at the board's direction, by the Department of State Lands under Commissioner Schwinden. The board granted the easement provided that Anaconda agreed to eleven stipulations designed to satisfy environmental concerns and protect the area's amenities.[40]

Anaconda had no qualms about the first ten stipulations. The final stipulation, however, was more stringent than had ever been applied to the mining industry. It required Anaconda, upon the completion of mining, to reclaim the mined and disturbed lands to the "best beneficial land use."[41] In essence, the Board of Land Commissioners was establishing the precedent requiring mine reclamation in Montana. Montana's legislature would not enact a statute mandating mine reclamation until the following year.

The Board of Land Commissioners remained under public pressure. Montana's burgeoning environmental groups ensured that the antimine drumbeat continued. They were quietly fed critical wildlife and fisheries information by scientists from within state agencies and the U.S. Forest Service who were opposed to the project. Antimine editorials appeared in prominent Montana newspapers. National environmental groups such as Trout Unlimited, Sierra Club, and National Wildlife Federation, as well as the League of Women Voters, panned Anaconda's proposal. At the same time, the mine's proponents weighed in with repeated guarantees that the nation needed copper and that the company was sensitive to the environment. Both sides utilized the press as much as possible.[42]

Behind the scenes, as the public furor waxed and waned, Anaconda realized two new and critical facts. First, and extremely important, senior geologists revised the estimates of the Heddleston project's ore reserves to much less than the original 200,000,000-plus tons. Almost no one outside the company was aware that Anaconda's Copper Production Evaluation Committee had decided, by mid-1970, that Heddleston's *proven* reserves totaled only 110,000,000 tons. Demonstrated copper and silver values had remained fairly constant in the reanalysis, but molybdenum values had declined sharply from 0.15 percent to 0.01 percent. In fact, the company's mine-planning engineers reestimated that the company's after-tax return on investment would be less than 3 percent if the company proceeded with mining the Heddleston ore body.[43] Realizing that the company had other properties that would potentially realize higher returns, Anaconda's executives decided the property did not justify the investment needed to open and operate the mine.[44]

The second piece of new information derived from groundwater test wells drilled in the upper Blackfoot River Valley and along lower Alice Creek. When combined with surface water rights already owned by Anaconda, the company realized it had access to sixty-five hundred gallons of water per minute, whereas the company's proposed fifteen thousand tons-per-day mining operation required just twenty-five hundred gallons per minute. Thus, just two months following the Board of Land Commissioners' decision, Anaconda recognized that it no longer needed the water-supply reservoir upon which the original easement request was based.[45]

In its final official public statement, Anaconda did not agree to the board's stipulations and withdrew its application for the easement. The board's stipulations gave the company an easy out. Accustomed to leaving mined land as open pits and barren waste dumps and mill tailings impoundments, Anaconda refused to agree to reclaim hundreds of acres in a manner that would not be decided for another twenty or thirty years.

The company allowed Montana to fret over the mine's future, never publicly acknowledging that a reanalysis of the ore body concluded that it was not large enough to justify a mine. The company let politicians and the public wonder whether environmental clamor had killed the project, when the salient fact was that the company simply decided, on the basis of business reasons, not to open the mine.[46]

Months later Anaconda and the state agreed that for the Heddleston project to ever proceed the company would have to reevaluate its plans and assist the state with needed environmental studies. Any viable revised plan must be compatible with the area's cutthroat trout and elk populations and protective of the river's water quality. Out of this agreement rose Anaconda's decision in 1971 to financially support Liter Spence's studies on the upper Blackfoot.[47]

Anaconda probably agreed to assist with financing these environmental studies because the company did not wish to admit that the ore body was too small to mine profitably and thereby discourage potential buyers. By 1972 the property's molybdenum reserve estimates had been again decreased by a factor of ten, although within the company existed the optimistic observation that exploration to date had been relatively shallow and that with more and deeper drilling, another one hundred million tons of richer ore might be proven.[48]

Two factors explain how and why these downward revisions in ore reserves took place, factors fundamental to mine planning throughout the world. The first is due to the availability of increased subsurface information as exploration continued. Completed by junior geologists and engineers, initial ore reserve estimates were the result of interpolating known assay values between exploration holes. But as the company cored more holes in 1969 and 1970 to fill in the original grid, new and more accurate assays came back with erratic results. Eventually, Anaconda learned that the ore body's mineralization was less consistent and more unpredictable than first thought.

The other factor explaining the downward revision in ore reserves was the application of more conservative assumptions within the Anaconda organization. The Copper Production Evaluation Committee was chaired by senior Anaconda metallurgist Leonard Powell and was composed of four to five other senior geologists and production and operations talents. The committee's specific responsibility was to evaluate and oversee all of Anaconda's mineral investments.[49] They applied more hard-nosed experience and utilized more conservative assumptions than less experienced field professionals. The "copper committee," or "the posse" as the committee was also known within the company, was less likely to make quixotic leaps of faith concerning an ore body's size and worth. This is not a condemnation of Anaconda's junior field personnel; Anaconda employed some of the best young mineral geologists in the world. But reassessments by senior professionals occur within all mining companies.

The reasons for the copper committee's innate conservatism were twofold. First, senior heads, not junior, were most threatened when corporate directors looked to authorize a mine's startup investment. Unduly favorable forecasts that did not succeed would bear more heavily on the careers of senior executives than on those lower in the ranks. Second, the company's ability to raise outside capital, even its bond rating, depended on its proven ore reserves. Just as bankers use cars as collateral for car loans, commercial banks employ mineral reserves to collateralize mining company operating loans and bond issues. Banks and creditors insisted upon specific and reliable mineral reserve estimates from Anaconda and forced the mining company to develop conservative practices. Lending institutions required Anaconda to annually recalculate its ore reserves to certify reserve adequacy for existing loan agreements.[50]

While Anaconda dealt internally with this new information, Montanans, for the first time, were insisting upon tighter environmental controls over hardrock mining. Anaconda was caught up in the simultaneous rise of Montana's environmental movement and liberal activism of the era. Several coalescing factors contributed to this, one of which was certainly the growing unhappiness of Montanans over Anaconda's decades of political power.

Another factor was mining-related but about coal, not metals. Montana has the greatest untapped coal reserves in the nation, located primarily beneath its eastern plains. By the late 1960s, several coal companies had begun strip-mining for in-state power generation and for shipment to Midwestern utilities. Reclamation laws in Montana were nonexistent at the time, but a grassroots environmental group, the Northern Plains Resource Council, battled for legislation to protect rural ranching communities and the environment against Montana's growing coal industry. Hardrock mining was caught up in this same legislative flurry.[51] Montanans had begun to view mining as more than just an industry that provided jobs. A healthy environment had become as important as a healthy economy.

Montana's environmental fervor grew concurrently with a national movement that became formidable through congressional passage in 1969 of the National Environmental Policy Act (NEPA). Two years later, Montana enacted its own version of NEPA: the Montana Environmental Policy Act (MEPA). More federal legislation, like the Clean Water Act in 1972, would follow. By the early 1970s, the din in Montana was directed specifically at mining; this ultimately resulted in the 1971 passage of the state's so-called hardrock act, or what is today referred to as the Metal Mine Reclamation Act.

Under Montana's 1971 hardrock act mining companies were required for the first time to reclaim their properties upon the cessation of mining. As the state's largest and most visible mining company, Anaconda felt the initial brunt of these changes. After all, Anaconda had essentially run Butte—some would say the entire state—since the turn of the century. The year 1970 marked the point from which the company no longer had its way with Montana's resources.

After 1969 Anaconda never mentioned the Heddleston project in its annual reports. Following 1970 Anaconda hardly mentioned the project to Montanans. By 1972 Anaconda had relocated its western corporate offices from Butte to Tucson, Arizona. Its Montana operations faded from the corporate consciousness.[52] Apparently, Anaconda's directors did not feel Heddleston was their salvation for losses occurring elsewhere.

In Chile, where Anaconda had actively developed and mined copper since the end of World War II, America's industrial clout collided with Third World socialist resolve. In December of 1970, only months after Anaconda dropped its Heddleston project, Chile's President Allende proposed constitutional amendments that would allow Chile to nullify its recently executed agreements with Anaconda and expropriate, without compensation, Anaconda's Chilean assets.[53]

On 16 July 1971, President Allende carried out his threats, nullified existing agreements with Anaconda, and expropriated the company's assets.[54] Anaconda had begun shifting its exploration emphasis toward the continental United States by the mid-1960s, but it was too late. The company's greatest copper ore reserves effectively vanished.[55] Anaconda attempted to recover some value from the Chilean government for its losses, but Allende's hand-picked Cabinet and his Special Copper Tribunal denied the claim on the grounds that Anaconda had taken "excessive profits" from Chile since at least 1955.[56]

Anaconda's 1971 annual report to its shareholders succinctly described what happened and its effect: "During 1971, Anaconda encountered the full force of political adversity in Chile. The expropriation of our Chilean investments had an impact of a magnitude that few corporations have ever had to absorb. It took away two-thirds of the company's copper production and much of its earnings."[57] Due primarily to Chile's expropriation of company assets, Anaconda reported a total loss for the year of more than $350,000,000.[58]

Having lost most of its copper-producing properties, Anaconda scrambled to reinvent itself. The company's plight brightened briefly in 1972 when it reported a small increase in industrial material sales and sold its Montana-based timberland and lumber mill.[59]

In April of 1972, in an attempt to sell its Heddleston properties, Anaconda hosted an industrywide show-and-tell in Butte. Practically every financially solvent mining company in America was invited. Although ASARCO still legally owned the property, the value of Anaconda's project lay in its leases and detailed knowledge of the ore body. Hardrock companies attended and politely considered the property, but none stepped forward with an offer.[60]

Over the next year, Anaconda's managers repeatedly attempted to interest industry comrades in taking on Heddleston. Numerous memoranda and executive directives encouraged Anaconda managers to entice Amoco Mineral Company, a subsidiary of Standard Oil of New Jersey, and others to step forward.[61] Perhaps these companies, recognizing Anaconda's lessening vitality and growing desperation, were waiting for a "fire sale." Potential buyers or partners always expressed optimism and interest, but Anaconda never found a taker.

Anaconda's gross revenues increased again in 1973, but net income declined 30 percent.[62] The following year resulted in record sales and the highest net earnings in almost a decade. Chile settled with Anaconda for the expropriation of its copper properties for $93.6 million and eventually settled all Anaconda claims by offering $253 million in interest-bearing promissory notes guaranteed by the Central Bank of Chile.[63] But these benefits were negated by a softening of the U.S. economy late in the year that caused the company to cut its base metal prices five times. The company's poor financial health was further exacerbated by federal wage and price controls.[64]

Conditions eroded even more in 1975. Sales declined, and the company reported a net loss of nearly forty million dollars. A nationwide recession affected all operating divisions. For the year, Anaconda's Montana mining and general mining divisions experienced an operating loss of nearly fifty million dollars.[65] At the same time, major Third World copper reserves were coming into production, subsidized by Western banks stuffed with assets derived from the lofty international oil prices of 1973 and 1974. Chile, Zambia, and Zaire leaped to the forefront of international copper producers. Their new mines enjoyed dramatically lower labor costs and practically none of the environmental protection costs associated with American mines.[66]

Anaconda's executives grumbled about new, federally mandated, domestic environmental controls, noting that its entire Natural Resources Group, which included all mining operations, spent 43 percent of its capital expenditures on "environmental issues."[67] Industrywide, copper-mining executives claimed that environmental protection cost them approximately $0.15 per pound.[68] Still, Anaconda soothed its shareholders: "Anaconda supports sensible environmental regulation. We continue to stress, however, that environmental overkill must be avoided, that environmental control regulations must be reasonable, and that industry must be given adequate time to develop and implement well-planned environmental programs."[69]

Then, in February of 1975, Anaconda announced big news: an "agreement in principle" to merge with Tenneco, a successful American petroleum and industrial products corporation. Before the Tenneco-Anaconda merger could be executed, however, a previously unknown entity, the Crane Company, announced that it would exchange five million shares of its stock for Anaconda's assets.[70]

In September of 1976, before the Tenneco-Anaconda merger could be implemented and as the company fought Crane's proposal in court, Anaconda again turned the hardrock mining industry upside down. Atlantic Richfield Company, known also as ARCO, one of the world's largest and richest oil companies, offered to make Anaconda a wholly owned subsidiary. When it heard the news, Tenneco terminated its merger talks with Anaconda, and the Crane Company essentially disappeared from public view. Anaconda's announced reasons for seeking the merger with ARCO were predicated primarily on frustration with turbulent copper prices and demand and declining prices in uranium and other products.[71] With respect to Anaconda's leased assets in the Heddleston district, the Anaconda/ARCO merger prospectus stated only, "Heddleston Deposit, Montana—Extensive exploration has confirmed *93 million tons* of material averaging 0.48% total copper. Deep drill holes in portions of the deposit have detected significant molybdenum values which could justify further study. Present economic conditions do not justify development of this deposit."[72]

Anaconda's shareholders approved the merger with ARCO on 20 October 1976. With the merger, an independent giant of the western mining industry disappeared. With it also vanished any immediate likelihood that the company would develop an open-pit copper mine next to the Mike Horse Mine. After the merger, Anaconda operated under orders issued by the principal executives of quite a different industry, and its presence in the Heddleston district largely evaporated, at least as far as mineral exploration was concerned. The company kept Bob Dent in the field for several years to assist with continuing water-quality and fishery studies along the upper Blackfoot River and its tributaries. Anaconda also cooperated with Helena National Forest in revegetating the network of exploration roads and drill pads it had constructed since 1964. And the company assumed reconstruction responsibilities following the Mike Horse tailings dam failure in June of 1975.

In preparing to sell its Heddleston project, Anaconda, as a wholly owned subsidiary of ARCO, undertook a new internal appraisal in January of 1981. The analyst determined that "Anaconda has spent approximately $7.9 million dollars to acquire and test this resource. [But] I can foresee no recoverable value based on the copper resource and have assigned a value of $0.0 in the summary of assets."[73] In other words, by 1981, world copper prices had tanked. From a high of $1.32 per pound in February of 1980, copper prices had dropped dramatically. Pegged largely to the value of its unwanted copper, the value of the Heddleston project suffered accordingly. Its value was based largely upon prevailing molybdenum prices of 3.2¢ per pound. Anaconda concluded that a sale price of between $11.4 million and $26.5 million was "not unreasonable."[74] Still, no buyers came forward. ARCO gave up. In November of 1981, ARCO relinquished its Heddleston leases to ASARCO.[75]

Meanwhile, ARCO permanently closed Anaconda's historic copper smelter in Anaconda, Montana, twenty miles west of Butte. Subsequently, ARCO shipped its Butte copper concentrate to Japan for smelting until 1983, when it halted mining in Butte's famous Berkeley Pit and abandoned the copper-mining business altogether. An Anaconda executive claimed later that during its final ten years the Butte mine's "labor and power costs had more than doubled in real terms. And its fuel bill quintupled."[76]

American copper producers had lost their international edge, perhaps permanently. By 1985 world copper prices averaged $0.62 per pound, while American copper mines produced the metal at an average cost of $0.76 per pound. Only America's richest, lowest-cost copper producers survived.[77] Given these circumstances, the probability of opening and profitably operating a new, low-grade copper ore body like Heddleston was near zero.

Anaconda's failed plans for the Heddleston district are little more than a footnote to the company's death throes. There is no credible reason to believe that by standing up to the copper mining giant Montana's young environmental movement drove a stake into Anaconda's corporate heart. If one must name a single culprit, the most appropriate target may be the Chilean government of 1970–71. Still, it is ironic that one of the world's most successful and best-known mining companies lost its life grip at the same time that it did *not* mine in Heddleston. Given the flurry of corporate activity in the Heddleston district between 1962 and

1970, it is easy to focus on the details of Anaconda's plans and Montana state politics. But looking beyond Anaconda and ARCO, what happened at the Mike Horse Mine and along the upper Blackfoot River during this interval?

In the 1960s and 1970s, environmental conditions in the river worsened. The prevailing corporate philosophy during these decades remained use-it-up-and-walk-away. In spite of the property's ownership and management by at least three major corporations—ASARCO, Anaconda, and ARCO—no individual, agency, or corporate entity openly discussed or attempted to clean up past abuses. The financial muscle existed, but no corporation voluntarily dips into its assets to clean up a mess caused decades earlier. It simply is not done. Business is business.

Environmental studies documented only existing conditions, but the existing environment was made up of visible devastation caused by past operations at the Mike Horse. Still, analysis of the consequences of the devastation was not attempted. Beyond repairing the dam and revegetating the network of exploration roads, no rehabilitation of any kind was planned or proposed.

9. Cleanup

It is not yet evident . . . whether the government, most likely the federal one, is willing to underwrite the enormous expense of cleaning up previous environmental pollution and damage. The industry can reasonably be expected to pay for current and future programs; it should not be expected to finance reclamation for the past two hundred years.—Duane A. Smith, *Mining America*

The use of CERCLA, CECRA, and associated terminology in this report is not and does not constitute an admission by ASARCO or ARCO that such regulations and guidance are legally applicable in the conduct or performance of activities at the UBMC [Upper Blackfoot Mining Complex]. In addition, the action by ASARCO and ARCO to proceed with remediation of the Anaconda and Mike Horse Mine areas is not an admission of responsibility or liability.—ASARCO work plan for the Mike Horse Mine area, 31 January 1994

You could bankrupt ASARCO and you aren't going to fix every problem in the State of Montana.—Chris Pfahl, ASARCO mining engineer

WHEN ASARCO REACQUIRED the Heddleston district claims from ARCO in 1981, the Blackfoot River gained a long-overdue reprieve. Unlike its predecessor, ASARCO had no immediate plans to mine in the district. Metal prices, especially for copper, were so low that mining companies were spending little or nothing to develop additional reserves in the American West. So quickly and thoroughly had subsidized copper producers from developing Third World nations overtaken America's copper-mining industry that the early and mid-1980s were nearly lethal to the American firms. Perhaps nowhere was this more evident than in the headwaters of the Blackfoot River, where silence replaced the earnest mineral exploration of a decade earlier. No company geologists traipsed the timbered mountainsides with Brunton compasses, air photos, and topographic maps in hand and surveyors in tow. No drill rigs roared in freshly cut forest clearings.

Oblivious to human endeavors, the Mike Horse Mine continued draining to the wounded Blackfoot River. ARCO had maintained both the dam and the Beartrap Creek diversion since the 1975 tailings dam failure, but no reclamation was undertaken in the district, and environmental data-gathering was limited to the occasional efforts of graduate students. The public had seemingly accepted the status quo and forgotten the upper Blackfoot River.

Unfortunately, at least one person had not forgotten George Kornec.

The shooting of George Kornec occurred at noon on a sunny July day in 1982.[1] George had been hired to run the physical plant on a small placer gold claim in the mountains west of Helena. When the bullet struck, George was standing on top of the plant, talking to the owner's twelve-year-old son. Initially, the boy thought something had blown up. George immediately knew he had been shot. The bullet severed the sciatic nerve in one leg, hit bone, and broke into pieces. One piece went through his stomach; another went into his other leg. Before an ambulance delivered him to a Butte hospital hours later, he required twenty-one pints of blood.

No motive has been determined for the shooting. It may have been a case of mistaken identity somehow related to the placer mine's ownership. A more spectacular suggestion is that George was shot by Ted Kaczynski—the infamous Unabomber, who lived near Lincoln. In any event, law enforcement authorities never arrested anyone for the shooting and George has not received a sheriff's update on the investigation in years. More than a decade after the incident, he describes it like an occupational hazard, as if he is disclosing a secret elk-hunting spot to a friend, then adds as an afterthought that sometimes the elk shoot back.

George spent months recuperating. Once he was able to get about on his own, he returned to the quiet and safety of Beartrap Gulch. Today, pinpricks do not generate a reaction in his left leg, and bullet fragments remain in his body.

"X-rays light up like a Christmas tree," George says, adding that he has given up gold mining.

As George was recovering, another Kornec returned to Montana. George was living in the refabricated Mike Horse Mine office-turned-house when Rosie moved back to Beartrap Gulch in

9. George Kornec advancing into the Kornec's Sammy K. tunnel in upper Beartrap Gulch, 7 September 1995. Photograph by author.

1983.[2] Together, the brothers turned to the family's unpatented claims. To the extent that George's leg allowed, they toiled in the Sammy K. tunnel with drilling and mucking machines purchased from used mining–equipment dealers around the state. If they could not afford a piece of equipment, they traded for it. When not developing their mine or making improvements to the house, they cut firewood for the five- and six-month-long winters. There was plenty of accessible firewood; the mountainsides overlooking lower Beartrap and Mike Horse Gulches had reforested naturally to lodgepole pine. And tucked away near the head of Beartrap Gulch were more than twenty acres of untouched Douglas fir—old growth—where aged specimens measure three feet or more in diameter and reach skyward eighty to ninety feet.

In the evenings, when not watching video movies or listening to the radio, the brothers simply sat and enjoyed the silence.

"Silence is golden," George likes to say.

A challenge to the silence surrounding the upper river arose in 1986 when the Big Blackfoot Chapter of Trout Unlimited finally exhausted its patience. Trout Unlimited is a nationwide, nonprofit organization dedicated to improving natural trout habitat. The Big Blackfoot chapter, based in Lincoln with active and influential members in Helena and Missoula, decided that with the trout fishery in the upper river getting worse, habitat rehabilitation in the Heddleston district was long overdue. Montana's Department of Fish, Wildlife and Parks agreed but claimed it lacked the funds and expertise to implement a remedy and referred the chapter to the only state agency with the apparent know-how: the Department of State Lands—the agency that was also responsible for regulating Montana's mining industry.

By the mid-1980s, Montana Department of State Lands had developed one of the most proactive and successful abandoned-mined land reclamation programs in the nation. A little-known facet of the federal Strip Mine Conservation and Reclamation Act (SMCRA), signed into law by Jimmy Carter in 1977, is that it established a funding mechanism to reclaim abandoned coal mines. The reclamation fund is supported by a tax on all coal mined in the United States and is administered by the federal Office of Surface Mining, which issues grants to individual states to carry out specific projects. The fund is devoted almost exclusively to reclaiming abandoned coal mines. Use of the fund to reclaim hardrock mines is prohibited except under very special circumstances. (Although central and western Montana is known better for its hardrock mining, early rail companies reaching across the West developed modest coalfields along their routes to fuel their steam-powered locomotives. Montana has supported some form of a coal-mining industry almost since statehood.)

Because it did not have access to the federal abandoned-mined-land reclamation fund, and because it did have Trout Unlimited's active and vocal support, Montana's 1987 legislature appropriated $107,000 to the Department of State Lands to reclaim the Mike Horse Mine and improve water quality in the upper Blackfoot River. The agency accomplished little, however, because a more detailed look at the problem revealed that $107,000 was inadequate for the task. Montana's 1989 legislature responded by appropriating an additional $300,000 to the Lewis and Clark County Conservation District for reclamation efforts at the Mike Horse. In concert with the county conservation district, the Department of State Lands subsequently initiated serious planning to address the most significant environmental problems in the Heddleston district.[3]

In June of 1990, Helena's *Independent Record* announced that the Department of State Lands was undertaking restoration efforts at the Mike Horse Mine to clean up "one of the worst abandoned mine sites in the Rockies." [4] Indeed, the Mike Horse had gained national notoriety over the years and was becoming a cause célèbre among state and national environmental activists. Oddly, the Department of State Lands indicated that its involvement arose because no other responsible party existed to conduct the cleanup and reclamation.

Strange as it seems, this was true, at least under Montana mining law. Montana's 1971 hardrock act required mining companies to reclaim only those mines permitted *after* the law's enactment. Mines abandoned or left inactive before the law's passage were exempt, which in effect memorialized hundreds of derelict sites throughout the state, regardless of the ongoing environmental consequences. Moreover, the hardrock act required only reclamation of land disturbed by mining. Water-quality degradation was another issue entirely and covered by different laws administered by a separate state agency.

When the *Independent Record* hit Helena's streets, the state's Department of Health and Environmental Sciences saw reason for concern. For while the Department of State Lands oversaw a multimillion dollar budget for the reclamation of abandoned coal (and very few metal) mines, the Department of Health and Environmental Sciences administered Montana's own scaled-down version of the federal Superfund law: the Comprehensive Environmental Cleanup and Responsibility Act, or CECRA. Under CECRA, persons or parties responsible for a "release" of a "hazardous or deleterious substance" that "may pose an imminent and substantial threat to public health, safety, or welfare or the environment" was, in state regulatory lingo, a "potentially liable person," or PLP. Montana's 1985 CECRA statute, like the older federal law, also contained firm language forcing responsibility on polluters. But if the Department of State Lands attempted to reclaim the Mike Horse Mine and the upper Blackfoot River, and in the process inadvertently disturbed residual mill tailings and harmed the river— given the objective, a real possibility—the state of Montana might well become a PLP under unforeseen CECRA or CERCLA actions.

When the Department of Health and Environmental Sciences

informed the Department of State Lands of the PLP implications, the latter placed its cleanup plans on hold. Little would prove more embarrassing to Montana than to unintentionally become a PLP at a nationally recognized abandoned-mine site. The Department of Health and Environmental Sciences also asked its sister agency why the latter claimed there was no PLP when everyone even tangentially involved with the hardrock mining industry knew that ASARCO owned the Mike Horse Mine and most of the Heddleston district.[5]

ASARCO watched while Montana's agencies wrestled with liability issues, project funding, and defining potential reclamation and water-treatment technologies. The company likely chose not to involve itself beyond an advisory capacity to the Department of State Lands purely for business reasons. In this context, ASARCO can hardly be blamed. American businesses exist to make money for their owners; it is the modus operandi of American capitalism. A corollary to the moneymaking process is not spending it needlessly. If Montana chose to remedy an environmental eyesore with tax dollars, why should the company voluntarily open its own wallet? Such a tight-fisted philosophy is not limited to the mining industry. Successful businesses differentiate between those expenses necessary to stay in business and those more pensively characterized as "moral obligations." Difficulties or reluctance to understand and accept this distinction underscores much of the tension between advocates of broadly mandated environmental programs and the business community. Business leaders are more likely to be accountants or attorneys than members of the clergy.

To further complicate the matter, environmental regulatory agencies, including those in Montana, operate under legislation directing them to protect human health and the environment. They function under broad public mandates, whereas industry functions primarily for private profit. Strong differences frequently surface between agencies attempting to interpret the statutes and companies regulated thereunder. Indeed, the shifting sands underlying business, government regulatory obligations, and environmental activists make ready comprehension of most sensitive environmental issues difficult.

After months of interdepartmental negotiations, the Department of State Lands canceled its planned cleanup of the Mike Horse Mine in early 1991.[6] Before a shovel of dirt was turned or a handful of grass seed cast, issues of liability and financial responsibility halted rehabilitation of the mine and the river's worst abuses. Eventually, the legislature assigned responsibility for the Mike Horse problem to the Department of Health and Environmental Sciences.[7] The ultimate question was finally asked: If ASARCO was the owner, why wasn't it conducting a cleanup? The answer was: ASARCO should be. No longer could the company remain on the sidelines. The department named ASARCO and ARCO "PLPS" under Montana's CECRA law in June of 1991 and informed the two firms that they were expected to conduct a cleanup.[8]

With this notification, the Mike Horse Mine and associated problems in the Heddleston district entered the hazardous waste regulatory arena. Prior to 1991, any mine reclamation attempted would have been considered an extension of normal mining practices. Once the mine waste was deemed hazardous, however, different statutes came into play. Federal and state regulatory agencies had concluded that huge volumes of low-toxicity mine waste met the legal definition of hazardous. Also, under the new approach, water-treatment issues could no longer be ignored or passed onto another agency. For ASARCO and ARCO it was a brand new game at the Mike Horse.

Seven months later, in February of 1992, the department issued a "special notice letter" to ASARCO and ARCO and inquired about their intentions.[9] At this point, ASARCO approached ARCO about joining forces. After all, the 1975 tailings dam failure occurred while ARCO controlled the Heddleston claims, and the widespread presence of mill tailings along the upper river was a major factor in Montana's decision to designate the Mike Horse area a CECRA site. The department believed that the unintentional discharge of mill tailings in 1975 qualified as a "release" of a hazardous substance under the CECRA statute. Under the legal theory of liability presented by both the federal Superfund law and Montana's CECRA, ARCO potentially bore as much liability as ASARCO. Knowing all this, ASARCO concluded that ARCO should help pay the bill.

ASARCO and ARCO did not initially acquiesce or agree to negotiate or participate with Montana. ASARCO resisted, in part, because it considered the Mike Horse to be "inactive," not abandoned, although few state employees accepted this distinction. Mostly, ASARCO and ARCO stalled because they feared being sucked into Montana's CECRA morass. Lofty cleanup costs, including paying the agency's management oversight costs, and the public stigma attached to hazardous waste sites in general, can wreak havoc on corporate personas and financial assets. Instead, through the inevitable involvement of attorneys, both companies employed an honored and time-tested tradition of both the legal profession and the hardrock mining industry.[10] A well-heeled company is discouraged from assuming responsibility and taking care of the problem when, instead, it can less expensively deny, delay, and obfuscate. It is business.

This contentious state of affairs continued until 1993, when two independent, yet complementary, factors changed. In Montana, a newly elected Republican governor appointed Bob Robinson to head the Department of Health and Environmental Sciences. Robinson believed he could overcome habitual agency inertia and implement cleanups around the state without involving the agency at every step. The other factor that broke the stalemate occurred within ASARCO when Chris Pfahl was assigned to manage the growing Mike Horse controversy.

Chris Pfahl, an ASARCO mining engineer, has spent his career in ASARCO's Northwest mining department. He worked a number of company mines in Idaho and Montana until congressional passage of the federal Superfund law. Since then, he has been involved with ASARCO's Superfund cleanups in Colorado and Idaho. He also knows the Heddleston district well.

Pfahl interacts with Montana's government agencies, hires consultants, and oversees the work on the ground. He splits his time among negotiating with contractors, keeping regulatory officials informed, and carrying on telephone conversations on dozens of related topics. In the Heddleston district, whatever is achieved or whatever goes wrong, he is on the spot.

Hardrock miners are a no-nonsense group and Pfahl fits the mold. He is direct to the point of being blunt. He is also articulate, which some might find surprising for a person who makes a living wresting rocks from the earth. Pfahl believes the federal Superfund law was never meant to be applied to western mining sites characterized by huge volumes of low-toxicity waste. Still, the law has gained industry's attention and he concedes that attitudes among miners have changed radically since the law's passage. According to Pfahl, two decades ago, mining companies did not include "shutdown costs"—environmental cleanup and reclamation costs—when performing financial feasibility studies on potential mining projects in this country. Now, they do.

CERCLA has even forced some mining companies to undertake site cleanups, regardless of whether they were responsible for a site's condition or the presence of hazardous mine waste. In the West, an abandoned mine's condition is frequently due to a company or individual that owned or operated the mine decades ago but no longer exists. Today, modern corporations may own it but have done little or nothing to aggravate its condition. ASARCO, in particular, has been hit hard. The company essentially monopolized the lead industry since the turn of the century and owned numerous mines, although many were never actually operated by the company. Under the Superfund law, however, that makes no difference.

According to Pfahl, ASARCO's post-1980 change in attitude manifested itself with the creation of a separate environmental department. Prior to this, the company's environmental professionals worked for the operations department. But because the latter's primary objectives were productivity and profit, environmental concerns, especially those that might slow productivity or incur costs, at least occasionally did not receive the recognition or financial support they deserved.

Pfahl's participation in the Heddleston district marked a major turning point for ASARCO. Somehow, he convinced his superiors that CECRA status under Montana law at the Mike Horse Mine was not inevitable and that assuming active leadership for the cleanup was in the company's best interests, *as long as* Montana agreed to ASARCO's actions without insisting upon veto authority over cleanup particulars.[11]

For Montana, the prospect of a company assuming unilateral control of a cleanup, without mandatory state agency direction, bordered on heresy. Montana's environmental regulatory community had long distrusted industry and refused to believe industry would do a proper job unless the state approved company plans and actions in advance. Much of this distrust is traceable to Anaconda's role in Montana government and politics prior to 1975. Anaconda lobbied tirelessly to keep Montana's environmental statutes and regulatory programs tame and toothless, and the state's cadre of regulators were raised with this history firmly in mind. Following Anaconda's demise, which left Montana with a world-class mess and the nation's largest federal Superfund site in Butte, these same regulators were not easily intimidated by any industry, particularly the mining industry.

In April of 1993, over the objections of his staff, which believed the state was being snookered into an unfavorable compromise, Bob Robinson reached a closed-door agreement with ASARCO's Pfahl and ARCO's Phyllis Flack that allowed the two companies to undertake a voluntary cleanup without acquiescing to the state's CECRA process. By late May, Robinson had written a letter to ASARCO and ARCO memorializing this agreement.[12] The companies agreed to abide by the spirit and intent of CECRA, but the agency's role was almost purely advisory.[13] For possibly the first time in Montana history, a company was to stipulate the means and methods by which it would correct a major environmental problem without first agreeing to state veto authority over these same means and methods. Montana's traditional insistence upon plan approval prior to a cleanup operation is not unique. Most western states insist upon similar controls.

The major stumbling block removed by this agreement was ASARCO and ARCO's acceptance of risk. In the past, and certainly under Superfund- and CECRA-directed cleanups, PLPs like ASARCO agreed to execute cleanups largely because the agencies "signed off" on the cleanup plans. The agencies would detail the plan's objectives and in return give the PLP limited protection against future fines and penalties if the agreed-upon "fix" failed. The cost to the PLP for the lessened consequences of failure was the greater time and expense it took to work under state direction, especially under Superfund or CECRA.

In exchange for project control of the Mike Horse cleanup, ASARCO assumed the up-front risk that its actions might not prove effective. Montana authorities would not be in a position to micromanage the site cleanup. But if ASARCO's cleanup proved ineffective, the company practically conceded fines for continuing water quality and CECRA violations.

Pfahl described ASARCO's expectations concerning its agreement with Robinson and the Department of Health and Environmental Sciences this way: "We don't need their sign-off going into it. If we do the work, and it's effective, why do we need them to ever approve the work? We don't care if the state likes what we're doing or dislikes what we're doing. We're willing to take the long-term commitment of a discharge permit, which has fines associated with it for non-compliance."[14] Pfahl's reference to a "discharge permit" provides a pivotal, though not uncommon, twist to company plans. Indeed, the question of such a permit is pertinent to practically *every* abandoned mine in the West with acidic drainage. The ugly truth is that hundreds of abandoned mines throughout the West violate the federal Clean Water Act and state statutory equivalents. Acid mine drainage violates established water-quality standards because, at a minimum, metal concentrations are lethal to fish and other aquatic life.

The issue has not been addressed because nearly everyone in the mining industry as well as federal and state water-quality regulatory programs knows about these violations yet does nothing to correct them. Suspicions of a deep-seated conspiracy would nonetheless be mistaken. It is not as simple as regulators allowing known violators to flout federal and state laws. Little has been done about the far-reaching problem because few believe that much can be done. The quandary of acid mine drainage in the West is one of the most intractable environmental challenges facing industry and government.

There are many reasons for this inaction. One of the most significant is that relatively few mines as prominent as the Mike Horse have identifiable owners with strong financial balance sheets. The vast majority of abandoned mines in the West either have no surviving owners, or the known owners do not possess the financial wherewithal to reclaim their mines and treat AMD in perpetuity. When state or federal agencies accuse owners of allowing environmental damages and water-quality violations to continue, the owners frequently claim that they did not cause the problem in the first place and that they only inherited the mine from some hypothetical Great-Uncle Otto. Under federal and state water-quality and hazardous waste laws, this is no defense; owners remain liable. But in most cases the hazardous waste cleanup morass truly affects only those with "deep pockets." Thousands of less affluent owners are, in legalese, "judgment proof."

Even if a solvent, responsible, and willing mine owner steps forward, little can be done to end acid mine drainage at many abandoned mines. Hefty initial construction costs and perpetual operation and maintenance expenses, the remoteness of many mines and great distances to available electrical power, scarcity of suitable land upon which treatment systems might be constructed, and the lack of cost-effective land- or water-treatment technologies, all conspire against dealing with the West's abandoned-mine problem. There is no easy fix, no miraculous, gee-whiz technology by which discharging mines can be rendered benign. Just because the chemistry of acidic mine waters is reasonably well-understood and straightforward does not mean it is easy or cheap to treat. Sophisticated water-treatment plants could be constructed at most mines and affected reaches of western streams and rivers, but in the collective opinion of experienced and knowledgeable regulators a practical and cost-effective way of constructing water-treatment operations for every discharging mine in the West does not exist. The number of needed facilities is in the thousands, the probable costs in the hundreds of millions of dollars. Without "deep pockets," who pays? The taxpayers, of course. And these particular animals have become increasingly unwilling to fork out billions for purposes they can live without, especially when many of the worst mine offenders are hidden deep in the mountains, out of sight, out of mind.

Another reason for the resounding inaction is latent complacency—latent in the sense that the problem has existed for so long that in many states the problem is perceived as an acceptable part of the state's history. When compared with competing demands on regulators' shrinking resources, citizen complaints are neither forceful nor frequent enough to raise the acid mine drainage issue to a higher regulatory consciousness. In this respect, the public is as responsible for inaction as the agencies. Almost everyone simply wishes the mines would disappear.

These reasons do not mean that mining companies and other owners of abandoned-mine sites obstinately refuse to deal with the issue. Their reticence is more complex than simple refusal. As one consultant to the mining industry said, "I have clients with wallets in hand who want to go do something at these sites, but they know that the moment they do, they'll be asked to do the impossible. So they're reluctant." [15] Well-intentioned owners are averse to voluntarily spending finite resources when they perceive a great probability that one of two things, or both, will occur. First, either the costs to rehabilitate the site and treat AMD will prove too high or the results will be less than they hoped. Second, regulatory involvement will prove so unreasonable, to their thinking, that the reward ultimately is not worth the effort. ASARCO and ARCO's willingness to assume responsibility and rehabilitate the Heddleston district is anomalous. They probably stepped forward from fear of the more punitive costs and burdens associated with outright defiance of federal and Montana hazardous waste laws.

While Pfahl, Phyllis Flack, and Bob Robinson were agreeing on how to proceed with a voluntary cleanup of the Heddleston district, the companies were overcoming their own corporate inertia. By midsummer of 1993, ASARCO and its Colorado-based consultant had crafted a comprehensive plan to return the mining district to something approaching a healthy condition. To begin, ASARCO applied in June for a state permit to discharge mine effluent to the Blackfoot River. Acid mine drainage from the Mike Horse had been draining to the river for years without treatment or a permit. By applying for a permit, ASARCO was giving notice that it intended to meet strict water-quality standards once its cleanup program was in place.

In October ASARCO submitted its two-pronged "master plan" to the state and federal agencies. First, and as quickly as possible, ASARCO and ARCO proposed to control the major sources of metals to the upper Blackfoot River. In addition to the Mike Horse Mine, major sources in the district included several other discharging adits, waste dumps, and tailings exposed where surface runoff could flush metal-enriched sediments or leachate into the river or its tributaries. To deal with these latter sources, the mine dumps and tailings would be reclaimed as quickly as possible. The companies estimated that this initial phase would require several years. Second, once the primary metal sources had been identified and corrected, residual sources of contamination would be addressed. The companies reasonably believed that dominant sources "masked" lesser sources and that these minor sources could not be identified until the first cleanup phase was complete.[16]

ARCO already possessed a major cleanup presence in Montana, having inherited Anaconda's Superfund mess that extended from Butte down the Clark Fork River nearly to Missoula, a distance of more than a hundred miles. But neither ASARCO nor Pfahl had attempted this form of voluntary cleanup before. Like ARCO, their experience paralleled the Superfund process. Although ASARCO and Pfahl sincerely believed their negotiated cleanup process would save the company both time and money, they would learn as they went along.

ASARCO and ARCO wasted no time in identifying the major metal contributors to the river. Not surprisingly, the Mike Horse Mine headed the list. The preliminary report provided no surprises: "The dominant environmental concern at the UBMC [Upper Blackfoot Mining Complex] documented by existing data is contamination of surface water by metal-enriched drainage from the Mike Horse adit. Discharge from this single source accounts for *more than 90%* of the mining-related loadings of metals to surface water resources of the UBMC."[17] The companies also identified acid mine drainage from the nearby Anaconda Mine and leachate and lesser quantities of acid mine drainage from other district adits as well as poorly delineated sources, like groundwater, stream sediments, and precipitates affected by past mining activities. Clearly, however, the principal problem was the Mike Horse Mine discharge.

From the beginning, Pfahl did not believe that cleanup of the Mike Horse and the Heddleston would require the development and application of innovative reclamation methods. As far as he and his consultants were concerned, standard mine reclamation technology combined with known water-treatment systems would prove adequate.[18] Most of these methods had never been implemented in the Heddleston district, but their use now made sense to Pfahl and his consultants. Simply stated, their guiding, two-step approach was to isolate metal sources and other solid mine wastes from uncontaminated surface- and groundwater and to treat the contaminated water.[19]

Isolation would be accomplished by recontouring and revegetating areas disturbed by mining (for example, mine-waste dumps and pockets of exposed, residual tailings) to increase surface-water runoff and decrease infiltration and the generation of leachate, plus the installation of adit *bulkheads*—plugs—to control mine water draining through acid-generating material either within or outside the mines.[20] This collection of techniques, loosely termed "hydrologic isolation," effectively meant that ASARCO and ARCO would excavate acid-generating mine waste from where it influenced surface-water quality and relocate it to engineered repositories, where the material would be isolated from precipitation and leaching. The surface of these so-called repositories would be shaped to a natural contour, covered with a topsoil, then reseeded. In theory, at least, isolation was to be permanent.

In early 1994, Pfahl mobilized general contractors to begin moving mine and mill waste to the designated Mike Horse repository. Knowing the reputation and history of the Kornec brothers in the district, he instructed his contractors to seek assistance from the Kornecs whenever the location of a buried or collapsed feature was in question, such as one of the upper two Mike Horse adits. George and Rosie complied willingly, thoroughly relishing an opportunity to exercise their knowledge of the area.[21]

From the outset of mining over a century ago, Joseph Hartmiller and his successors dumped most of their mine waste outside the no. 3 adit in a manner that created a horizontal work area. As the mine expanded, more and more waste was brought to the surface and the pad was extended into Mike Horse Gulch. About the time they recognized that filling the gulch bottom and blocking the stream was more effort than it was worth, they recognized a need to extend the bench northward toward the mill site. Over the following decades, much of the mine's waste was used as fill for building foundations and for the ore car–tracks leading to the mill.

With so much mine waste already located adjacent to the Mike Horse adit, ASARCO elected to enlarge the area to create a new Mike Horse repository for the district's remaining waste. Because moving any quantity is more costly than leaving it where it is, project economics likely drove ASARCO's decision, at least in part. ASARCO also planned to construct a portion of its Mike Horse adit discharge water-treatment facility on the repository surface and believed that relocating the repository would render its water-treatment plans more difficult to implement.

The Department of Health and Environmental Sciences questioned locating the district's primary mine-waste repository adjacent to Mike Horse Creek and based its opposition on several factors, including a concern that the repository might prove unstable, plus its desire that ASARCO maintain an exacting degree of hydrologic isolation between acid-generating mine waste and the creek. Constructing the repository in this location would also make it more difficult for ASARCO to implement the department's recommendation that ASARCO mix lime, a neutralizing agent, with Anaconda Mine waste being hauled to the new repository. The department believed that amending the mine waste with lime provided greater assurance that it would not become acidic in the future.

To avoid the first of these potential problems, the department recommended that ASARCO construct its waste repository elsewhere in the district. After months of unexplained delay, ASARCO finally provided engineering calculations proving that enlarging the bench on the mountainside above the stream presented no real danger. The bench would be stable and not slump into the stream. ASARCO further argued that its property ownership within the district limited its options and that constructing a repository on undisturbed ground ran counter to its mission.[22]

Believing its advice and recommendations were being ignored, the department responded with a 1 November 1994 letter from Bob Robinson that stated: "The CECRA Program and its technical consultants believe that, given the climatic, hydrologic, and soils conditions at the Mike Horse site, there is a good possibility that the hydraulic controls that ASARCO has designed into the waste repository will not succeed in preventing the development of acid rock drainage over time."[23] In the end, ASARCO and ARCO largely ignored the department's concerns regarding the Mike Horse repository. Under formal CECRA-guided cleanups, ASARCO would have ignored the department's concerns at its peril. However, the terms of their unusual agreement with Robinson allowed the two companies to ignore the department's recommendations, since they assumed the risk of adverse regulatory consequences if the concerns ever proved valid.

In spite of this disagreement, the department continued to provide ASARCO and ARCO with substantive comments and advice on their plans. The department was able to draw heavily on expertise from its sister agency, the Department of State Lands, as well as technical experts in the state's university system. The department would not go away. By the end of 1995, ASARCO had moved the bulk of the district's newly designated mine waste to the Mike Horse repository. Filled, it rises 35 feet above Mike Horse Gulch and measures 350 to 400 feet long and 150 to 200 feet across. Most of the new waste came from near the Anaconda Mine, where for years it resided precariously between the mine portal and the Blackfoot River.[24]

Downriver from the Anaconda Mine, the two companies and the department identified several smaller mounds of mine waste requiring removal and isolation and agreed that another repository should be built near the mouth of Paymaster Gulch. The sources of waste for this repository were the Paymaster Mine and the Edith and no. 3 tunnels. The Edith and no. 3 waste dumps dated from Anaconda's 1967 copper and molybdenum exploration.[25]

Dealing with mine waste that was both exposed and visible was the easiest and least challenging of Pfahl's tasks. Mining engineers make their living moving dirt and rock in the most inexpensive and efficient manner; that the dirt and rock being moved in the Heddleston district was considered hazardous by regulatory authorities altered Pfahl's plans and procedures very little. Far more challenging was plugging the discharging mine adits.

Adit plugs have been employed for decades in mines throughout the world to control the flow of water into or out of mines.[26] In the Heddleston district, two mines clearly warranted plugging: the Mike Horse and the Anaconda. In both cases, the plugs would have to be constructed as part of a larger system designed to control and treat mine drainage. Drainage from the Anaconda Mine was more acidic and of poorer quality than that from the Mike Horse, but the flow was far less. The Anaconda was also a much smaller mine. The real challenge for Pfahl's engineering mind was plugging the Mike Horse Mine.

Before designing the plug, Pfahl wanted to inspect the mine firsthand. Wearing hip boots and miners' hard hats and head-lamps, Pfahl and two of his consultants pulled open the doors covering the entrance to the no. 3 adit and proceeded into the mountain, their lamp beams driving tunnels of light into the darkness. Yellowboy coated the adit walls and the men's hands quickly acquired the same hue. Seven to eight hundred feet into the mine, moving cautiously in water that neared the top of their boots, they reached a point where wooden structures hung above them and drifts branched both left and right. This was likely where the adit intercepted the Little Nell Vein system. Observing water welling up from below, Pfahl's companions wondered if stopes of the no. 4 level were beneath them. Not wanting to flounder in frigid mine waters of unknown depth, they elected to go no farther. Pfahl proceeded alone—until he waded into waist-deep yellowboy. Wisely concluding they had enough information, the trio retreated to daylight.[27]

The following year, Pfahl designed and oversaw construction of the Mike Horse Mine plug, although not before Montana State University's Reclamation Research Unit—technical consultants to the Department of Health and Environmental Sciences—devised an interesting add-on. Beginning 325 feet into the mine, ASARCO's contractors packed a 75-foot reach with several hundred tons of crushed limestone. The limestone was an intrinsic component of the overall water-treatment plan.

Two hundred fifty feet from the portal, after scraping the yellowboy from the adit walls and ceiling, workers placed large boulders in the passageway between wooden forms about 6 feet apart. Weather- and corrosion-resistant HDPE (high density polyethylene) piping was laid from the inner side of the plug to the mine portal. Once the piping was in place, workers pressure-grouted the space between the wood forms with a specially designed cement mixture. The adit plug was designed to withstand at least 120 feet of hydraulic *head*, meaning that the mine could flood and the water level rise to a depth of 120 feet behind the plug before the plug might theoretically fail. In reality, Pfahl and his consultants intended the mine to flood only to a maximum of

90 feet, a depth that would be controlled by pressure valves installed in the HDPE pipe. In fact, Pfahl and his consultants wanted the water levels to fluctuate between 60 and 90 feet; they planned to use the flooded mine as an underground reservoir.[28]

Flooding previously dry portions of a mine serves to decrease the amount of oxygen available to exposed pyrite and other reactive sulfides. Eliminating oxygen can halt pyrite oxidation before it begins, but two factors remain problematic. Water, especially that entering the mine from the surface, contains enough dissolved oxygen to oxidize pyrite, even under water. And there is no way to know precisely where in the mine the most significant and troublesome pyrite oxidation has taken place or whether it will worsen. ASARCO hopes that flooding a greater portion of the mine will be beneficial in the long run.

The flooded mine and adit plug can be envisioned as a partially buried, eight-story apartment building that can only be entered from the top three floors. Water filling the building would flood the floors from the bottom up until escaping from the lowest of the three floors open to the outside. Plugging the exit from the floor equivalent to the no. 3 adit means that water would continue rising toward its next lowest escape level. Maintaining a fixed range in hydraulic head behind the plug allowed Pfahl to keep a comparatively constant flow through the HDPE discharge pipe, prevent water from rising high enough to drain from the no. 2 level, and use the difference in water levels within the mine as a reservoir.

Unfortunately, plugging the adit does not ensure that the mine can be used like a bathtub, where the adit plug functions like a rubber stopper. Mountains are not impermeable. Even if the adit plug works as designed, some leakage may occur. The question is where. ASARCO completed the Mike Horse adit plug and closed the gate valves on the HDPE pipe in late 1995. As mine water levels rise, ASARCO and the department watch closely for seeps on the nearby mountainside.[29] The likelihood of seeps centers on the fractured nature of the bedrock hosting the Mike Horse ore deposit. For nearly a century, groundwater drained freely from the mine because the open adit provided the path of least resistance. Water levels never rose high enough in the mine to "force" the water through fractures connecting the mine with the ground surface. As the water level rises behind the plug, this could change.

Cramped between the timbered, south-facing nose of Anaconda Hill and the Blackfoot River and extending from the Anaconda Mine down and along the river's first few hundred yards, sits a series of ponds in the center of the narrow valley. It is impossible to miss them; they are the most visible component of ASARCO's efforts to restore some measure of health to the upper Blackfoot River. They are also the terminus of the longest water-treatment facility in the American West, beginning with the crushed limestone behind the Mike Horse adit plug and ending over five thousand feet later where the ponds discharge to the river.

The ponds constitute an artificial wetland. Pfahl hopes they will help convert the metal-laden flows from the Mike Horse and Anaconda Mines into water capable of supporting trout. He has high expectations: "I truly believe this is one of the most unique, high-tech water-treatment setups ever built anywhere on Earth. It's the highest tech, low-tech water-treatment plant ever built. It uses no electricity, it uses no chemicals, and clean water is going to come out."[30] The use of artificial wetlands to treat AMD was developed chiefly in the coal-producing regions of Appalachia.[31] ASARCO's efforts in the Heddleston district represent one of just several attempts to implement this technology in the Northern Rockies. The technology borrows from nature by utilizing processes not unlike those operating within the river's upper and lower swamps.[32]

Water treatment begins where acid mine water comes into contact with the limestone packed behind the Mike Horse adit plug. There, in the neutralizing geochemical environment of calcite (the predominant mineral that makes up limestone), the water's pH is raised in a presumably oxygen-free environment. Because most metals are less soluble in neutral-pH water than in either highly acidic or highly alkaline conditions, the metals precipitate from solution. By the time water exits the mine through the HDPE pipe, a portion of the metal load has already been left behind.

The HDPE pipe extending through the adit plug leads to a concrete "meter vault," where a pressure-relief valve controls mine discharge. It opens and closes when pressure corresponds to eighty-eight and seventy-eight feet, respectively, of hydraulic head behind the adit plug. From the meter vault, a four-inch HDPE pipe leads to a cinder-block structure about three hundred feet north of the adit. During winter months, the building is heated with propane, the only outside power source required by the entire treatment process—and the source of Pfahl's considerable pride. The building houses a jet pump used to aerate the mine effluent. Aerated water immediately flows into an adjacent pretreatment pond that sits atop the original Mike Horse waste dump in front of the adit portal. The pond is lined with a thick, nearly impermeable HDPE liner designed to safely contain hazardous substances far more dangerous than acid mine drainage. The jet pump discharges about one hundred gallons per minute to the pond, which holds about six hundred thousand gallons. The "residence time" of water in the pond is about three to four days, during which the neutralized and oxygenated water precipitates a sludge composed primarily of iron hydroxides. Other metals readily adsorb to solids, so it is safe to reason that other metals are trapped in the sludge as well. This is an important step in the treatment process; ASARCO and state regulatory professionals want the fewest possible precipitating metals going into and hindering the artificial wetland. The pretreatment pond can be cleaned of accumulated metallic sludge. Most of the constructed wetlands cannot.

Sludge from the pond is removed periodically and spread on an adjacent, lined "sludge drying bed" to air dry. Once dry, the sludge will be moved to a waste repository, most likely the one next to the Paymaster Mine. The pond is expected to generate about ten thousand cubic feet of dried sludge per year.[33]

The two-year disjunction between completing the pretreatment pond in 1994 and the artificial wetlands in 1996 was due partially to ASARCO's intentions and partially to government refusals. The complete water-treatment system requires the wetlands to be fully effective, yet ASARCO pushed ahead with the pretreatment pond system because it wanted to begin some treatment as quickly as possible. Unfortunately, the wetlands could not be constructed on ASARCO's schedule and in the desired location.

ASARCO's original plan called for mine water to be piped from the pretreatment pond to a phase I wetland, where additional

10. ASARCO's pretreatment pond near the portal of the Mike Horse Mine, 30 September 1997. The pond has been drained for maintenance. Worker in foreground is wading in metallic hydroxides that have precipitated and settled from the mine's acidic waters. Montana Department of Environmental Quality.

metal removal would occur before the water was run to a phase II wetlands for final treatment. A kink in ASARCO's plan developed when Helena National Forest would not allow construction of the phase I wetlands on forest land. (ASARCO owns nearly all patented claims in the Heddleston district, but *un*patented surface is still managed by the Helena National Forest.) Wetlands require flat, or nearly flat ground, a scarce resource in most western mining districts, including the Heddleston. Ground conditions appropriate for these two artificial wetlands phases existed only along lower Beartrap Creek, above its confluence with Anaconda Creek, and below the Anaconda Mine along the Blackfoot River. ASARCO owns the river frontage, but lower Beartrap Creek is controlled by the U.S. Forest Service.

Helena National Forest reacted to ASARCO's proposal with substantial skepticism. As trustee of national forest land owned by the citizens in common, the agency was understandably reluctant to host a so-called hazardous waste facility. To the forest service, it made no difference that the wetlands were to improve water qual-

11. ASARCO's artificial wetlands constructed along the upper Blackfoot River, 18 June 1996. These ponds are the final step of ASARCO's treatment of the Mike Horse Mine's acidic waters. Montana Department of Environmental Quality.

ity; it mattered only that potentially unsafe accumulations of metals would collect on its land. As a matter of national policy, the forest service does not permit placement of hazardous materials on its land.

ASARCO attempted several times to obtain the forest service's permission to construct the phase I wetlands along lower Beartrap Creek, but without success. Eventually, in 1995, ASARCO deferred its original two-phased approach, at least temporarily, and began construction of a single wetlands next to the Anaconda Mine.[34] ASARCO connected the pretreatment pond at the Mike Horse Mine and the new wetlands with a 4-inch HDPE pipeline. Although it was not a challenging engineering assignment, the pipeline's design and construction commanded meticulous attention to detail and knowledge of construction techniques appropriate for harsh conditions. Pfahl's consultants buried the pipe 3 feet deep. In all, the pipeline dropped 322 feet over a linear distance of nearly 5000 feet. Acid mine drainage from the nearby Anaconda Mine was also piped to the wetland, a substantially easier task.

Four "cells," or small ponds, covering just three and one-half acres, make up the artificial wetland. The first pond has three subcells. The first subcell is lined so that precipitated iron and other metals may occasionally be pumped out, dried, and relocated to a waste repository. The second subcell is a "compost curtain" composed of 50 percent eco-compost, 25 percent gravel, and 25 percent calcite. It provides a final filter for precipitating iron. The third subcell is essentially a gravel bed that permits water to move through it and onto the next cell. Water flows laterally through the gravel, which contains crushed limestone mixed with peat to create an anaerobic, alkaline environment. Common sedges, a water-loving plant known to thrive in a metal-rich medium, are planted in the gravel.

The second and third ponds are larger than the first and repeat the gravel bed process. The final pond differs markedly from the first three. Treatment ends here with a sort of polishing process. The water flows open to the air so that accumulated hydrogen sulfide gas can dissipate. Alternating gravel berms extend out from the pond sides, forcing the water to meander from one side of the pond to the other as it moves closer to its discharge point. By lengthening the flow path of the treated water, the berms increase the residence time within the final cell.

Finally, nearly nine hundred feet from the inlet to the wetland, after undergoing treatment from the adit plug to vegetated gravel beds, acid mine drainage from the Mike Horse empties innocuously into the Blackfoot River. ASARCO's consultants expect this water-treatment system to reduce metal loads in the river up to 90 percent. They are confident much greater removal efficiency would result if the forest service would agree to a land swap so another artificial wetlands could be constructed.[35]

ASARCO's optimism is not universal. Montana's Department of State Lands has experimented extensively with artificial wetlands and no longer uses them in its own mine reclamation programs.[36] Although it observed improved water quality and a 60 percent reduction in metal loads in acid mine drainage, water discharged from artificial wetlands does not meet state or federal water-quality standards. Aquatic life and fish may not thrive in the treated water.

Whether cutthroat trout downriver appreciate ASARCO's efforts has yet to be determined. The river will almost unquestionably improve. The questions are how much, when, and will it be enough? By mid-1998, discharge from the artificial wetlands nearly met most water-quality standards for trout and other aquatic life.[37] Only zinc concentrations were proving stubborn, and zinc is notoriously toxic to trout. ASARCO's wastewater-discharge permit for its artificial wetlands commits the company to meeting protective water-quality standards by 1 October 2000.

ASARCO is a healthy financial target, the Mike Horse Mine is readily accessible, and the Blackfoot River possesses a near-rabid following of environmental activists. These factors contributed to the chain of events that led to ASARCO's cleanup efforts in the Heddleston district. But the coalescence of such factors is uncommon among the West's abandoned mines. ASARCO has clearly demonstrated what commitment can accomplish, but the company's involvement is anomalous. Few mining companies or individuals volunteer to redress the industry's historic environmental failures because of impediments presented by remote sites, perpetual maintenance costs, absence of power sources, scarcity of suitable land, demanding water-quality standards, and the lack of economical water-treatment technologies. Regulatory agencies like those in Montana are limited by their do-it-if-you-can-find-deep-pockets approach. Continuing down this path will surely result in thousands of abandoned-mine problems in the West remaining ignored.

10. The Divide

*The philosophy that got us into trouble is not the philosophy that is going
to get us out of trouble.* —Wes Jackson

Buy land. They aren't making any more. —Will Rogers

I AM ON THE DIVIDE AGAIN. It rained hard the past two nights,
and this morning an opaque mist fills the valleys and blots out
the horizon. Gray clouds hang above the hills and valleys to the
south and to the north above the broken outline of the Scapegoat
Wilderness. To the east, fat cumulus rise from the plains like
nineteenth-century canvas-sided Conestoga wagons. Towering
clouds are uncommon this time of year, but these rise many thousands of feet. Their undersides are black and angry, their summits incandescent.

An annual cycle is ending in the high country. The air has an
edge to it that warns fall is close, winter not far behind. In spite of
recent rain, the jeep track I walk is dry and hard from the effects
of wind and sun at seven thousand feet. Butterflies swarm silently
around me without obvious ambition. Some are gold trimmed
with black; others are dun and black. The only sounds are the wind
and the clicking of grasshoppers. Grasses and flowers have gone
to seed, although daisies, harebell, and bedstraw still blossom. A
few months ago, glacier lilies bloomed in the lee of snowbanks.
Now, curled brown leaves are all that remain.

I come to a padlocked forest service gate across the road. A sign
announces that the area behind the gate is closed permanently to
jeeps, dirt bikes, and quadratracks, and to snowmobiles during
big game hunting season between mid-October and the end of
November. Nevertheless, the sign concedes the area to foot traffic.
The selective closure indicates that it provides security for big
game, nonmotorized recreational experiences, and habitat for
threatened or endangered wildlife. Deciding I must fit into one
of these categories, I walk around the gate and continue. The jeep

trail bends to the southeast, contours a slope, then climbs and loops back east and north. I arrive atop a nearly bald summit marked "7497" on my map. Lichen-covered bedrock litters the crest. It is flaky and fissile and breaks easily. At the highest point, someone has constructed a cairn from six or eight large chunks.

The parklike summit meadow is several hundred feet across. Grotesque specimens of twisted and gnarled whitebark pines squat everywhere. Decades of gales have peeled away the bark. Long dead, tortured by time and wind, and less than fifteen feet tall, they remind me of terra-cotta warriors guarding the tombs of ancient China. I put my boot against the trunk of the largest pine and push. It resists, seems to push back. Like the clay guards, these pines intend to honor a commitment. I drop my pack, settle against one worn trunk, and pull lunch into my lap. At this moment, I would rather be here than anyplace else on Earth.

The Mike Horse is invisible, tucked behind a timbered ridge two miles away. Logging clearcuts have carved divots from forest-clad mountains to the west, while over my shoulder lie wheat fields, threads of highway, and shiny steel farm buildings. Fragments of pampered wildness lie near, but almost everything beneath an infinite sky differs from what it once was. The human hand is obvious. I doubt Meriwether Lewis would recognize the river valley he ascended two centuries ago. Norman Maclean, the Blackfoot River's most eloquent psalmist, might howl.

The Mike Horse Mine's metals and acids are finite, of course. Someday they will be gone. Already one scientist has suggested that a significant portion of the total may have drained into the river.[1] It is not a long step from that reckoning to a recommendation that we leave the mine alone and allow nature to cleanse itself over the next millennium or two. But the logical extension of this argument is to allow spent nuclear fuel to decay by its own atomic clock without protecting ourselves or making amends with nature. Both are unwise and reckless propositions. We must draw lines somewhere, protect what we can, repair what we cannot. Pure geographic discovery on the surface of this planet is over.

But I am being maudlin. There is no reason to expect absence of change. Humanity's crush dictates change as surely as a hungry stomach growls. It is an ancient irony: change is the only constant.

Leaving the summit, I descend into an old forest-fire burn that

12. Upper Blackfoot River drainage, 1 April 1995. The far ridge on the left is the Continental Divide. The Mike Horse Mine lies several miles behind the timbered ridge descending from the right. Photograph by author.

started on the Divide and scorched several acres before drifting eastward. Life has come full circle. The fire released nutrients stored in the living trees and forest litter. Now, bunchgrass reaches nearly to my thighs and charred stumps squat like misshapen mushrooms among young pines ten feet tall. Farther on, I spy the Mike Horse, an old friend from which I have learned much. Overgrown mine roads crisscross the mountainside above its adits. Although I cannot see it, I know its tailings pond shimmers in the afternoon sun at the foot of a cliff of maroon shale.

Twenty years ago, a friend of mine supported his student bride by constructing snow fences along Wyoming's Interstate-80, a desolate stretch of highway prone to high winds and nasty winters. For months, Peter commuted sixty miles every morning to build snow fences so that winter travelers might avoid an unscheduled night in Rawlins or Medicine Bow, or worse, on the icy front seat of the family Chevy.

Peter still mimics his foreman's constant use of a single phrase, "The century belongs to the doers, not the thinkers."

The manifesto was dispensed with gusto, as if frenetic action was an appropriate antidote to considered performance. Do not think too much, he intoned, or those doing, not considering, will pass you by. It was his irritating, catchall way of ending a lunch break or spurring his crew to finish one more fence before quitting time. It seemed the only thing he knew to articulate. After recounting this story, Peter always smiles ruefully and wags his head. A thoughtful guy, he wonders why, if thinking was so bad, did they so frequently have to rebuild or relocate a fence?

A single maxim can stay with you long after you leave the scene of its relevance. I wonder this: If hardrock miners of the past 150 years had done more thinking before doing, would there be a half-million abandoned mines in this country? Or would they have proceeded as they did in any event? Montana, Idaho, Nevada, Colorado, Arizona, and California encompass hundreds of abandoned mines in the same league as the Mike Horse. Not all are as bad; some are worse. The truly offensive may rise to the stature of a federal Superfund site, but the vast majority are treated like ugly stepchildren. If we ignore them long enough, maybe they will disappear.

For all the capital invested, jobs generated, wages paid, and the pittance of new wealth created, it is a shame that the Mike Horse is known best for its blight on the Blackfoot River. ASARCO likely spends more now to repair the consequences of this single mine than it ever profited during the mine's seven-year prime. Surely, the company must question history's fairness. All this and taxpayers received just several hundred dollars in patenting fees and nothing at all for the minerals. I cannot avoid astonishment that the richest nation in the broad span of human ambition has allowed one industry to go unchecked for so long. It is as if our collective wealth exists because so many aged bills remain unpaid.

The town of Mike Horse, Montana, has come and gone as well. Its once-inhabitants are now aging men and women, their wages long since spent on diapers and groceries. Mine buildings have been torn down. Equipment has been scrapped or moved to the next hot mining district. It is a story line both unique to Mike Horse and common to the West.

The questions are obvious. How could early miners have exhibited such little respect for the land? How could they have used and then discarded a mountain valley and part of a river? Perhaps they assumed they were opening up a wilderness; maybe they believed they were rough-edged capitalists leading America westward. But I find it difficult to attach patriotic objectives to their efforts. Like so many of us, they were guided by survival and self-interest, not altruism. Hardrock miners of the past left a legacy of wreckage because reclamation and protection of water resources were unnecessary and avoidable expenses. They received the land for damn near free, paid no royalties and few taxes, then walked away because it cost them less than repairing the damage. No one made them do otherwise.

It is hard to blame them. In addition to being miners, they were businessmen. If the government—their government and our government—placed no value on the land, why should they? Any businessman who knowingly provides a raw material to another below his own cost and with unknown future liability is considered a fool in the business community. Doing so, he consumes and someday depletes his assets. By this definition, America has been a fool.

Businessmen who would not take advantage of such largess would likewise be considered fools by their peers. It is business.

Only if America cares enough are changes possible. The most sweeping reforms proposed for the General Mining Law of 1872 include an end to the patenting process, a royalty on minerals extracted from federal lands, and a program to reclaim the nation's abandoned mines and return abused streams and rivers to health.

Patenting, the archaic process whereby individuals or companies acquire title to federal lands and minerals for a pittance, was adopted to help open and populate the West and provide miners with an avenue to obtain clear title to discovered minerals. In this sense, the 1872 mining law was more a land use law than a mining law. In an effort to at least temporarily remedy the statute's most generous subsidy, Congress has, since 1994, annually suspended this statutory right.[2] A permanent end to the patent right is a likely inclusion in any final reform legislation, but that the suspension must currently be renewed each year places this beast on a tenuous chain.

In any event, the West no longer needs congressional encouragement to develop its wide-open spaces. If you doubt this, visit Denver, Phoenix, Salt Lake City, or Las Vegas. The Rocky Mountain

West's population has increased apace in the past century and continues to grow.

The other two components of long-overdue reform remain buried in congressional caucus rooms. Contending factions argue over the definition of a fair royalty. Dollars to be paid to the federal treasury under competing proposals vary by a factor of ten. Regardless, it is transparently in the interests of the mining industry to fight and delay *any* meaningful royalty. It can be expected to oppose all royalties as fiercely and for as long as possible. Royalties will increase operating costs, which must be passed along to reluctant customers. And business is business.

The major obstacle to an effective program to correct the worst perversions of past mining operations is the lack of funding. Mineral royalties could finance such a program, so these two reforms might proceed hand in hand. Only a sharply focused, well-funded program can address and overcome the regulatory and technological difficulties inherent in reclaiming the West's abandoned mines and treating their polluted waters. As for mineral lands already transferred from the federal estate and patented, imposition of an abandoned-mine reclamation fee may be appropriate. Until a focused program is in place, cleanups will be limited to the worst or most public circumstances, where they will be executed under complex and expensive hazardous waste laws poorly suited to western mines.

Hardrock miners have exploited the 1872 law for more than a century, a law born of nineteenth-century beliefs and business practices. Mining technology and business practices have grown with the times, but the law, mired in post–Civil War boosterism, has not. For any reform to be effective, it must be predicated on a basis understood by modern business minds. Today, mining companies pay bonds to ensure reclamation when mining is complete. But bonding primarily covers reclamation of the earth and guarantees little about future water quality. To expect miners to act in the best interests of the environment on the basis of moral suasion is dementia of the most naive sort. Create a business environment that values land and water, and miners will protect and restore them.

I have spoken with many mining men and women. With few exceptions, over cold beer in smoky bars, they acknowledge the savage past of their industry. They also want to do better than their predecessors. Only one or two deny mistakes were made. To these few, western landscapes strewn with the rusting debris of mines and miners are simply an unavoidable cost of economic growth. Such individuals fortunately seem to be a minority. In fact, some industry leaders finally acknowledge that problems exist and that something needs to be done.[3] But how long must we wait?

It is time to leave. Instead of retracing my steps along the Divide and over the bald summit, I choose the hypotenuse. Discovering a faint trail leading toward the summit's north face, I follow it onto a steep, timbered slope. The track is vague and the hillside slick, and the sole evidence that humans ever walked here is an occasional ax blaze on trees. Only deer and elk use the trail now, and judging by its wear, rarely.

There is no evidence that logging or fire ever occurred in this highest and most remote corner of the Beartrap Creek watershed. There are no stumps in this old growth. Even so, the forest is unimpressive. Few of the familiar pine and fir rise above thirty feet. Disfiguring clumps of growth cling to many pine branches— mistletoe, a parasite common to stressed lodgepole stands. I stop and peer through a jungle of jackstrawed blowdowns. A mile off, the Mike Horse tailings pond reflects the evening light.

My reckoning is accurate. The path yields to angled sunlight and I exit the timber onto the jeep road below the padlocked forest service gate. Sundown is not far. In the dim valleys below me, ranchers' yard lights create eccentric pinpoints in the reaching darkness. Beside me, trees throw lengthening shadows. Above me, the sky is as clear and blue as a jay squawking along the Blackfoot River.

As I near my truck, a lone spruce grouse struts onto the road before me and stops in profile. I softly chuck a small rock at it. I miss, but the bird will not fly. Composed and deliberate, it saunters back into the trees. I pause and stretch, anticipating my descent down the steep jeep road in the dark and wondering if someone driving the highway will notice my headlights bouncing across the mountainside. Will he or she ponder the path I am on and where I have been?

These mountains and canyons still embody mining country—

here, where sunlight burnishes the rocks and where the wind pours over the Divide. George and Rosie Kornec still believe in it. Anaconda's strike of the 1960s lies untapped, waiting. And ASARCO remains mired in a district that bustles only with those who would mend it. No one hopes more than I that they succeed.

I know a mining engineer, a man with hardrock experience throughout the West. He has crawled and waded through many of the abandoned adits and drifts of the Heddleston district. He once told me that there is nothing exceptional about the Mike Horse and claims it is no different than hundreds of other abandoned mines in the West.

Indeed.

Notes

Much of what I have written about the Mike Horse Mine and the people
and events that make up its environmental history calls on observations and lessons drawn from my own experience. Additional information included in the text was compiled from various government,
academic, and company files, and more was obtained from discussions
with, and interviews of, knowledgeable government regulators and
company officials. Of course, the Kornec brothers of Lincoln, Montana,
were invaluable.

INTRODUCTION

To give some background on the first epigraph, I should note that Agricola, a sixteenth-century Saxon physician, was also interested in mining
and metallurgy. His classic statement is widely cited within the mining
and geology professions, although the complete, translated text is out-
dated. Nonetheless, the quote provides a wonderful perspective on mining and geological thought during his era. Also see William C. Peters, *Exploration and Mining Geology* (New York: John Wiley & Sons, 1978), 1–3.

    1. Stephen F. Arno, "Whitebark Pine," in *Northwest Trees* (Seattle: The
Mountaineers, 1977), 26.

    2. Numerous references, both common and obscure, address this por-
tion of Montana's prehistory. Perhaps the best known and most accessible is Michael P. Malone, Richard B. Roeder, and William L. Lang, *Montana: A History of Two Centuries*, rev. ed. (Seattle: University of Washington
Press, 1991). Also see Olin D. Wheeler, *The Trail of Lewis and Clark, 1804–
1904*, vol. 2 (New York: G. P. Putnam's Sons, 1904), 293; Noah Brooks, *First
Across the Continent* (New York: Charles Scribner's Sons, 1901), 313; and
Hubert Howe Bancroft, "History of Washington, Idaho, and Montana:
1845–1889," in *The Works of Hubert Howe Bancroft*, vol. 31 (San Francisco:
History Company, 1890), 605.

1. BEGINNINGS

    1. Duane A. Smith, *Mining America: The Industry and the Environment,
1800–1980* (Niwot: University Press of Colorado, 1993), 1.

    2. America's mining history, especially Montana's, is covered in a va-

riety of sources, some better and more comprehensive than others. I have not attempted to summarize or list all of them because the scope of western mining history is well beyond that of this book. Information included in this chapter was taken from Malone, Roeder, and Lang, *Montana*. Also see Otis E. Young Jr., *Western Mining: An Informal Account of Precious-Metals Prospecting, Placering, Lode Mining, and Milling on the American Frontier from Spanish Times to 1893* (Norman: University of Oklahoma Press, 1970); and Carl Ubbelohde, Maxine Benson, and Duane A. Smith, *A Colorado History*, 7th ed. (Boulder CO: Pruett Publishing, 1995).

3. Charles F. Wilkinson, *Crossing the Next Meridian* (Washington DC: Island Press, 1992), 38.

4. Malone, Roeder, and Lang, *Montana*, 64–67.

5. Montana Department of State Lands, Abandoned Mines and Reclamation Bureau, *Abandoned Hardrock Mine Priority Sites*, by Pioneer Technical Services and Thomas, Dean and Hoskins, summary report, March 1994, 1–5.

6. Various Montana and federal agencies have attempted to document the value of mineral production to early local and state economies. The federal agency originally charged with this responsibility was the U.S. Bureau of Mines. In Montana, reports have typically been prepared by the Bureau of Mines and Geology. See Montana College of Mineral Science and Technology, *Metallic Mineral Deposits of Lewis and Clark County, Montana*, by Henry G. McClernan, Montana Bureau of Mines and Geology Memoir 52 (Butte MT: 1983); Malone, Roeder, and Lang, *Montana*, 71, 185–92; and James Arthur MacKnight, "The Mines of Montana, Their History and Development to Date" (paper prepared for the National Mining Congress, Helena MT, 12 July 1892), 6. All provide estimates of mineral production in early Montana. Other experts have concluded that "Mine production data for the period prior to 1904 is generally nonexistent or unavailable." United States Department of Interior, *Mines and Prospects of the Butte 1° × 2° Quadrangle, Montana*, by James E. Elliott et al., open-file report 86-0632, U.S. Geological Survey (Denver, 1986), 9.

7. John Byrne and John J. Barry, *Fourteenth Annual Report of the Inspector of Mines of the State of Montana* (Helena MT, 1902), 24.

8. MacKnight, "The Mines of Montana, Their History and Development to Date," 5.

9. Malone, Roeder, and Lang, *Montana*, 242.

10. Much of this discussion is summarized from Wilkinson, *Crossing the Next Meridian*, 34–50. Also see L. Thomas Galloway and Karen L. Perry, "Mining Regulatory Problems and Fixes," in *Golden Dreams, Poisoned*

Streams, edited by Philip M. Hocker (Washington DC: Mineral Policy Center, 1977), 202–3; as well as John L. Neff's detailed legal discussion in "The Miners Law—Part I," *California Geology* (November–December 1994): 152–57; and Neff, "The Miners Law—Part II," *California Geology* (January–February 1995): 10–21.

11. These figures derive from a comprehensive assessment of the national abandoned-mined land problem prepared by the Mineral Policy Center. Those with more interest in the extent of the problem in the American West would do well to begin with James S. Lyon, Thomas J. Hilliard, and Thomas N. Bethell, *Burden of Gilt* (Washington DC: Mineral Policy Center, 1993).

12. Western Interstate Energy Board, *Inactive and Abandoned Noncoal Mines: A Scoping Study*, vol. 1, prepared for the Western Governors' Association Mine Waste Task Force, August 1991.

13. Wilkinson, *Crossing the Next Meridian*, 33.

14. Lyon, Hilliard, and Bethell, *Burden of Gilt*, 6.

15. The larger figures are presented in Lyon, Hilliard, and Bethell, *Burden of Gilt*, 25. The lower estimates are from Montana Department of State Lands, Abandoned Mines Reclamation Bureau, *Abandoned Hardrock Mine Priority Sites*, by Pioneer Technical Services, summary report, December 1994, 1–2. The considerable difference between these two estimates is likely due to conflicting definitions of what constitutes an abandoned mine site.

2. DISCOVERY

1. The facts surrounding Joseph Hartmiller's discovery seem to be unknown. The version presented here is pieced together from two sources. One is a published history of the Lincoln, Montana, area: *Gold Pans and Singletrees* (Fairfield MT: Anderson Publications, 1994), 260. The other source is oral. As I researched the Mike Horse Mine and its environmental history, I came to know two remarkable brothers, George and Dan "Rosie" Kornec, whose lives and family history have been entwined with the Mike Horse Mine and Heddleston Mining District since World War I. I spent hours talking with and listening to the Kornec brothers, beginning in September of 1995 and continuing through October of 1996. George recounted the story of Hartmiller's strike to me on 4 September 1995. George was married to Joseph Hartmiller's granddaughter and had numerous occasions to hear the story of her grandfather's discovery around his in-laws' table.

2. Young, *Western Mining*, 21. A mining historian of some repute, Young lends little credence to stories like Hartmiller's, which credit an

animal for the accidental discovery of rich lodes. Hartmiller's discovery, as told by George Kornec, bears noteworthy resemblance to one of the typical, yet unlikely, versions described by Young. In fact, Young concludes that "if the animal's antics had not resulted in discovery, a systematic search certainly would have." Striking similarities exist between the version recalled by George Kornec and the more compact account contained in the area's published history.

3. For information regarding the forest fire history of the Heddleston Mining District, I am indebted to Jack Kendley, Helena National Forest silvaculturalist, whom I interviewed 19 January 1996. Concerning the role prospectors and miners played in initiating forest fires, a surprising number of histories mention this occurrence only as an afterthought. For example, see Duane A. Smith, *Mining America*, 13.

4. A variety of published geological information is available to the lay reader. A fundamental understanding of Montana geology can be obtained in David Alt and Donald W. Hyndman, *Roadside Geology of Montana* (Missoula MT: Mountain Press Publishing, 1986). For more detailed information concerning the geology and geological history of the Heddleston Mining District and nearby area, refer to Montana College of Mineral Science and Technology, *Metallic Mineral Deposits*; U.S. Department of Interior, *Metalliferous Deposits of the Great Helena Mining Region, Montana*, by J. T. Pardee and F. C. Schrader, U.S. Geological Survey Bulletin 842 (Washington DC: Government Printing Office, 1933), 87–108; U.S. Department of Interior, *Geologic Map of the Rogers Pass Area, Lewis and Clark County, Montana*, by James W. Whipple, Melville R. Mudge, and Robert L. Earhart, U.S. Geological Survey Miscellaneous Investigation Series Map I-1642 (Denver, 1987); and U.S. Department of Interior, *Physiography and Glacial Geology of Western Montana and Adjacent Areas*, by W. C. Alden, U.S. Geological Survey Professional Paper 231 (Washington DC: Government Printing Office, 1953).

5. *Gold Pans and Singletrees*, 260; George Kornec, conversation with author, 4 September 1995.

6. The Silver Panic of 1893 was a major international economic event that warrants serious historical research in its own right. Here, I have provided a generalized sketch of what its impact probably was on prospectors and miners working in a remote Montana mining district. For further reading on the panic, see Bill Skidmore, *Treasure State Treasury: Montana Banks, Bankers and Banking, 1864–1984* (Helena: Montana Bankers Association, 1985), 46–52; and Malone, Roeder, and Lang, *Montana*, 192.

7. Isaac F. Marcosson, *Metal Magic, The Story of ASARCO* (New York: Farrar,

Straus and Company, 1949), 150–51. American Smelting and Refining Company went by the acronym ASARCO until 1975, when the company formally changed its name to Asarco. However, because the fully capitalized spelling, ASARCO, is still widely seen and used within the mining industry, and for the sake of consistency, ASARCO is used throughout this book.

8. Rowland King, mining engineer, to F. W. Rader, president, Sterling Mining and Milling Company, 31 March 1921, Montana Department of Health and Environmental Sciences Upper Blackfoot Mining Complex, file no. 18-01-03-10, photocopy; "Story of Lincoln, 1860's–1989," n.p., 21 February 1995, Montana Department of Health and Environmental Sciences Upper Blackfoot Mining Complex, file no. 18-01-03-01, photocopy, 41; Chester T. Kennan, mining geologist and engineer, "The Big Blackfoot Lead-Silver District, Lewis and Clark County, Montana," Spokane, Washington, [1926?], ASARCO company records of the Heddleston Mining District, Wallace, Idaho.

9. The early mining and mineral production history of the Heddleston district has been summarized in several places: *Gold Pans and Singletrees*, 259; U.S. Department of Interior, *Metalliferous Deposits*, 87–88; and McClernan, *Metallic Mineral Deposits*, 31–36.

10. Mike Horse Mining Company, articles of incorporation, 21 June 1902, Montana Secretary of State Office, Helena.

11. General Land Office, Mineral Survey no. 10371, files of the U.S. Bureau of Land Management State Office, Billings, Montana.

12. Hartmiller's dealings with nearby claim owners and eventual business partners were unraveled from undifferentiated photocopies of documents in the Montana Department of Health and Environmental Sciences Upper Blackfoot Mining Complex files. Information concerning other lode claims included in the initial consolidation of the burgeoning Mike Horse Mine are from Mineral Survey no. 10371.

13. Koehler S. Stout, "Mine Methods and Equipment," in *Handbook for Small Mining Enterprises*, Montana Bureau of Mines and Geology Bulletin 99 (Butte: Montana College of Mineral Science and Technology, 1976), 85.

14. My assessment that Hartmiller and his partners initially drilled by hand is based largely upon the absence of any historical record of a steam boiler, compressor, and other equipment at the mine at that time. Such equipment was not documented at the Mike Horse until around World War I. The revolutionary role played by the use of steam and then by compressed air in drilling in hardrock mines is summarized in Terry Cox, *Inside the Mountains: A History of Mining around Central City, Col-*

orado (Boulder CO: Pruett Publishing, n.d.), 30–33. Also see Young, *Western Mining*, 204–11.

15. For wonderfully vivid descriptions of hand-drilling and blasting techniques, I am indebted to David Newman, an Elliston, Montana, hardrock miner with whom I spoke on 12 December 1995, and to Stout, a retired professor of mining engineering from the Montana College of Mineral Science and Technology with whom I had a conversation 19 January 1996. Also see Young, *Western Mining*, 182–85.

16. Byrne and Barry, *Fourteenth Annual Report*, 50.

17. Byrne and Barry, *Fourteenth Annual Report*, 4.

18. Kennan, "The Big Blackfoot Lead-Silver District," 10–11.

19. U.S. Department of Interior, *Metalliferous Deposits*, 88.

20. Kennan, "The Big Blackfoot Lead-Silver District," 21.

21. J. A. Grimes, "Report on the Mike Horse Mine and the Heddlestone [*sic*] Mining District, Lewis and Clark County, Montana," 15 May 1915, Anaconda Geological Documents Collection, University of Wyoming, Laramie, file 31106.

22. King to Rader, 31 March 1921; *Gold Pans and Singletrees*, 261; U.S. Department of Interior, *Metalliferous Deposits*, 94.

23. King to Rader, 31 March 1921.

3. HARD TIMES AND EARLY SIGNS

1. For the formation of the Sterling Mining and Milling Company, see their articles of incorporation, 19 August 1919, Montana Secretary of State Office, Helena; Kennan, "The Big Blackfoot Lead-Silver District," 15. On the purchase of the mine, see *Gold Pans and Singletrees*, 261.

2. Kennan, "The Big Blackfoot Lead-Silver District," 15–21.

3. U.S. Department of Interior, *Metalliferous Deposits*, 94; Sterling Mining and Milling Company, annual reports for 1920–26, Montana Secretary of State Office, Helena.

4. U.S. Patent no. 969729, files of the U.S. Bureau of Land Management State Office, Billings, Montana.

5. Kennan, "The Big Blackfoot Lead-Silver District."

6. Sterling Mining and Milling Company, annual report for 1927, Montana Secretary of State Office, Helena.

7. Of course, the absence of relevant corporate or state records does not prove that organized mining ventures were not operating in the Heddleston district during the depression, nor does it prove that the Mike Horse Mine was inactive at the time. Unfortunately, looking for available and published sources on the Mike Horse Mine and the district for this period is like stepping into a black hole. My inference that

"informal" mining likely took place is based upon my conversations with individuals who lived in Montana's mining districts during this time: George and Rosie Kornec, numerous conversations between 4 September 1995 and 22 October 1996; John J. Thompson Jr., conversation, 17 January 1996; and Newman, conversations, 1 December 1994 and 12 January 1995.

8. This brief account of the early history of the Kornec family in the Heddleston district was pieced together from talks with George and Rosie Kornec in their home on Beartrap Creek, one-half mile above the Mike Horse Mine, 4 and 7 September 1995, 17 January 1996, and 22 October 1996.

9. Kennan, "The Big Blackfoot Lead-Silver District," 14.

10. Photographs no. 92-58 (set of five), Archive MC 239, Montana Historical Society Photographic Archives, Helena; Thompson, conversation, 17 January 1996; and Rosie Kornec, conversation, 17 January 1996. Rosie Kornec and Thompson assisted with dating the photographs.

11. A very conservative estimate of the volume of rock removed from the Mike Horse Mine by 1940 was calculated by multiplying the 1919 recorded lengths of the mine's three levels—2625 feet—times the typical adit dimensions of the era—5 feet by 7 feet. The resulting figure—about 3400 cubic yards—was doubled to allow for drifts and stopes.

12. U.S. Department of Interior, *Metalliferous Deposits*, 97.

13. U.S. Department of Interior, *Metalliferous Deposits*, 107.

14. For example, see Duane A. Smith, *Mining America*, chapter 7.

4. REBIRTH

1. Repeated inquiries of Rosie and George Kornec and of Thompson, all of whom grew up in or near the town of Mike Horse, failed to provide greater specificity. The Kornecs had lived nearby for about five years. Thompson moved to the town of Mike Horse with his father in 1940.

2. Deed Book 99, Lewis and Clark County, Montana, 20 October 1930, 26.

3. Charles C. Goddard Jr., "Report on the Mike Horse Mine, Heddleston Mining District, 19 Miles East of Lincoln, Lewis and Clark County, Montana, October, 1940," Anaconda Geological Documents Collection, University of Wyoming, Laramie, file 31106.

4. Miscellaneous Book 37, Lewis and Clark County, Montana, 17 October 1940, 546.

5. Goddard, "Report on the Mike Horse Mine," 5.

6. *Gold Pans and Singletrees*, 263.

7. Miscellaneous Book 38, Lewis and Clark County, Montana, 10 May 1940, 37.

8. Mike Horse Mining and Milling Company, articles of incorporation, 19 December 1940, Montana Secretary of State Office, Helena.

9. Miscellaneous Book 37, Lewis and Clark County, Montana, 31 December 1940, 613.

10. Miscellaneous Book 37, 17 October 1940, 546.

11. Miscellaneous Book 38, Lewis and Clark County, Montana, 8 June 1942, 535.

12. For the description of the ore dressing process presented in this chapter, which is applicable to both the original 1916 mill and subsequent improvements added by Mike Horse Mining and Milling Company, I relied upon Montana College of Mineral Science and Technology, *A Guide to Mineral Processing*, by Gordon L. Zucker and Hassan E. El-Shall, Montana Bureau of Mines and Geology Special Publication 85 (Butte, 1982), 1–18. Details concerning the 1916 mill layout and equipment are from King to Rader, 31 March 1921; and Rosie Kornec, who elaborated on mill layout and operations for both the 1916 and 1941 mills, conversations, 4 September 1995 and 22 October 1996. Additional information concerning the 1941 mill improvements are from C. P. Pollock and Keith Whiting, "Report on the Mike Horse Mining and Milling Company and Adjacent Groups, Heddleston Mining District, Lewis and Clark County, Montana," September 1944, ASARCO company records of the Heddleston Mining District, Wallace, Idaho, 5.

13. George and Rosie Kornec, conversations, 4 and 7 September 1995.

14. Pollock and Whiting, "Report on the Mike Horse Mining and Milling Company and Adjacent Groups," 5; *Gold Pans and Singletrees*, 263.

15. Mike Horse Mining and Milling Company, untitled report, 15 April 1941, Montana Secretary of State Office, Helena; *Gold Pans and Singletrees*, 263; Pollock and Whiting, "Report on the Mike Horse Mining and Milling Company and Adjacent Groups," 5.

16. *Gold Pans and Singletrees*, 264.

17. Rosie Kornec, conversation, 7 September 1995; *Gold Pans and Singletrees*, 263.

18. Pollock and Whiting, "Report on the Mike Horse Mining and Milling Company and Adjacent Groups," 6.

19. Rosie Kornec and I estimated the dimensions of the 1941 mill while we reviewed photographs from the period.

20. Montana College of Mineral Science and Technology, *A Guide to Mineral Processing*, 7.

21. Montana College of Mineral Science and Technology, *A Guide to Mineral Processing*, 8–18.

22. Pollock and Whiting, "Report on the Mike Horse Mining and Milling Company and Adjacent Groups."

23. Historical Research Associates, "Potentially Responsible Party Search of Selected Mining Properties in the Vicinity of the Mike Horse Mine, Lewis and Clark County, Montana," by T. Weber Greiser and Daniel F. Gallacher, 9 April 1991, Montana Department of Health and Environmental Sciences Upper Blackfoot Mining Complex, file no. 18-01-05-01, photocopy. The reported purchase price of one million dollars is from Rosie Kornec, conversation, 4 September 1995.

24. Deed Book 137, Lewis and Clark County, Montana, 7 August 1945, 331.

25. Mike Horse Mining and Milling Company, report, 10 August 1945, Montana Secretary of State Office, Helena.

26. *Gold Pans and Singletrees*, 264–67; "Story of Lincoln, 1860's–1989," 41; Thompson, "As I Remember the Mike Horse Mine," n.d., Montana Department of Health and Environmental Sciences Upper Blackfoot Mining Complex, unnumbered files; Thompson, conversation, 17 January 1996.

27. Pollock and Whiting, "Report on the Mike Horse Mining and Milling Company and Adjacent Groups," 8–11.

28. ASARCO, untitled memorandum, 18 July 1949, ASARCO company records of the Heddleston Mining District, Wallace, Idaho.

29. U.S. Bureau of Mines, *Minerals Yearbook 1949* (Washington DC: Government Printing Office, 1950), 17.

30. U.S. Bureau of Mines, *Minerals Yearbook 1950* (Washington DC: Government Printing Office, 1951), 16.

31. ASARCO[?], oversize plans and cross sections of the Mike Horse Mine, Montana, 31 January 1952, Anaconda Geological Documents Collection, University of Wyoming, Laramie, Document 125404.04; ASARCO, untitled memorandum, 12 August 1952, ASARCO company records of the Heddleston Mining District, Wallace, Idaho.

32. Brian Hansen, a professional engineer with McCulley, Frick and Gilman of Missoula, Montana, a consultant to ASARCO, interview by author, 16 January 1996; George and Rosie Kornec, conversations, 17 January and 22 October 1996.

33. U.S. Bureau of Mines, *Minerals Yearbook 1952* (Washington DC: Government Printing Office, 1953), 26.

34. D. C. Springer to P. I. Conley, 26 August 1957, ASARCO company records of the Heddleston Mining District, Wallace, Idaho, photocopy, 3.

35. Dick Rogers, telephone interview with author, 13 June 1995; Springer to Conley, 1.

36. Springer to Conley, 1–5.

37. Miscellaneous Book 37, 17 October 1940, 546.

38. Lease agreement between ASARCO and Norman Rogers, 1 April 1958, ASARCO company records of the Heddleston Mining District, Wallace, Idaho.

5. THE DAM

1. Duane A. Smith, *Mining America*, 112–22; Stout, telephone conversation, 11 October 1996.

2. Jeremy Mouat, "The Development of the Flotation Process: Technological Change and the Genesis of Modern Mining, 1898–1911," *Australian Economic History Review* 36 (March 1996): 3–31.

3. Rosie Kornec, conversation, 22 October 1996; Stout, telephone conversation, 11 October 1996; Anaconda Company, "Design Report on Repair of Tailings Embankment, Mike Horse Mine, Near Lincoln, Montana, for The Anaconda Company," by Dames & Moore, 18 September 1975, Montana Department of Health and Environmental Sciences Upper Blackfoot Mining Complex, file no. 18-01-02-10, photocopy, 3.

4. Helena National Forest, "Mike Horse Dam Reconstruction Environmental Analysis Report," August 1975, Montana Department of Health and Environmental Sciences Upper Blackfoot Mining Complex, file no. 18-01-02-10, photocopy, 4–8; Anaconda Company, "Design Report on Repair of Tailings Embankment," 3.

5. Rosie Kornec, conversation, 17 January 1996.

6. George and Rosie Kornec, conversations, 4 and 7 September 1995; Thompson, conversation, 17 January 1996.

7. Helena National Forest, "Mike Horse Dam Reconstruction Environmental Analysis Report," 4–5.

8. Thompson, conversation, 14 January 1999.

9. Helena National Forest, "Mike Horse Dam Reconstruction Environmental Analysis Report," 6–7.

10. Helena National Forest, "Mike Horse Dam Reconstruction Environmental Analysis Report," 7. Also see Anaconda Copper Mining Company, miscellaneous correspondence, memoranda, and "Details of Expenses," 1963–66, Anaconda Geological Documents Collection, University of Wyoming, Laramie, document 125404.04, file 619.

11. Jerry Stern to Anaconda Copper Mining Company, 16 November 1964, Anaconda Geological Documents Collection, University of Wyoming, Laramie, document 125404.04, file 619.

12. C. W. Potter to Goddard, 28 December 1964.

13. Dent, conversation, 3 January 1996.

14. Thompson, conversation, 17 January 1996.

15. Neil Peterson, Lincoln District ranger, memorandum to file, 2 November 1972, Anaconda Geological Documents Collection, University of Wyoming, Laramie, file 703.

16. Anaconda Company, untitled memorandum, 6 December 1972, Anaconda Geological Documents Collection, University of Wyoming, Laramie, file 703.

17. Helena National Forest, "Mike Horse Dam Reconstruction Environmental Analysis Report," 7; George and Rosie Kornec, conversation, 7 September 1995.

18. Thompson, conversation, 17 January 1996; George and Rosie Kornec, conversations, 4 and 7 September 1995, 17 January 1996, and 22 October 1996.

19. Rosie Kornec, conversation, 17 January 1996.

20. George Kornec, conversation, 7 September 1995.

21. My postulated sequence of events leading to the failure of the Mike Horse tailings dam is a compilation and synthesis of a variety of reports and firsthand accounts: Montana Department of Health and Environmental Sciences, "Field Surveillance of the Mike Horse Mine Tailings Pond Spills," by Mike Pasichnyk, Helena, Montana, 25 June 1975, Montana Department of Health and Environmental Sciences Upper Blackfoot Mining Complex, file no. 18-01-02-19, photocopy; Helena National Forest, "Mike Horse Dam Reconstruction Environmental Analysis Report," 4–8; Anaconda Company, "Design Report on Repair of Tailings Embankment," 3–4; Dent, conversation, 3 January 1996; Thompson, conversation, 17 January 1996; George and Rosie Kornec, conversations, 4 and 7 September 1995, and 17 January 1996.

22. Thompson, conversation, 17 January 1996.

23. Dent, conversation, 3 January 1996.

24. Montana Department of Health and Environmental Sciences, "Field Surveillance of the Mike Horse Mine Tailings Pond Spills."

25. Helena National Forest, "Mike Horse Dam Reconstruction Environmental Analysis Report," 1.

26. Anaconda Company, "Design Report on Repair of Tailings Embankment," 4.

27. Helena (Mont.) Independent Record, 29 June 1975.

28. Helena (Mont.) Independent Record, 30 June 1975. Also see Missoulian (Mont.), 28 and 30 June 1975 and Great Falls (Mont.) Tribune, 27 and 29 June 1975.

29. Dent, conversation, 3 January 1996; Montana Department of Health and Environmental Sciences, "Field Surveillance of the Mike Horse Mine Tailings Pond Spills"; Liter E. Spence to the author, 17 March 1997.

30. Helena National Forest, "Mike Horse Dam Reconstruction Environmental Analysis Report, 8; Montana Department of Health and Environmental Sciences, "Field Surveillance of the Mike Horse Mine Tailings Pond Spills"; Montana Department of Fish and Game in cooperation with the Anaconda Company, "Upper Blackfoot River Study: A Premining Inventory of Aquatic and Wildlife Resources," by Spence, December 1975, Helena, Montana, v.

31. Montana Department of Fish and Game, "Effects of the June, 1975 Mike Horse Tailings Dam Failure on Water Quality and Aquatic Resources of the Upper Blackfoot River, Montana," 15 December 1997, Helena, Montana.

32. Spence, to author, 17 March 1997.

33. Dent, conversation, 3 January 1996.

34. Helena National Forest, "Mike Horse Dam Reconstruction Environmental Analysis Report," 1, 17.

35. Anaconda Company, "Design Report on Repair of Tailings Embankment."

36. Anaconda Company, "Design Report on Repair of Tailings Embankment," 7.

37. Anaconda Company, "Design Report on Repair of Tailings Embankment." 6–24.

38. Anaconda Company, "Report on Construction Inspection, Mike Horse Dam and Spillway, Near Lincoln, Montana, for The Anaconda Company," by Dames & Moore, 5 January 1976, Montana Department of Health and Environmental Sciences Upper Blackfoot Mining Complex, file no. 18-01-02-10, photocopy.

39. Montana Department of Fish and Game, "Upper Blackfoot River Study," v.

40. Dent, telephone conversation with author, 15 December 1995, and conversation with author, 3 January 1996; Mike Pasichnyk, telephone conversation with author, 15 December 1995. Following the dam failure, Pasichnyk was Montana's first regulatory official on the scene.

41. Kevin Keenan, telephone conversation with author, 19 December 1996. Keenan oversaw regulatory enforcement for the Montana Department of Health and Environmental Sciences, Water Quality Bureau, at the time of the Mike Horse tailings dam failure.

42. Malone, Roeder, and Lang, *Montana*, 323, 367–68.

43. Keenan, telephone conversation, 19 December 1996.

6. AN OPEN PORTAL

1. ASARCO[?], oversize plans and cross sections of the Mike Horse Mine, Montana.

2. This discussion of AMD, its characteristics, origins, and control, is summarized from a variety of sources and emphasizes the role AMD plays in the West's abandoned mines and mining districts. The topic is quite broad, however, and today's mining industry and regulatory agencies deal with it almost daily, with greater to lesser degrees of success. See Donald D. Runnells, Thomas A. Shepherd, and Ernest E. Angino, "Metals in Water: Determining Natural Background Concentrations in Mineralized Areas"; U.S. Department of Interior, *Metal Biogeochemistry in Surface-Water Systems—A Review of Principles and Concepts*, by John F. Elder, U.S. Geological Survey Circular 1013 (Washington DC: Government Printing Office, 1988), 32; U.S. Department of Interior, *Geochemistry of Ground Water in Mine Drainage Problems*, by Ivan Barnes and F. E. Clarke, U.S. Geological Survey Professional Paper 473-A (Washington DC: Government Printing Office, 1964), A4; Ohio State University Research Foundation, *Acid Mine Drainage Formation and Abatement*, prepared for U.S. Environmental Protection Agency, 1971, 9; U.S. Department of Interior, *Acid Mine Drainage: Control and Abatement Research*, by Ann G. Kim et al., U.S. Bureau of Mines Information Circular 8905 (Pittsburgh PA: 1982); Ohio State University Research Foundation, *Sulfide to Sulfate Reaction Mechanism: A Study of the Sulfide to Sulfate Reaction Mechanism as It Relates to the Formation of Acid Mine Waters*, prepared for Federal Water Pollution Control Administration and U.S. Department of Interior, February 1970, FWPCA grant no. 14010 FPS; Mellon Institute, Carnegie-Mellon University, *Microbial Factor in Acid Mine Drainage Formation*, prepared for Federal Water Quality Administration and U.S. Department of Interior, July 1970, FWQA grant no. 14010 DKN; R. L. Nelson, M. L. McHenry, and W. S. Platts, "Mining" in *Influences of Forest and Rangeland Management on Salmonid Fishes and Their Habits*, American Fisheries Society Special Publication 19, 1991, 425–27.

3. U.S. Department of Interior, *Metalliferous Deposits*, 108.

4. Montana College of Mineral Science and Technology, *Metallic Mineral Deposits*, 36.

5. Montana Department of State Lands, *Addendum to Cultural Resource Inventory and Evaluation of Selected Abandoned Hardrock Mine Sites in West-*

ern Montana, 1985: Four Hard Rock Mine Sites in the Heddleston District, Lewis and Clark County, Montana, by GCM Services, July 1989, 3.

6. U.S. Department of Interior, *Metalliferous Deposits,* 108.

7. U.S. Department of Interior, *Metalliferous Deposits,* 108.

8. George and Rosie Kornec, conversations, 4 September 1995 and 17 January 1996.

9. This discussion of ARD's characteristics and origins is based on discussions I had with George Furniss in person and on the telephone (18 January, 18 June, and 23 October 1996), as well as several of his research publications. For further reading, see Furniss, "Natural Acid Drainage Baseline Water Quality of Paymaster and Stevens Creek, Heddleston District, Lewis and Clark County, Montana," working paper, Missoula, Montana, 1996, and Furniss and Nancy W. Hinman, "Iron Oxide Deposits Resulting from Natural Acid Drainage Record Holocene Environment of Paymaster Creek, Heddleston District, Lewis and Clark County, Montana" (abstract and poster presented at the annual meeting of the Geological Society of America, Denver CO), *Abstracts with Programs* 28.7 (October 1996).

7. PLANTING FISH

1. U.S. Department of Interior, *Physiography and Glacial Geology of Western Montana and Adjacent Areas,* 106.

2. Discussion of the natural history of the west-slope cutthroat trout is summarized from Patrick C. Trotter, *Cutthroat, Native Trout of the West* (Boulder: Colorado Associated University Press, 1987), 1–33, 56–71. Some readers may note that the west-slope cutthroat is referred to elsewhere as *Salmo clarki lewisi,* whereas I use *Oncorhynchus clarki lewisi.* The latter is the more current and accepted nomenclature among fishery taxonomists. For further reading, see Leo F. Marnell, "Cutthroat Trout in Glacier National Park, Montana" in *Our Living Resources, A Report to the Nation on the Distribution, Abundance, and Health of U.S. Plants, Animals, and Ecosystems,* edited by Edward T. LaRoe, et al., 153–54 (Washington DC: Government Printing Office, 1995).

3. John Fraley, "Further Adventures of a Travelin' Fish," *Montana Outdoors,* May–June 1994, reprinted by Montana Department of Fish, Wildlife and Parks; Don Peters, Montana Department of Fish, Wildlife and Parks, telephone conversation with author, 12 April 1996; Montana Bull Trout Scientific Group, *Blackfoot River Drainage Bull Trout Status Report,* prepared for the Montana Bull Trout Restoration Team, June 1995.

4. Don Peters, telephone conversation, 15 March 1996; Spence, to author, 17 March 1997.

5. Pat Van Eimeren, Flathead National Forest (Mont.) fishery biologist, to author, 1 September 1998.

6. Fraley, "Further Adventures of a Travelin' Fish."

7. Don Peters, telephone conversation, 12 April 1996.

8. Trotter, *Cutthroat, Native Trout of the West*, 12, 18, 24.

9. Don Peters, telephone conversation, 15 March 1996; Montana Department of Fish, Wildlife and Parks, "Fish Planting Report" (Helena MT: n.d.), Montana Department of Fish, Wildlife and Parks fishery records, photocopy).

10. Don Peters, telephone conversations, 15 March 1996 and 12 April 1996.

11. Ed MacHaffie, "Fishing Notes for the Year 1911," photocopy, provided by Stan Bradshaw, Helena, Montana.

12. Thompson, conversation, 17 January 1996.

13. Grimes, "Report on the Mike Horse Mine."

14. George and Rosie Kornec, conversation, 17 January 1996.

15. Detailed fishery information about the Blackfoot River's upper watershed, pre-1970, that indicates specifically which trout species existed, how many, and where is lacking. Nonetheless, reasoned speculation suggests that these streams would have been habitable to trout at the time. See Montana Department of Fish and Game, "Upper Blackfoot River Study," 52; Don Peters, telephone conversation, 15 March 1996.

16. Trotter, *Cutthroat, Native Trout of the West*, 1–33, 56–71.

17. U.S. Environmental Protection Agency, Office of Water Regulations and Standards, *Quality Criteria for Water 1986*, (Washington DC: Government Printing Office, 1986); Janet Decker-Hess, "Impact on the Aquatic Ecosystem by Mining in the Mike Horse Area, Heddleston Mining District, Lewis and Clark County, Montana" (master's thesis, University of Montana, 1978), 136–39; Montana Department of Fish and Game, "Upper Blackfoot River Study," 83; Johnnie N. Moore, S. N. Luoma, and Don Peters, "Downstream Effects of Mine Effluent on an Intermontane Riparian System," *Canadian Journal of Fisheries and Aquatic Sciences* 48.2 (1991): 225, 228–30; Van Eimeren, to author, 1 September 1998.

18. U.S. Environmental Protection Agency, *Quality Criteria for Water 1986*.

19. For general discussions of natural water-sediment-metal relationships, see U.S. Department of Interior, *Metal Biogeochemistry in Surface-Water Systems* and U.S. Department of Interior, *Study and Interpretation of the Chemical Characteristics of Natural Water*, 3rd ed., by John D. Hem, U.S. Geological Survey Water-Supply Paper 2254 (Washington DC: Government Printing Office, 1989).

20. Montana Natural Resource Damage Litigation Program, *Aquatic Resources Injury Report, Appendices A–H: Aquatics Resources Injury Assessment*, prepared by Mark Kerr, January 1995, Helena, Montana, including "Acute Toxicity in Pulse Events: Relative Sensitivity of Brown and Rainbow Trout to Pulses of Metals Typical of the Clark Fork River," by Harold Bergman (appendix B): 16; "Influence of Acclimation/Adaptation on Toxicity: Differential Tolerance and Resistance of Brown and Rainbow Trout to Water-Borne Metal Concentration Typical of the Clark Fork River," by Bergman (appendix C): 19; "Determine the Extent to Which Rainbow Trout and Brown Trout Avoid or Prefer Water Quality Characteristic of the Clark Fork River," by Dan Woodward and Bergman (appendix C): 24–25; "Chronic Toxicity of Cadmium, Copper, Lead, and Zinc to Rainbow Trout and Brown Trout at Concentrations and Forms Present in Water and Aquatic Invertebrate Food Chains in the Upper Clark Fork River," by Woodward, Bergman and Charles Smith (appendix E): 25; and "The Physiological Impairment of Fish Caused by Chronic Exposure to Metals at Concentrations Typically Found in Clark Fork River Food and Water," by Bergman (appendix F): 23–24.

21. Montana Department of Fish and Game, "Upper Blackfoot River Study."

22. Montana Department of Fish and Game, "Upper Blackfoot River Study," 41.

23. Montana Department of Fish and Game, "Upper Blackfoot River Study," 26.

24. Montana Department of Fish and Game, "Upper Blackfoot River Study," 23, table 2.

25. Montana Department of Fish and Game, "Upper Blackfoot River Study," 52, 81.

26. Montana Department of Fish and Game, "Upper Blackfoot River Study," 52–53.

27. Spence, conversation with author, 11 January 1996.

28. Don Peters, telephone conversation, 12 April 1996.

29. Shirley Ashby, telephone conversation with author, 18 March 1996.

30. Paul Roos, telephone conversation with author, 18 March 1996.

31. Montana State University and MSI Detoxification, *Hydrogeochemical, Vegetational and Microbiological Effects of a Natural and a Constructed Wetland on the Control of Acid Mine Drainage*, by D. J. Dollhopf et al., Reclamation Research Publication 88-04 (Bozeman MT, 1988), 16.

32. Montana State University and MSI Detoxification, *Effects*, 2–3.

33. Montana State University and MSI Detoxification, *Effects*, 5.

34. Montana State University and MSI Detoxification, *Effects*, 4–5.

35. Moore, Luoma, and Don Peters, "Downstream Effects of Mine Effluent on an Intermontane Riparian System"; Moore, "Mine Effluent Effects on Non-Point Source Contaminants in the Blackfoot River, Montana," report to the Lewis and Clark City-County Health Department and the Montana Department of Health and Environmental Sciences, Water Quality Bureau, n.d., Missoula, Montana, Montana Department of Health and Environmental Sciences Upper Blackfoot Mining Complex, file no. 18-01-02-17, photocopy.

36. Moore, Luoma, and Don Peters, "Downstream Effects of Mine Effluent on an Intermontane Riparian System," 222.

37. Moore, Luoma, and Don Peters, "Downstream Effects of Mine Effluent on an Intermontane Riparian System," 223.

38. Moore, "Mine Effluent Effects on Non-Point Source Contaminants in the Blackfoot River" 27, 31; Moore, conversation with author, 25 October 1996.

39. Moore, Luoma, and Don Peters, "Downstream Effects of Mine Effluent on an Intermontane Riparian System," 229.

40. Moore, Luoma, and Don Peters, "Downstream Effects of Mine Effluent on an Intermontane Riparian System," 230.

41. Moore, Luoma, and Don Peters, "Downstream Effects of Mine Effluent on an Intermontane Riparian System," 230.

42. Moore, conversation, 25 October 1996.

8. WHEN GIANTS DIE

1. Anaconda Company, "Geology of the Heddleston Copper-Molybdenum Deposit, Lewis and Clark County, Montana," by Richard N. Miller et al., n.d., Butte, Montana, Montana Department of Health and Environmental Sciences Upper Blackfoot Mining Complex, file no. 18-01-03-12, photocopy, 6.

2. Anaconda Company, "Geology of the Heddleston Copper-Molybdenum Deposit," 5.

3. U.S. Bureau of Mines, *Minerals Yearbook 1954* (Washington DC: Government Printing Office, 1955), 28; U.S. Bureau of Mines, *Minerals Yearbook 1955* (Washington DC: Government Printing Office, 1956), 30; Montana College of Mineral Science and Technology, *Directory of Known Mining Enterprises, 1959*, by F. A. Crowley, Montana Bureau of Mines and Geology Bulletin 14 (Butte, 1960), 22; Montana College of Mineral Science and Technology, *Directory of Mining Enterprises for 1964*, by Crowley, Montana Bureau of Mines and Geology Bulletin 46 (Butte, 1960), 20.

4. Vincent D. Perry, "Anaconda Geology, Its Origins, Achievements,

and Philosophy," July 1979, Anaconda Geological Documents Collection, University of Wyoming, Laramie, document file 3102, 11.

5. Anaconda Company, "Summary of Heddleston District Work by the Anaconda Company from May 1961 to Date," 16 August 1971, Anaconda Geological Documents Collection, University of Wyoming, Laramie, document file 702.

6. Anaconda Company, "Geology of the Heddleston Copper-Molybdenum Deposit," 9.

7. Springer to Conley, 2.

8. Edward P. Shea to E. I. Renouard, 1 July 1964, Anaconda Geological Documents Collection, University of Wyoming, Laramie, document file 619.

9. Shea to Renouard, 1 July 1964.

10. Anaconda Company, "Summary Report, Heddleston Property, Lewis and Clark County, Montana," March 1972, Anaconda Geological Documents Collection, University of Wyoming, Laramie, document file 703; Anaconda Company, "Details of Expenses for Geological Examination of Properties in Lewis and Clark County, from August 1962 to December 31, 1965," 31 December 1965, Anaconda Geological Documents Collection, University of Wyoming, Laramie, document file 619.

11. *Helena (Mont.) Independent Record*, 4 August 1964, Anaconda Geological Documents Collection, University of Wyoming, Laramie, document file 619.

12. Anaconda Company, "Summary of Heddleston District Work by the Anaconda Company from May 1961 to Date."

13. K. L. Howard Jr., "An Evaluation of the Heddleston Property, Montana," 20 January 1981, Anaconda Geological Documents Collection, University of Wyoming, Laramie, document file 31028, document .08.

14. Anaconda Company, annual report for 1964, Anaconda Geological Documents Collection, University of Wyoming, Laramie. All Anaconda Company annual reports from 1951 to 1975 are housed in document file 1419.02.

15. Anaconda Company, annual report for 1965.

16. T. G. Fulmor, untitled memorandum, 12 August 1965, Anaconda Geological Documents Collection, University of Wyoming, Laramie, document file 619.

17. Anaconda Company, annual report for 1965.

18. Shea, untitled memorandum, 26 July 1966, Anaconda Geological Documents Collection, University of Wyoming, Laramie, document file 701. The memorandum identifies the family as Cornich, not Kornec. Given the proximity of the Kornec family's claims to Anaconda's explo-

ration operations as well as references to the incident by George and Rosie Kornec, it is likely that Shea meant the Kornec family. The memorandum names a Bill and Don Cornich. Bill and Don Kornec are Rosie and George's brothers.

19. Anaconda Company, Surplus Equipment Department, transfer statement, 2 September 1966, Anaconda Geological Documents Collection, University of Wyoming, Laramie, document file 619; George Kornec, conversation, 4 September 1995.

20. Anaconda Company, "Anaconda's Ore Resources, 1972–1974," 1972, Anaconda Geological Documents Collection, University of Wyoming, Laramie, document file 4022.01A.

21. Anaconda Company, proposed mine plan, 16 July 1965, Anaconda Geological Documents Collection, University of Wyoming, Laramie, document file 123801.34.

22. *Wallace (Idaho) Miner*, 4 May 1967, Anaconda Geological Documents Collection, University of Wyoming, Laramie, document file 701.

23. Anaconda Company, annual report for 1966.

24. Anaconda Company, annual report for 1967.

25. Goddard to M. K. Hannifan, 15 November 1967; Hannifan to J. G. Hall, 27 November 1967; John Hall to Hannifan, 30 November 1967, Anaconda Geological Documents Collection, University of Wyoming, Laramie, document file 701.

26. Anaconda Company, "Progress Report, Heddleston Project, November, 1967," Anaconda Geological Documents Collection, University of Wyoming, Laramie, document file 701.

27. R. D. Piper to Goddard, 11 January 1968, Anaconda Geological Documents Collection, University of Wyoming, Laramie, document file 26706.01.

28. Anaconda Company, annual report for 1968; Anaconda Company, "Summary of Heddleston District Work by the Anaconda Company from May 1961 to Date."

29. Anaconda Company, annual report for 1969.

30. Anaconda Company, "Environmental Impact of Mining and Milling, Heddleston Area, Montana," n.d., Anaconda Geological Documents Collection, University of Wyoming, Laramie, document file 31028, document .02.

31. Frank Laird Jr., telephone conversation with author, 11 January 1997. Laird was a senior Anaconda executive with its environmental operations during this period; John North, chief legal counsel, Montana Department of Environmental Quality, telephone conversation with author, 14 January 1997; Monte Mason, chief, Minerals Manage-

ment Bureau, Montana Department of Natural Resources and Conservation, telephone conversation with author, 14 January 1997; Mason to John North, 15 September 1994, Montana Department of Natural Resources and Conservation, Trust Land Management Division, photocopy.

32. Governor Ted Schwinden, telephone conversation with author, 17 February 1997, and conversation with author, 19 February 1997.

33. Laird, telephone conversation; Mason to John North, 15 September 1994.

34. Laird, telephone conversation, 11 January 1997; Anaconda Company, "Environmental Impact of Mining and Milling."

35. Anaconda Company, "Environmental Impact of Mining and Milling."

36. *Down to Earth*, August 1994, 4. *Down to Earth* is the monthly newsletter of the Montana Environmental Information Center, Helena, Montana.

37. Laird, telephone conversation, 11 January 1997; Anaconda Company, "Environmental Impact of Mining and Milling."

38. James Nathan Miller, "Bad Scene at the Mike Horse Mine," *Empire Magazine, Denver Post*, 10 January 1971, 16–21.

39. Mason to North; Schwinden, telephone conversation, 17 February 1997; Schwinden, conversation, 19 February 1997; *Down to Earth*, 4.

40. Mason to North; Schwinden, telephone conversation, 17 February 1997; Schwinden, conversation, 19 February 1997.

41. Laird, telephone conversation, 11 January 1997.

42. *Down to Earth*, 4; Miller, "Bad Scene," 16–21.

43. Laird, telephone conversation, 11 January 1997; Anaconda Company, "Summary of Metal Resources Heddleston District," n.d., Anaconda Geological Documents Collection, University of Wyoming, Laramie, document file 702; Anaconda Company, "Summary Report, Heddleston Property, Lewis and Clark County, Montana," March 1972, Anaconda Geological Documents Collection, University of Wyoming, Laramie, document file 703; Anaconda Company, "Mineral Properties, The Anaconda Company, 1971, 1974 and 1979," mineral property summary, 14 December 1971, Anaconda Geological Documents Collection, University of Wyoming, Laramie, document file 4023.

44. Laird, telephone conversation, 11 January 1997.

45. Anaconda Company, "Summary of Heddleston District Work"; "Environmental Impact of Mining and Milling"; Anaconda Company, untitled memorandum, 20 July 1970, Anaconda Geological Documents Collection, University of Wyoming, Laramie, document file 702.

46. Laird, telephone conversation, 11 January 1997; Schwinden, telephone conversation, 17 January 1997.

47. Laird, telephone conversation, 11 January 1997; James Posewitz, conversation with author, 14 March 1995. At the time, Posewitz was actively engaged in Montana Department of Fish and Game's review of Anaconda's Heddleston plans.

48. Anaconda Company, "Mineral Properties, The Anaconda Company, 1971, 1974 and 1979."

49. Laird, telephone conversations with author, 11 January 1997 and 30 September 1998.

50. Anaconda Company, "Anaconda's Ore Resources, 1972–1974," 1 January 1976, Anaconda Geological Documents Collection, University of Wyoming, Laramie, document file 4022.01B.

51. Malone, Roeder, and Lang, *Montana*, 394–95; Charles Van Hook, telephone conversation with author, 29 September 1998. Van Hook was active with Montana environmental organizations during this period; John North, telephone conversation with author, 29 September 1998.

52. Laird, telephone conversation, 11 January 1997.

53. Anaconda Company, annual report for 1970.

54. Anaconda Company, annual report for 1971.

55. Anaconda Company, annual report for 1970.

56. Anaconda Company, annual report for 1972.

57. Anaconda Company, annual report for 1971.

58. Anaconda Company, annual report for 1972.

59. Anaconda Company, annual report for 1972.

60. Anaconda Company, untitled memorandum, n.d., Anaconda Geological Documents Collection, University of Wyoming, Laramie, document file 703.

61. Anaconda Company, miscellaneous letters, February–June 1973, Anaconda Geological Documents Collection, University of Wyoming, Laramie, document file 703; Anaconda Company, "Mineral Properties, The Anaconda Company, 1971, 1974 and 1979."

62. Anaconda Company, annual report for 1973.

63. "Anaconda's Ore Resources, 1972–1974."

64. Anaconda Company, annual report for 1974.

65. Anaconda Company, annual report for 1975.

66. William H. Miller, "What Killed King Copper?" *Industry Week*, 28 October 1985, 44–48.

67. Anaconda Company, annual report for 1975.

68. Miller, "What Killed King Copper?" 46.

69. Anaconda Company, annual report for 1975.

70. Anaconda Company, annual report for 1975.

71. Anaconda Company, Anaconda/ARCO merger prospectus, 15 September 1976, Anaconda Geological Documents Collection, University of Wyoming, Laramie, document file 5107.

72. Anaconda Company, Anaconda/ARCO merger prospectus, 83.

73. Howard, "An Evaluation of the Heddleston Property, Montana," 20 January 1981, Anaconda Geological Documents Collection, University of Wyoming, Laramie, file 31028, document .08.

74. Howard, "Evaluation of the Heddleston Property."

75. Historical Research Associates, "Potentially Responsible Party Search," 7.

76. Miller, "What Killed King Copper?" 45.

77. Miller, "What Killed King Copper?" 46–47.

9. CLEANUP

1. The description of the ambush of George Kornec and its aftermath is based upon conversations with George, 4 and 7 September 1995, 17 January 1996, and 14 January 1999. The inference that Ted Kaczynski may have been responsible for the shooting was reported in the *Missoulian (Mont.)*, 13 December 1998.

2. Rosie Kornec, conversation, 4 September 1995.

3. Department of State Lands, Abandoned Mined Land Bureau, fact sheet, November 1990, Montana Department of Health and Environmental Sciences Upper Blackfoot Mining Complex, file no. 18-01-01-16.

4. *Helena (Mont.) Independent Record*, 19 June 1990.

5. Montana Department of Health and Environmental Sciences, miscellaneous correspondence, 1990–91, Montana Department of Health and Environmental Sciences Upper Blackfoot Mining Complex, file no. 18-01-01-16; Chris Pfahl, conversation with author, 15 January 1996.

6. Montana Department of Health and Environmental Sciences, miscellaneous correspondence, 1990–91.

7. Judy Reese, Montana Department of Environmental Quality, memo to author, 16 May 1997.

8. Reese, memo, 16 May 1997.

9. Reese, memo, 16 May 1997.

10. Pfahl, conversation, 15 January 1996; Hansen, conversation with author, 25 October 1996.

11. Pfahl, conversation, 15 January 1996.

12. Reese, conversation, 17 February 1995; Robert J. Robinson to Pfahl, 26 May 1993.

13. Pfahl, conversation, 15 January 1996; Reese, conversation, 17 February 1995; Robinson to Pfahl, 26 May 1993.

14. Pfahl, conversation, 15 January 1996.

15. Hansen, conversation with author, 25 October 1996.

16. ASARCO and ARCO, *Draft Master Plan for Remedial Actions at the Upper Blackfoot Mining Complex*, 22 October 1993, Montana Department of Health and Environmental Sciences Upper Blackfoot Mining Complex, file no. 18-02-09, photocopy.

17. ASARCO and ARCO, *Draft Master Plan*, 4.

18. Pfahl, conversation, 15 January 1996.

19. W. C. Rust, McCulley, Frick and Gilman, to Pfahl, 22 October 1993.

20. ASARCO and ARCO, *Draft Master Plan*, 8–9.

21. Rosie Kornec, conversation, 22 October 1996.

22. Reese, telephone conversation with author, 19 May 1997; Robinson to Pfahl, 26 May 1993; Reese, memo, 16 May 1997; Hansen, conversation with author, 25 October 1996.

23. Robinson to Pfahl, 26 May 1993.

24. ASARCO and ARCO, *Upper Blackfoot Mining Complex (UBMC), Anaconda and Mike Horse Mine Waste Materials, Identification of Remedial Actions and Work Plan for Implementation of Remedial Action*, prepared by McCulley, Frick and Gilman, January 1994, 6-12.

25. ASARCO and ARCO, *Upper Blackfoot Mining Complex Draft 1995 Remedial Design Report*, prepared by McCulley, Frick and Gilman, March 1995, 5-2.

26. Hansen, conversation, 16 January 1996.

27. Hansen, conversation, 16 January 1996.

28. Pfahl, telephone conversation with author, 29 January 1997; ASARCO and ARCO, *Upper Blackfoot Mining Complex*; Hansen, conversation, 16 January 1996.

29. Hansen, telephone conversations with author, 16 January 1996 and 31 January 1997.

30. Pfahl, conversation, 15 January 1996.

31. M. A. Girts and R. L. P. Kleinmann, "Constructed Wetlands for Treatment of Acid Mine Drainage: A Preliminary Review" (paper presented at the National Symposium on Mining, Hydrology, Sedimentation and Reclamation, Lexington KY, 1986).

32. John Koerth, Montana Department of Environmental Quality, telephone conversation with author, 24 February 1997.

33. Hansen, telephone conversations, 25 October 1996 and 31 January 1997; ASARCO and ARCO, *Upper Blackfoot Mining Complex Draft 1995 Remedial Design Report*; Hansen, fax to author, 5 February 1997.

34. Pfahl to Charlie Hester, U.S. Forest Service, 22 October 1993; Pfahl, telephone conversation with author, 29 January 1997; Reese, memo, 16 May 1997.

35. ASARCO and ARCO, *Upper Blackfoot Mining Complex Draft 1995 Remedial Design Report*, prepared by McCulley, Frick and Gilman, March 1995, 5-12–5-17; Frank Sanders to Bryan McCulley, McCulley, Frick and Gilman, memorandum titled "Results of Site Visit to UBMC Regarding Design of Wetland Treatment Systems for Mike Horse and Anaconda Mine Discharges and Related Data Needs," 1 September 1993; Hansen, conversation, 16 January 1996; Hansen, conversation, 25 October 1996; Hansen, telephone conversation, 31 January 1997; ASARCO and ARCO, *Draft Master Plan*.

36. Koerth, telephone conversation, 24 February 1997.

37. Reese, telephone conversation, 21 September 1998.

10. THE DIVIDE

1. ASARCO, Northwestern Exploration Division, *Water Characteristics of the Upper Blackfoot River with Inactive Mine Workings*, prepared by Margarete Kalin, Boojum Research, 4 April 1990, 14, Montana Department of Health and Environmental Sciences Upper Blackfoot Mining Complex File No. 18-01-02-14, photocopy.

2. Philip M. Hocker, president, Mineral Policy Center, quoted in Susan A. Brackett, "Reform for the 21st Century," *Clementine* (spring–summer 1997): 7.

3. Mineral Policy Center, *MineWire*, 30 January 1999, 2.

Index

abandoned mines, 14–15, 71
acid mine drainage (AMD): bacteria and, 94; characteristics of, 92; Clean Water Act and, 159–65, 173; ferric and ferrous iron and, 94; ferric hydroxide and, 93, 95, 113; *Ferrobacillus ferrooxidans*, 94; *Ferrobacillus sulfooxidans*, 94: Heddleston district and, 92–103, 112–24; metals mobilized by, 93–95; neutralization of, 95–97; sulfuric acid and, 93; *Thiobacillus Thiooxidans*, 94; wetlands and, 120–24, 168–73; yellowboy and, 94
acid rock drainage (ARD), 101–3
adit, 28–30, 42
Alder Gulch, 10
Alice Creek, 137–40
AMD. *See* acid mine drainage
American Smelting and Refining Company. *See* ASARCO
Anaconda Copper Mining Company (also Anaconda Minerals Company), 46–47, 58, 72; Montana assets of, 84; Copper Production Evaluation Committee, 140–42; corporate difficulties of, 74, 131–46; Heddleston Mining District and, 117–18, 126–48, 165; Mike Horse tailings dam failure and, 73–85
Anaconda Creek, 3, 6, 54, 64, 83, 88, 113, 118
Anaconda Mine, 5, 42, 88, 98, 162, 164–71
Anderson, Reece, 10
ARCO (Atlantic Richfield Company), 146–49, 155–65

ARD. *See* acid rock drainage
argillite, 19, 20, 64
arsenopyrite, 20
ASARCO (American Smelting and Refining Company): Anaconda Copper Mining Company and, 126–29, 144–48, 158; Blackfoot River cleanup and, 149–73, 178; formation of, 25; Mike Horse Mine purchase by, 53–54, 90; Mike Horse tailings dam and impoundment and, 71, 84–85; Norman Rogers's negotiations with, 59; smelters, 32, 47, 53
Ashby, Shirley, 119
Atlantic Richfield Company (ARCO), 146–49, 155–65

Beartrap Creek, 3, 6, 17, 38, 41, 64; cleanup of, 150–71; diversion of, 68–69, 74, 79; diversion reconstruction of, 82–83; flood of June 1964 and, 72; flood of June 1975 and, 75–85; mining and minerals processing impacts on, 113–24
Belt Supergroup, 22
Blackfoot River, 3, 19, 22, 25, 33, 37, 40, 48, 57, 88; Anaconda and, 134–41, 146; cleanup of, 149–73; fishery history, 109–17; flood of June 1964 and, 119; flood of June 1975 and, 78–85, 117–20; indigenous game fish of, 108–9; metals in, 112, 121–25
Black Ore lode claim, 28
BLM (Bureau of Land Management), 14
bornite, 20

207

Boyer, S. L., 28
bulkhead, adit plug, 163, 165–72
Bureau of Land Management
(BLM), 14
Butte Mining District, 11, 128
Butte MT, 12, 147
Byrne, John, 31

cadmium, 123
Cadotte Pass, 4, 33
calcite, 95, 168
Calliope Lode, 25
Carbonate Mine, 5
CECRA (Montana Comprehensive
Environmental Cleanup and
Responsibility Act), 153–64
Central Montana Highway, 114
CERCLA. See Comprehensive Envi-
ronmental Response, Compen-
sation, and Liability Act
chalcopyrite, 20
Chicago, Milwaukee, and St. Paul
Railway, 33, 36
Chile, 74, 131–36, 143–45
Civil War, 11, 13
Clark Fork, 3, 162
Clean Water Act, 115, 143, 159,
165
Coeur d'Alene Mining District,
36, 54
comminution, 49–50
Comprehensive Environmental
Response, Compensation, and
Liability Act (CERCLA, or Super-
fund), 14–15, 156–62, 178
concentrate, 32, 50–52, 147
Congress: minerals development
policy and 1866 act of, 12
Continental Divide (Divide), 1, 38,
41, 134, 175, 177, 181
Cook & West, 36
copper, 56, 59, 93, 117, 126–41,
146–47
Crane Company, 145–46
creeks. See Alice Creek; Anaconda
Creek; Beartrap Creek; Mike
Horse Creek; Pass Creek; Pay-

master Creek; Sandbar Creek;
Willow Creek; Wolf Creek

Dent, Bob, 80–83, 146
Detroit lode claim, 28
diorite, 20, 64
Dobler, Michael, 27
Dollhopf, Douglas, 120–21, 123
drill, pneumatic, 30
Dwyer, John, 47, 53

East Helena MT, 25, 29, 32, 35, 47,
53, 107
electric power, 48, 51–52
Estill, Edgar, 47, 53

Federal Mines, 54
ferricrete, 102
Finlay, Francois, 10
Flesher Pass, 32, 100
Flesher Pass Road, 119–20
forest fires, 20, 112–13
Fuchs, Conrad, 28
Furniss, George, 100–103

galena, 20
gangue, 49, 52
General Mining Law of 1872, 12,
13, 26, 85; reform of, 179
Goddard, Charles C., Jr, 46–47, 50–
52, 60, 126–32
gossans, 100
Great Depression, 36, 40, 45
Great Falls MT, 6, 25, 31–32, 36, 53,
114
Great Northern Railway, 32
Grimes, J. Alden, 32–33, 36
groundwater: Mike Horse Mine
and, 91, 167; pumping of, 57
Gruhle, Henry, 27
gulches. See Alder Gulch; Mike
Horse Gulch; Moly Gulch; Paymaster Gulch; Shoue Gulch;
Swamp Gulch

hand-steel, single- and double-
jacking, 30

Hartmiller, Joseph, 17–20, 23–35, 126
Heddleston, William, 25
Heddleston Mining District (Heddleston district), 5, 19, 21–25, 36, 68; Anaconda and, 126–41, 146–47; cleanup of, 154–73; copper and molybdenum ore body of, 80, 117, 127–41; major mining in, 57, 126–27; mineral production of, 126; water quality and, 118–24
Helena MT, 6, 10, 12, 25, 32, 54, 119
Helena National Forest, 69, 72–73, 78, 81, 146, 170–72
high-grading, 31
Hog All claim, 26
Hog All Vein, 59
hydraulic head, 166–69

Independent Record (Helena), 78–79, 130, 153
Intermediate Vein, 55

jaw-crusher, 49

Kaczynski, Ted, 150
Kennan, Chester T., 36
Kennecott Copper Company, 130
Kleinschmidt, Harrison, 129
Koontz, Robert, 28
Korean War, 56–57
Kornec, Dan (Rosie), 39–41, 68–69, 76, 113, 150–51, 163
Kornec, George, 39–41, 70, 76, 113, 132, 150–51, 163
Kornec, Margaret, 70, 75–76
Kornec, Samuel, 39–40, 51, 69–70
Kornec, Samuel, Jr., 51
Kornec family, 37–39, 66, 132

Lander's Fork, 4, 79, 111, 118
lead, 56, 59, 93, 126
Lewis, Meriwether, 4, 176
Lewis and Clark Pass, 4
Liberty Mining Company, 34

limestone, 21, 168
Lincoln MT, 25, 33, 48, 54, 119
Little Nell lode claim, 28
Little Nell Vein, 55
logging, 112–13, 176
Luoma, Sam, 121–24

MacGilvara, Boo, 47
MacHaffie, Ed, 110–12, 117
Maclean, Norman, 176; A River Runs Through It, 5
marcasite, 20; acid mine drainage and, 93–97
Marty, Lee, 69–70
MEPA (Montana Environmental Policy Act), 143
metals: Blackfoot River and, 112–14, 121–24; occurrence in natural waters and, 116; removal by wetlands and, 120–24; toxicity to wildlife and, 121; trout toxicity and bioaccumulation, 116–17, 119; water quality standards, 115–16; west-slope cutthroat trout and, 114–15
Midnight Copper Mining Company, 129
Mike Horse Creek, 51, 57, 59, 63, 65–68, 91; flood of June 1975 and, 75
Mike Horse Gulch, 41, 50, 55, 57, 65, 91, 163
Mike Horse lode claim, 26
Mike Horse Mine, 5, 15, 29, 33; acid mine drainage and, 98, 112–16, 118–24; Anaconda and, 126–32, 146; ASARCO's purchase and operation of, 53–57; cleanup of, 150–73; closure of, 71; groundwater in, 91; Kornec family and, 37, 40–41; main portal of, 89–90; rebirth of, 46–53; World War II and, 42–45
Mike Horse Mining and Milling Company: formation of, 47–48, 126; mining start-up of, 51–53, 65; sale of, 54

Mike Horse Mining Company, 26–27, 33–34
Mike Horse MT, 54, 178
Mike Horse Road, 37, 87, 131
Mike Horse tailings dam, 63, 65, 69; engineering inspection of, 72; failure of, 77, 155; headcutting of, 72; original siting of, 66–67; size of, 71; reconstruction of, 82–84
Mike Horse Vein, 20, 25, 55, 56, 90, 126
mill, ball, 50
mill, concentrating, 48, 52
mill, gravity, 50
mine development, 31
mineral, 93, 116; sulfide (sulfur-bearing) minerals, 20, 93
mines. *See* Anaconda Mine; Carbonate Mine; Mike Horse Mine; Paymaster Mine
mining claims: lode, 13, 25, 69; patented, 68; unpatented, 14, 68
mining district, 11
Missoula MT, 12, 36, 114
molybdenum, 117, 129–41, 147
Moly Gulch, 41, 131
Montana blackspot. *See* trout, westslope cutthroat
Montana Board of Land Commissioners, 137–40
Montana Bureau of Mines and Geology, 98
Montana Comprehensive Environmental Cleanup and Responsibility Act (CECRA), 153–64
Montana Department of Fish and Game, 79
Montana Department of Fish, Wildlife and Parks, 111, 117, 121, 152
Montana Department of Health and Environmental Sciences, 79, 153–66; Bob Robinson and, 156–64
Montana Department of State Lands, 152–55, 165

Montana Environmental Policy Act (MEPA), 143
Montana Fish and Game Commission, 109
Montana Metal Mine Reclamation Act, 143
Montana Power Company, 51–52, 84
Montana State University Reclamation Research Unit, 120, 166
Montana Water Resources Board, 138
Moore, Johnnie, 121–24
mucking, muck, 29–30

National Environmental Policy Act (NEPA), 81, 143
National Wildlife Federation, 139
no. 2 level, 57, 167
no. 3 adit or tunnel, 33, 51, 55–56, 90, 112, 163, 166–67
no. 4 level, 53, 56, 91, 166
no. 6 level, 55–56, 91
no. 8 level, 55–56, 91
Northern Plains Resource Council, 142

O & M Mines Company, 33–34
O'Connor, Walt, 39–40
Old Mike, 19, 24
ore, concentrating, 31–32
ore and ore reserves, 19, 133, 140–42

Padbury, George, 25, 27
Paramount Estates, 129
Pass Creek, 6, 25, 65, 78, 83, 113, 118
passes. *See* Cadotte Pass; Flesher Pass; Lewis and Clark Pass; Rogers Pass
patent, 12–13, 179
Paymaster Creek, 97–103; acid rock drainage and, 101–3; George and Rosie Kornec's description of, 99
Paymaster Gulch, 98

Paymaster Mine, 5, 98–100, 129,
	165, 169
perimeter discharge method, 67
Perry, Vincent D., 127
Peters, Don, 121–24
Peterson, Neil, 73
Pfahl, Chris, 156–73
Pine Hill lode claim, 28
placer mining, 25, 51
Pleistocene epoch, 22, 106–7
porphyry, 23, 128
Porter, Robert, 51, 53
Potter, Charlie, 76
Powell, Leonard, 141
premiums, 53–54, 56
Prickly Pear Junction, See East Hel-
	ena MT
pyrite, 20, 42, 52, 78, 112, 167; acid
	mine drainage and, 93–97; acid
	rock drainage and, 100–103

quartz, 19–20

reserves, proven, 31
Robinson, Bob, 156–64
Rogers, Norman, 58, 72, 126; Ana-
	conda's negotiation with, 73,
	129; 1958 lease agreement and,
	60; Norman Rogers Mining
	Company and, 58
Rogers Pass, 1, 25, 114
roll crusher, 49
Roos, Paul, 119
Rothermel, Frank, 27
Rothermel, William, 26
royalty payments, royalties, 47, 59,
	180

Sandbar Creek, 100
Scapegoat Wilderness, 175
school trust lands, 138
Schwinden, Ted, 137, 139
sedimentation, 113; trout produc-
	tion and, 114–16, 122
selective flotation, 52, 57
shaft, 28–29
shaking table, 50

Sherman Silver Purchase Act of
	1890, 24
Shoue Gulch, 78, 113, 118
Silver Camp, 32, 64
Silver City MT, 53, 107, 134
Silver Panic of 1893, 24
size of liberation, 52
slimes, 66
Spence, Liter, 117–19, 141
sphalerite, 20
spillway, emergency flood, 72, 77,
	82–84
Stampfly, Sam, 46–47, 60
Sterling lode claim, 28
Sterling Mining and Milling Com-
	pany, 35–36; bondholders of, 46,
	50, 54
Stern, Jerry, 73
Strip Mine Conservation and Recla-
	mation Act, 152
Stuart brothers, 10
Superfund. See Comprehensive En-
	vironmental Response, Compen-
	sation, and Liability Act
Swamp Gulch, 120

tailings and tailings dam, 50–52,
	113, 117, 119, 124, 146
tailings ponds, 14, 69, 71, 75
Tenneco, 145–46
tetrahedrite, 20
Thompson, John, 73–78
Thompson, John, Jr., 73–78, 112–13
timbers, 29
trout: brook, 109–10, 113, 118–24;
	bull, 109–11, 113–14; German
	brown, 110; rainbow, 110
trout, west-slope cutthroat, 79–
	80; characteristics and historic
	range of, 108–11; metals and,
	115; mining impacts on, 113,
	118–24; spawning and, 114,
	119
Trout Unlimited, 139, 151–52

U.S. Bureau of Fisheries, 109
U.S. Bureau of Mines, 11

U.S. Environmental Protection
   Agency, 14, 115
U.S. Forest Service, 138–39
U.S. Geological Survey, 42, 121, 138

vein: 19, 41

Wallace Miner (Idaho), 134
wastewater treatment, 54
Watt, Mr., 66–67
wetlands, role in metals removal,
   120–21
whitefish, mountain, 109

White Hope Mine Inc., 38
Wilkinson, A. E., 46–47
Willow Creek, 100
winze, 53, 91
Wolf Creek, 5
Wolf Creek MT (town), 5, 25, 32
Woodahl, Robert, 137
World War II, 40, 42, 45, 56, 59

yellowboy, 94–95, 99, 101, 108, 166

zinc, 56, 59, 93, 123, 126